Coup d'État

Also by Jerome R. Corsi, PhD.

Silent No More:
How I Became a Political Prisoner of Mueller's "Witch Hunt"

Dr. Corsi Investigates:
Why The Democratic Party Has Gone Communist

Goodnight Obama:
A Parody

Coup d'État

EXPOSING DEEP STATE
TREASON AND THE PLAN TO
RE-ELECT PRESIDENT TRUMP

JEROME R. CORSI

POST HILL
PRESS

A POST HILL PRESS BOOK
ISBN: 978-1-64293-437-3
ISBN (eBook): 978-1-64293-438-0

Coup d'État:
Exposing Deep State Treason and the Plan to Re-Elect President Trump
© 2020 by Jerome R. Corsi

Cover art by Cody Corcoran

Post Hill Press
New York • Nashville
posthillpress.com

Published in the United States of America

*Dedicated to my attorneys
David Gray and Larry Klayman,
whose expert professional legal advice
was indispensable in my successful fight
to prevent Mueller
from indicting and imprisoning me—
a fate that would have silenced me
and prevented me
from writing this book.*

*Now, free of Mueller's corrupt investigation,
I am SILENT NO MORE*

*While praying the traitors are brought to justice,
we pray God's will be done:
in the end, God always wins!*

Table of Contents

Introduction

This is perhaps the most important book I have ever written. It is one I never imagined I would have to write.

In these pages, I present shocking evidence that the Obama administration used false allegations secretly sourced from opposition research written by foreign operatives that was funded by Hillary Clinton's presidential campaign and by the Democratic National Committee to launch a Justice Department counterintelligence espionage investigation against Donald Trump, the GOP's presidential candidate. The counterintelligence operation was extended into the first year of Donald Trump's presidency, at which time the Justice Department also launched a criminal case. The DOJ only closed the counterintelligence and criminal investigations against the president when the Mueller Office of Special Counsel failed to result in indictments in March 2019.

The truth is that former secretary of state Hillary Clinton and then president Barack Obama orchestrated a Deep State coup d'état designed to prevent Donald Trump from being elected president. When that failed and Trump won the election, the Clinton-Obama team morphed the Justice Department counterintelligence operation into a coup d'état aimed at impeaching Trump. To be specific, by "Deep State" I mean those legacy employees in the federal government—especially those in the CIA, the National Security Agency (NSA), the Office of the Director of National Intelligence, as well as the DOJ and the FBI—who opposed Donald Trump on partisan ideological grounds. These bureaucrats, loyal to the globalist appeal of leftist policies espoused by Hillary Clinton in her 2016 presidential run, took it upon their own authority first to conspire to deny Donald Trump the presidency, and then, once Trump surprised them by winning the election, to remove him from office by impeachment or though the provisions of the Twenty-fifth Amendment for the removal of the president.

As I demonstrate in chapter after chapter, the Obama administration's intelligence agencies, including the CIA and the NSA, along with the Obama administration federal justice system, including both the Department of Justice acting in a prosecutorial capacity and the FBI acting in an investigative capacity, conspired to commit numerous criminal miscarriages of justice, including fabrication of evidence and suborning of perjury to portray Trump as a Russian agent, or, failing that, as a guilty party determined to block a Justice Department criminal investigation.

In the end, obstruction of justice charges against Trump emerged out of the failed Office of Special Counsel's counterintelligence investigation. When the Office of Special Counsel under Robert Mueller failed to produce any evidence of Trump or his campaign being involved in alleged "Russian collusion" to defeat Hillary Clinton in 2016, Mueller went public with a statement that attempted to encourage Congress to begin impeachment hearings over allegations that Trump had obstructed Mueller's investigation. In doing so, Mueller disregarded the conclusion of Attorney General William Barr that the instances of possible obstruction of justice did not meet the probable cause threshold needed to seek indictments against President Trump or his close associates. At the time of this writing, hate-Trumpers of the Clinton-Obama hard left are continuing their efforts to remove Trump from office by launching impeachment hearings conducted by Representative Jerry Nadler (Democrat, New York), chairman of the House Judiciary Committee, and by Representative Adam Schiff (Democrat, California). When Mueller's appearance before the House Judiciary Committee failed to achieve Nadler's goal to support a House vote to begin impeachment proceedings, Schiff took over as the anti-Trump Deep State conspirators morphed Russiagate into Ukrainegate. Substituting Ukraine for Russia, Schiff pursued the claim that President Trump had threatened to withhold foreign aid from Ukraine unless Ukraine's newly elected president, Volodymyr Zelensky, cooperated with Trump in digging up dirt in Ukraine on former Vice President Joe Biden, then a leading candidate for the Democratic presidential nomination in 2020.

I will show in this book that the fingerprints of foreign intelligence agencies—including, most importantly, British intelligence—were all over perhaps the greatest political scandal in American history, alternatively characterized as "Russiagate" and "Spygate," and now "Ukrainegate."

Never before in our history has one political party made such serious criminal efforts to defeat the presidential candidate of the opposing political party. When that failed, the Democrats and their Deep State conspirators refocused their criminal efforts to deny a duly elected president the Constitutional right to assume the powers and duties of that office without unrelenting threats of impeachment.

I am in a particularly good position to write this book because I experienced firsthand the partisan hate-Trump political nature of Mueller's Office of Special Counsel investigation.

My mission here is to expose the hard left, making it clear that in their ideological zeal, Deep State "patriots" in 2016 engaged in treasonous crimes designed to pull off a coup d'état aimed at removing Trump from the presidency.

Clinton failed. Mueller failed.

Now, with the help of God, the Deep State will also fail.

That is why I am writing this book.

Chapter One

DEEP STATE TREASON

The central premise of this book is that Deep State actors operating as senior officers in U.S. intelligence agencies, including the CIA, and the U.S. justice system, with both the FBI and the Department of Justice involved, engaged in a coup d'état designed to make sure Donald Trump lost the presidential election in 2016. In the unlikely event Trump might be elected, the Deep State conspirators morphed their efforts into impeachment strategy as an "insurance policy." The insurance policy was designed to make sure Trump would be removed from office either through impeachment or by his being declared mentally incompetent under the auspices of the Twenty-fifth Amendment.

What distinguishes this analysis is not only my first-hand experience with the Mueller investigation, but the years of investigative reporting I have devoted to uncovering and exposing criminal governmental misconduct. Donald Trump's candidacy and election have set off in America's political left an intense hatred often described as Trump Derangement Syndrome. In the pages of this book, I seek to prove that unelected bureaucratic officials in the nation's justice and intelligence agencies acted on their personal political preferences to weaponize law enforcement in a conscious effort to go outside the law to destroy the presidential candidate of the Republican Party. I will argue that in their zeal, these unelected officials used the powers of the federal government to subvert the Constitution, hatching what has become a treasonous coup d'état aimed at removing Donald Trump from the presidency despite no evidence Donald

1

Trump has committed any "high crime or misdemeanor" that would warrant his removal from office.

Hillary Clinton's defeat in the 2016 presidential election came as a devastating and unanticipated shock to those on the hard left, including those in the U.S. federal bureaucracy who had expected her to win. The expectation of the hard left was that eight years under a Hillary Clinton presidency would advance, if not complete, the fundamental transformation of America into the socialist state that had been forecast by Barack Obama as he was about to win the presidency in 2008. Donald Trump's election as president in 2016 accelerated the rate at which the Democratic Party openly has embraced socialism, along with a disdain for the Constitution and the rule of law that has emboldened them with a "higher loyalty" that over human history has been deemed treason when their efforts to remove the head of state fail.

Robert Mueller's Downfall

In writing my 2018 *New York Times*-bestselling book entitled *Killing the Deep State: The Fight to Save President Trump*, I predicted that Robert Mueller's investigation as special counsel would fail to produce probable-cause evidence proving that Trump or anyone in his campaign had colluded with Russia, or that Trump had obstructed justice by interfering in the special counsel's investigation.[1] That has now happened. Mueller produced no evidence that resulted in a criminal indictment of any American for colluding with Russia in the 2016 presidential campaign. The various indictments of Trump associates that Mueller produced were either for tax fraud, as in Paul Manafort's case, or for lying to federal investigators, as in the case of Lieutenant General Michael Flynn and others, including George Papadopoulos. The two indictments Mueller brought against Russians involved no Americans.

The irony is that if Hillary Clinton had won the 2016 election, none of the Deep State actors involved in the treasonous coup d'état would ever have come to light. Had Clinton been inaugurated as president on

---

1   Jerome R. Corsi, *Killing the Deep State: The Fight to Save President Trump* (West Palm Beach, FL: Humanix Books, 2018).

January 20, 2017, Donald Trump most likely would have been allowed to return to his Trump Tower home to live life as a celebrity billionaire. With Clinton in power, the coconspirators of the 2016 coup d'état could feel comfortable that their treasonous plot would never be brought to justice. Put simply, those supporting Hillary Clinton, as well as Clinton herself, never imagined that she would lose.

August 28, 2018: The Day My Life Changed

In my 2019 bestseller, *Silent No More: How I Became a Political Prisoner of Mueller's "Witch Hunt,"*[2] I document my nightmare experience with the Mueller prosecutors and the FBI agents on his team. When Mueller's team finally blew up my two-month ordeal of suffering though forty hours of "voluntary interviews," the prosecutors threatened to indict me for lying to federal officials.

After the FBI showed up on my doorstep with a subpoena on August 28, 2018, three days before my seventy-second birthday, I resolved that since I had done nothing wrong, I would cooperate. Voluntarily, I handed over to the FBI the laptop computers I had been using since 2016, as well as all my external drive backup devices, plus all the usernames and passwords to my email accounts, and my cell phone. Truthfully, I believe the FBI already had all the information I handed over. Every aspect of my life was in those computers, my cell phone, and my email accounts, ranging from personal relations with family to business consulting information and financial records.

The IRS began auditing me in 2004, when I coauthored the Swift Boat book *Unfit for Command: Swift Boat Veterans Speak Out Against John Kerry*. That book contributed to Kerry losing the 2004 presidential election against then president George W. Bush, who was running for his second term in office.[3] Fortunately, my wife and I have always had highly competent and honest tax accountants, and we have meticulously report-

---

2 Jerome R. Corsi, *Silent No More: How I Became a Political Prisoner of Mueller's "Witch Hunt"* (New York, NY and Nashville, TN: Post Hill Press, 2019).

3 John E. O'Neill and Jerome R. Corsi, *Unfit for Command: Swift Boat Veterans Speak Out Against John Kerry* (Washington, D.C.: Regnery Publishing, 2004).

ed all income and paid all taxes due. We have no foreign bank accounts, and I have never worked for any foreign government.

I now believe that I was a target of the FBI's illegal electronic surveillance—approved by the Foreign Intelligence Surveillance Act (FISA)—especially given my working relationship during the 2016 campaign reporting on and working with Roger Stone. I suspect I have been under National Security Agency (NSA) electronic surveillance since 2004, when I coauthored *Unfit for Command* and worked on the Swift Boat campaign opposing the presidential candidacy of then senator John Kerry. The three prosecutors on Mueller's team who interrogated me—Aaron Zelinsky, Jeannie Rhee, and Andrew Goldstein (the former chief of the public corruption unit under U.S. Attorney Preet Bharara's office for the Southern District of New York)—seemed to know everything about me, including the content of my cell phone calls.

Mueller's Faulty Theory Exposed

Mueller's entire Russian collusion case came down to proving that I had introduced Julian Assange of WikiLeaks to Roger Stone, a longtime advisor to Donald Trump. Mueller's theory was that I had introduced Stone to Assange, and that Stone (in telephone contact with Trump) colluded with Assange as to how and when to release the emails Russia had stolen from the Democrats so as to do the most harm to Hillary Clinton's presidential campaign. The problem was that I had never communicated with Julian Assange or WikiLeaks.

The lead prosecutor interrogating me was Jeannie Rhee, a lawyer who had served as legal counsel for the Clinton Foundation. Rhee demeaned my religion. "Doctor Corsi, you are asking us to believe that in July 2016, when you took a trip to Italy with your wife for your twenty-fifth wedding anniversary, God intervened and performed a miracle in your mind telling you Assange had [John] Podesta's emails," she said in an angry voice. I responded that I did not appreciate her ridiculing God, but that if she was asking if I had figured out on my own in July and August 2016 that Assange had Podesta's emails, the answer was direct and honest: "Yes. I figured it out without any communication with Julian Assange or with WikiLeaks."

What concerned the FBI in the Mueller investigation can be traced back to a family trip my wife and I took in July and August 2016 to celebrate our twenty-fifth wedding anniversary. On that trip, relaxing from the demands of everyday writing, I had time to think. Of all things, I concluded that Julian Assange and WikiLeaks had obtained the emails stolen from Podesta, Clinton's 2016 presidential campaign chairman. I further deduced that Assange would make these emails public in October 2016, as that year's "October surprise," calculated to hit Clinton's presidential campaign with a death blow. The first batch of stolen emails Assange had released on July 22, 2016, focusing on then DNC chairperson Debbie Wasserman Schultz and the plan she implemented with Hillary Clinton to deny Bernie Sanders the Democratic presidential nomination. Soon after that, Assange let it be known he had additional "Clinton emails" to release. But it was not known what additional emails Assange had, or when he would make them public.

I connected the dots and deduced, or possibly I just guessed and was lucky, but I was sure on my Italy trip that the additional stolen emails that Assange possessed were Podesta's emails. I also reasoned that Assange would release the Podesta emails in October because that timing would not give Hillary time to recover, especially if Assange dripped out the emails, releasing them in a serial fashion—a few emails every day—right up until the November 6 election. I had been studying Podesta and Assange for some dozen years in my work as an investigative journalist. From what I knew of Podesta, I firmly believed that if I was right and WikiLeaks published the Podesta emails in October 2016, they would be extremely damaging to Clinton's presidential ambitions. By phone and email, I conveyed my conclusions from Italy to many people, including Stone.

Although I had no proof, I was absolutely certain I was right. Knowing I could not prove I was right or even explain to others how I came to this conclusion, I wrote several emails that made it sound as if I had a source. From the time I was a child, my father would counsel me to tell him when I came to conclusions regarding facts I could not prove, but he advised me not to share these insights with others at school. Often in my life, my leaps of intuition, or what I think are conclusions derived from a process of deduction, have turned out to be good guesses that have been surprisingly on-target and correct—as they were in July and August 2016.

My personal experience with Mueller's team gave me important insight into the mean political bias that pervaded every aspect of Mueller's investigation. In my forty hours of interrogation, Mueller's team showed no interest in anything except finding a crime that Trump had committed. Repeatedly, the prosecutors refused information I had about Clinton. "Doctor Corsi, we are uninterested in your theories that the Russians did not steal the DNC emails," Mueller's prosecutors insisted. Or, on a separate subject, they were equally insistent. "Please spare us your research on Huma Abedin's forwarding Hillary Clinton's classified emails from the State Department to her private email account on Yahoo."

Judging from the questions Mueller's prosecutors asked me, I concluded the FBI (and very possibly the NSA) had monitored my emails and phone calls while I was in Italy with my wife and family. Mueller's prosecutors told my attorney David Gray that the FBI was convinced I must have had direct contact with Assange because I appeared to have known all about Assange having Podesta's emails while I was in Italy. The information I was communicating from Italy about Assange and Podesta's emails turned out to be so precisely correct that the FBI was convinced that I could not have come to these conclusions by myself. Mueller's prosecutors pointed out to David Gray that when I was in Italy during July and August 2016, I was predicting correctly that the stolen Podesta emails would contain admissions by Podesta that Clinton was suffering some form of mental impairment that made her far more ill than her campaign was willing to admit publicly. I was predicting the Podesta emails would contain damaging information about Clinton Foundation frauds, as well as internal DNC grumbling that Hillary was a disappointing candidate. While I have attended, as part of the audience, various public meetings Podesta has chaired in Washington, D.C., I have never spoken to Podesta nor have I communicated with him by phone or email.

In my forty hours of questioning, the three prosecutors and the FBI became increasingly aggressive and abusive, refusing to accept my explanation that I had never had any contact with Assange or WikiLeaks, either directly or indirectly. Mueller's team simply refused to believe I was sufficiently smart to have figured this out myself. I expressed this predicament after Mueller submitted his final report in an op-ed piece titled "When Prescience Was a Crime" that I published in the *Washington Times*.[4]

After I rejected what I considered a fraudulent plea deal Mueller's prosecutors had prepared for me to sign, the prosecutors threatened to bring criminal indictments against me in federal court, seeking to imprison me for the rest of my life. The truth is, Mueller ended his investigation without bringing any charges against me. The only way I would have gone to prison is if Mueller had managed to scare me into pleading guilty to a crime I did not commit. Mueller's prosecutors knew I had committed no crime. But they desperately needed me to plead guilty, admitting I had connected Stone to Assange, even though that was not true. I refused to go before a federal judge and swear before God to a crime I had not committed. Failing to get this key piece of "evidence" from me, Mueller lacked a critical piece needed to complete the pre-conceived "Russian collusion" hoax.

William Barr Shuts Mueller Down

On Friday, March 22, 2019, Attorney General William Barr notified Congress that Special Counsel Robert Mueller had submitted the final report of his investigation to Barr's office. Two days later, on Sunday, March 24, in a four-page letter addressed to Congress, Barr summarized the conclusions of Mueller's investigation into Russian collusion in the following two simple points:

1. The Special Counsel's investigations do not find that the Trump campaign or anyone associated with it conspired or coordinated with Russia in its efforts to influence the 2016 election.

---

4 Jerome R. Corsi, "When Prescience Was a Crime," Analysis/Opinion, *Washington Times*, May 2, 2019, https://www.washingtontimes.com/news/2019/may/2/the-mueller-push-for-acceptance-of-a-plea-deal-was/.

2. The Special Counsel did not draw a conclusion—one way or the other—as to whether the examined conduct constituted obstruction.[5]

Given Mueller's inability to draw a conclusion on the collusion allegations, Barr took the matter into his own hands. In his March 24, 2019, letter to Congress, Barr wrote that the special counsel's decision not to draw any legal conclusions left the decision up to him, as attorney general, to determine whether the conduct described in Mueller's five-hundred-page report constituted probable cause that a crime had been committed.

Once again, Barr stated his conclusion simply and clearly:

> After reviewing the Special Counsel's final report on these issues; consulting with Department officials, including the Office of Legal Counsel; and applying the principles of federal prosecution that guide our charging decisions, Deputy Attorney General Rod J. Rosenstein and I have concluded that the evidence developed during the Special Counsel's investigation is not sufficient to establish that the President committed an obstruction-of-justice offense.

Almost immediately, President Trump began expressing his satisfaction with these conclusions. On Sunday, March 24, 2019, at 3:42 p.m., Trump tweeted a message that made it clear he considered that Barr's

---

5   "Letter from Attorney General Barr to the House and Senate Judiciary Committees regarding the conclusion of the Special Counsel's report," Department of Justice, March 22, 2019, https://www.justice.gov/ag/page/file/1147986/download. See also: "Letter from Attorney General Barr to the House and Senate Judiciary Committees regarding the Special Counsel's report," Department of Justice, March 24, 2019, https://www.justice.gov/ag/page/file/1147981/download. See also: "Read Attorney General William Barr's Summary of the Mueller Report," *New York Times*, March 24, 2019, https://www.nytimes.com/interactive/2019/03/24/us/politics/barr-letter-mueller-report.html.

summary of the Mueller report had completely removed from him the cloud of any criminal charges. Trump's tweet read:

> No Collusion, No Obstruction, Complete and total EX-ONERATION. KEEP AMERICA GREAT![6]

Barr's four-page letter set off a firestorm. Starting during the 2016 presidential campaign, CNN and MSNBC had begun a daily drumbeat hyping every tidbit of new information suggesting that Trump had colluded with Russia, turning every questionable scrap of gossip into near certain proof that Trump was a Russian asset who stole the election from Hillary. Twenty-four hours a day, the Russia-collusion hype was promoted by leftist talk show hosts and guests alike. If Barr's summary of Mueller's report was accurate, Never Trumpers had spent approximately the past two years depicting Trump as a traitor on the basis of supposition, rumor, and innuendo. Millions were hooked into the Russia-collusion hysteria, only to be left sadly disappointed by Barr's conclusion that Mueller had found no evidence of collusion with Russia and insufficient evidence of obstruction to declare that Trump (or any of his associates) had committed a crime.

Did Rosenstein Propose to Wear a Wire in Conversations with Trump?

In September 2018, the *New York Times* reported that in the spring of 2017, in the aftermath of Trump firing then FBI director James Comey, Deputy Attorney General Rod Rosenstein had suggested in meetings and conversations with various Justice Department and FBI figures that he might wear a wire to record future conversations he envisioned having with President Trump.[7] Rosenstein's goal was to record President Trump to obtain evidence of Trump's supposed mental incompetence, which the

---

6 Donald Trump (@realDonaldTrump), Tweet, March 24, 2019, https://twitter.com/realdonaldtrump/status/1109918388133023744?lang=en.

7 Adam Goldman and Michael S. Schmidt, "Rod Rosenstein Suggested Secretly Recording Trump and Discussed 25th Amendment," *New York Times*, September 21, 2018, https://www.nytimes.com/2018/09/21/us/politics/rod-rosenstein-wear-wire-25th-amendment.html.

Justice Department could then use to press for the removal of Trump from office under the Twenty-fifth Amendment.

The *New York Times* reported that Rosenstein, only two weeks into his job as deputy attorney general, was at that time overseeing Mueller's Russia investigation (after Attorney General Jeff Sessions's recusal). Rosenstein was upset that, when President Trump fired Comey, he cited a memo that he had asked Rosenstein to write that was critical of Comey's handling of the Hillary Clinton email investigation. In the controversial memo, Rosenstein wrote: "I cannot defend the Director's [Comey's] handling of the conclusion of the investigation of Secretary Clinton's emails, and I do not understand his refusal to accept the nearly universal judgment that he was mistaken."[8] By doing so, Rosenstein joined the Deep State conspirators in their effort to remove Trump from office. But Rosenstein felt no animus when FBI Director Comey "pardoned" Hillary.

Recall that on July 5, 2016, FBI Director James Comey gave a statement on national television regarding Secretary Clinton's use of a private email server. In this statement, Comey made it clear the FBI had not found sufficient legal grounds upon which to indict Clinton of a criminal offense. "Although we did not find clear evidence that Secretary Clinton or her colleagues intended to violate laws governing the handling of classified information, there is evidence that they were extremely careless in their handling of very sensitive, highly classified information," Comey said in a key sentence.[9] Comey continued to note that in the final judgment of the FBI, "no reasonable prosecutor" would bring such a criminal case because all of the cases prosecuted under the statutes regarding the handling of national security classified material involved some element of "clearly intentional and willful mishandling of classified information."

8 "White House Announces Firing of James Comey," *New York Times*, May 9, 2017, https://www.nytimes.com/interactive/2017/05/09/us/politics/document-White-House-Fires-James-Comey.html?module=inline.

9 "Statement by FBI Director James B. Comey on the Investigation of Secretary Hillary Clinton Use of a Personal E-mail System," FBI National Press Office, Washington, D.C., July 5, 2016, https://www.fbi.gov/news/pressrel/press-releases/statement-by-fbi-director-james-b-comey-on-the-investigation-of-secretary-hillary-clinton2019s-use-of-a-personal-e-mail-system.

Attorney Gregg Jarrett, in his book titled *The Russia Hoax: The Illicit Scheme to Clear Hillary Clinton and Frame Donald Trump*, points out the fatal flaw in Comey's logic. He correctly argues that "nowhere in U.S.C. 793(f) of the Espionage Act which governs the 'grossly negligent' handling of classified information does it state that a defendant must have intended to break the law in order to be charged or found guilty."[10] Jarrett stresses that the language of the statute is unmistakable in that no intent is required. He points out that this was a deliberate decision by Congress when it revised and expanded the law decades after its original passage in 1917. In revising the law, Congress added this language to provide a lesser alternative to willful conduct—namely, gross negligence.

After he had been fired from the FBI, Andrew McCabe gave an interview to CBS's *60 Minutes* in which he affirmed that Rosenstein had been serious about wearing a wire. "I never get searched when I go into the White House," Rosenstein said. "I could easily wear a recording device. They wouldn't know it was there." When the story first broke in September 2018, Rosenstein tried to dismiss it, claiming he was just being sarcastic when he made the suggestion. "He was absolutely serious," McCabe insisted. "And in fact, he brought it up in the next meeting we had. I never actually considered taking him up on the offer. I did discuss it with my general counsel and my leadership team back at the FBI after he brought it up the first time."

McCabe also recalled that Rosenstein, when he was considering wearing the wire, asked FBI officials how many cabinet members they thought would vote under the Twenty-fifth Amendment to remove Trump from office. "So I listened to what he had to say," McCabe continued to CBS, minimizing his involvement in the effort to use the Twenty-fifth Amendment to remove Trump. "But, to be fair, it was an unbelievably stressful time. I can't even describe for you how many things must have been coursing through the deputy attorney general's mind at that point."[11]

---

10 Gregg Jarrett, *The Russia Hoax: The Illicit Scheme to Clear Hillary Clinton and Frame Donald Trump* (New York: Broadside Books, HarperCollins Publishers, 2018), p. 28.

11 Laura Jarrett, "Former Acting FBI Director: 'Rosenstein Offered to Wear a Wire into the White House,'" CNN, February 17, 2019, https://www.cnn.com/2019/02/17/politics/mccabe-fbi-rosenstein-wire/index.html.

FBI attorney Lisa Page wrote a contemporaneous memo to herself that remained at the FBI after she was fired, documenting Rosenstein's comments in a manner that corroborates memos McCabe wrote at the time. Page's memo confirmed McCabe's insistence that Rosenstein had been serious about the suggestion.[12] Evidently, Rosenstein did seriously consider wearing a wire in the presence of Trump in the days immediately following Comey's firing, and before the appointment of Mueller as special counsel. Clearly, Trump's release of Rosenstein's memo on Comey upset Rosenstein. In the days after Comey's firing, Rosenstein expressed anger about how the White House had used him to rationalize the firing, saying the experience damaged his reputation. The *New York Times* reported that those speaking with Rosenstein said Rosenstein was "shaken," "unsteady," and "overwhelmed" after Comey's firing. One person told the *Times* that Rosenstein sounded "frantic, nervous, upset, and emotionally dis-regulated."[13] These feelings that President Trump had abused his trust evidently contributed to Rosenstein's decision to appoint a special counsel to investigate allegations advanced by the DOJ and the FBI charging that Trump had colluded with Russia to steal the 2016 election from Hillary.

Mueller Takes a Swipe at Trump

On Wednesday, May 29, 2019, Mueller decided to emerge from his silence by reading on national television a ten-minute statement apparently designed to sustain the political pressure on President Trump. In a startling statement regarding volume two of the report concerning the obstruction investigation, Mueller said, "As set forth in our report, after

---

12 Laura Jarrett, "What Happened Between Rosenstein and McCabe Before Mueller Was Appointed?" CNN, September 22, 2018, https://www.cnn. com/2018/09/22/politics/divergent-stories-may-16-rosenstein-mccabe/ index.html. See also: Laura Jarrett, Jeremy Herb, and Kevin Liptak, "Sources: Rod Rosenstein Discussed Secretly Taping Trump," CNN, September 24, 2018, https://www.cnn.com/2018/09/21/politics/rosenstein-mc-cabe-trump-wire/index.html.

13 Michael S. Schmidt and Adam Goldman, "'Shaken' Rosenstein Felt Used by White House in Comey Firing," *New York Times*, June 29, 2018, https:// www.nytimes.com/2018/06/29/us/politics/rod-rosenstein-comey-firing. html?module=inline.

that investigation, if we had confidence that the President clearly did not commit a crime, we would have said that."[14]

This comment drew a sharp rebuke from Charles C. W. Cooke, editor of *National Review*. "Innocence is the default position in this country," Cooke wrote. "If a person doesn't have enough evidence that someone committed a crime…he is obligated to presume his innocence. 'Not exonerated' is not a standard in our system, and it shouldn't be one in our culture, either."[15]

Mueller continued to refer to the Department of Justice Office of Legal Counsel (OLC) guidance forbidding the indictment of a sitting president. Again referencing whether Trump had obstructed justice, Mueller said the following in his press conference: "We did not, however, make a determination as to whether the President did commit a crime." Mueller explained that the OLC guidance was responsible for his team's taking this course, arguing that "a President cannot be charged with a federal crime while he is in office. That is unconstitutional. Even if the charge is kept under seal and hidden from public view—that too is prohibited."

Andrew C. McCarthy, a former assistant U.S. attorney for the Southern District of New York, sharply criticized Mueller, pointing out that "if his [Mueller's] default position was that the OLC guidance prevented him from doing the prosecutor's job—which is to decide sufficiency-of-evidence questions—he should not have accepted the appointment."[16] McCarthy interpreted what Mueller said as this: "Mueller believes there is enough evidence to indict, he decided he could not do so under the guid-

14 "Special Counsel Robert S. Mueller III Makes Statement on Investigation into Russian Interference in the 2016 Presidential Election," U.S. Department of Justice, May 29, 2019, https://www.justice.gov/opa/speech/special-counsel-robert-s-mueller-iii-makes-statement-investigation-russian-interference.

15 Charles C. W. Cooke, "'Not Exonerated' Is Not a Standard Any Free Country Should Accept," *National Review*, May 29, 2019, https://www.nationalreview.com/corner/not-exonerated-is-not-a-standard-any-free-country-should-accept/.

16 Andrew C. McCarthy, "Mueller's Press Conference Makes the Impeachment Tightrope Tougher to Walk for Democrats," *National Review*, May 29, 2019, https://www.nationalreview.com/2019/05/robert-mueller-press-conference-impeachment-politics-democrats/.

ance, and he intentionally left the matter for Congress to resolve—with the advice that felonies may have been committed." McCarthy correctly observed that Mueller was handing off the obstruction investigation to Congress, virtually urging Congress to begin impeachment proceedings, realizing, as McCarthy noted, that "Congress does not need a prosecutable criminal offense in order to impeach."

Mueller stated that there was nothing in his press conference statements other than what was already included in his 448-page report. If this was the case, why did he feel it was necessary to come to the podium on national television to make this statement? Obviously, Mueller, or some of Mueller's investigators (Andrew Weissmann, one of the most controversial prosecutors on Mueller's team, comes to mind immediately) felt that Trump and Barr had gone too far in concluding that President Trump had been exonerated by the Mueller investigation.

Truthfully, Mueller did not need to write a 448-page report that contains only dead-end information largely about persons not indicted for any crime. By suggesting that Congress was the appropriate place to adjudicate the obstruction "episodes," Mueller was making it clear that his investigation was political in nature. At law, Trump was right: the Mueller report did exonerate him from criminal prosecution on the Russia-collusion accusations and Barr exonerated him on obstruction charges. But Mueller, by going public like this, threw the gauntlet down for the Democrats in Congress to ramp up the impeachment hearings.

Mueller and the Continuing Cover-Up

Mueller, in reading his ten-minute statement, looked like a defeated man: pale, with no emotion in his voice, a person leaving his last hurrah having disappointed constituencies who wanted him to vindicate Hillary Clinton. If Trump did not collude with Russia, then Russia did not steal the election from Clinton, and Trump was not a traitor sitting in the president's chair.

Viewed critically, Mueller was part of the cover-up, assigned a role to limit his investigation to the Trump campaign. As early as October 19, 2018, some five months before the release of Mueller's final report, supporters of Hillary Clinton, hyped by the mainstream media, anticipated the release of Mueller's report would be "among the most thrilling events of their lives." The Mueller report had delivered a huge blow to Clinton and her supporters.[17] When the Mueller report failed to produce the criminal charges against Trump that were anticipated, the Clintons and their coconspirators knew the cover-up must continue. The Deep State remained determined that the DOJ must never be permitted to investigate the origins of the Russia-collusion charges. The Deep State continues to fear that any honest DOJ investigation will reveal the criminal, and potentially treasonous, activities of Barack Obama and Hillary Clinton— crimes that overshadowed in seriousness the crimes Obama and Hillary had committed by engineering numerous and continuing cover-ups in Clinton's email scandals.

As we shall see, there are serious reasons to doubt that any agency as corrupt as the Obama-created CIA, NSA, DOJ, or FBI should be trusted to investigate themselves. In the aftermath of the Mueller report, new evidence undermining the Mueller investigation has emerged. A key reason I am writing this book is to make sure the cover-up does not continue.

Why I Feel Vindicated

From Thanksgiving 2018 until Saint Patrick's Day 2019, when Attorney General Barr started making it clear that Mueller was done and there would be no more indictments resulting from the Mueller probe, my wife and I expected that any day the FBI could show up to arrest me. "Will the FBI storm the house and arrest you like the FBI did in Florida with Roger Stone?" members of the family and friends would ask. I answered that I could not rule it out. My wife and I would wake up at 4:00 a.m. to look out the window to see if FBI agents were assembling outside the house to break down the front door, ransack the house, and put me in handcuffs.

For weeks on end, CNN had a car parked on the street outside our home, waiting to see if they could catch me being led out of the house by the FBI on film, with me in handcuffs like a criminal and my wife and

---

17 Darren Samuelsohn, "Mueller Report PSA: Prepare for Disappointment," Politico, October 19, 2019, https://www.politico.com/story/2018/10/19/mueller-investigation-findings-914754.

family left behind, crying and afraid. The price Mueller forced us to pay as a family was not only psychological; it was economic. The legal bills rapidly escalated into six figures. At the same time, I lost my job as an investigative reporter, and all my consulting contracts were canceled by clients afraid that their business relationship with me would invite the FBI to put them under surveillance.

When the Mueller investigation closed with no indictments or convictions for Russian collusion or for obstruction of justice, I felt vindicated that I had told Mueller the truth. If the FBI had the evidence to prove in court that I had lied during my forty-hour interrogation, I am sure I would have been indicted and brought to trial before a federal judge and jury in Washington. That never happened.

Chapter Two

HILLARY CLINTON HIRES FUSION GPS

At the heart of the Russia-collusion allegations was a document that became known as the "Steele dossier," written by Christopher Steele—a former British intelligence officer who had worked as a British spy in Russia—and a U.S. opposition research firm known as Fusion GPS. Former *Wall Street Journal* reporter Glenn Simpson and two of his ex-colleagues who had left the newspaper founded in 2011 the Washington-based Fusion GPS as a research-for-hire firm.

The Steele Dossier: The Heart of the Clinton/ Obama 2016 Attempted Coup

We now have proof that in 2016, the Steele dossier was funded in large part by Hillary Clinton's presidential campaign and the Democratic National Committee. Clinton's campaign and the DNC passed the funds through a contract between Fusion GPS and Perkins Coie, a law firm representing Hillary Clinton's presidential campaign and the DNC during the 2016 presidential campaign. We can also prove that the FBI was involved in funding Fusion GPS. Top levels of the FBI and the Department of Justice used the Steele dossier to obtain legal permission to conduct electronic surveillance on the Trump campaign.

Despite concerns over the document's validity, people at top levels of the FBI and DOJ signed off on using the Steele dossier as a key part of their application to the U.S. Foreign Intelligence Surveillance Court (known generally as the FISA Court). The FISA Court is a secretive federal court established in 1978 to authorize and oversee surveillance warrants against foreign spies working in the United States; its power can extend to authorizing surveillance of U.S. citizens working with these foreign spies. The Steele dossier was widely used to establish collusion with Russia by the Trump campaign as the central thesis of the Clinton/Obama coup d'état. The Steele dossier was used by the FBI and DOJ to create the code-named Operation Crossfire Hurricane investigation that was the precursor to the Mueller probe. The highest levels of the U.S. intelligence community used the Steele dossier to buttress the joint intelligence community's assessment in 2016 that the Trump campaign was in cahoots with Russia to steal the presidential election.

Interestingly, investigative reporter Lee Smith in his 2019 book titled, *The Plot Against the President*, points out that the FBI/DOJ Operation Crossfire Hurricane was not named after the Rolling Stones' classic song, but after the 1968 Penny Marshall film by the same name as the Stones' song, *Jumpin' Jack Flash*. In the Cold-War-era comic film, the fictional Terry Doolittle, a bank officer played by Whoopi Goldberg, detects a cryptic computer message from a user identified as "Jumpin' Jack Flash" that traces to Jack, played by Jonathan Pryce, a fictional British spy being chased by Soviet KGB agents. Through the course of the movie, Doolittle manages to help the British agent escape the KGB. As Steele points out, the FBI/DOJ code Operation Crossfire Hurricane alludes to the political "storm" of Trump's candidacy and presidency from which the former British spy, Christopher Steele, escapes, here with the help of the FBI playing in real life the Whoopi Goldberg role.

The Steele dossier was also key to CIA director John Brennan's decision to create an interagency "fusion cell" tasked in mid-2016 to investigate Russian interference in the presidential election. This highly secretive ad hoc group reported initially only to Obama. The group, known informally as the "fusion cell," produced a series of papers for the White House on Russian interference in the U.S. 2016 presidential election. Agendas for the secret interagency task force meetings during the summer and fall of 2016 were sent in envelopes to FBI Director James Comey, Attorney

General Loretta Lynch, and National Security Advisor Susan Rice. A classified 2016 document that Brennan had hand-delivered to Obama in a sealed envelope contained information from someone Brennan described only as "a source close to Putin." The informant is believed to have been a Russian source that Brennan recycled out of the Steele dossier. Gradually, Brennan expanded the circle within the Obama administration to include Vice President Joe Biden. Various cabinet members, including Secretary of State John Kerry, began receiving sealed envelopes disclosing the agenda for "fusion cell" meetings. The envelopes containing the agendas were considered so secret that subordinates were not authorized to open the envelopes. Sometimes the agendas were withheld until invited participants had taken their seats in the White House Situation Room.[18]

The sordid story of the Steele dossier reveals the apparent willingness of anti-Trump officials positioned by the Obama administration at the highest levels of the U.S. intelligence and justice systems, with the full knowledge of the Obama White House and the explicit approval of the Clinton campaign, to use opposition research known to be false to develop the Russia-collusion hoax and to spy on the presidential campaign of the opposition party. That a dossier known to be false was used by the Obama DOJ to obtain authorization from a secretive federal court to conduct covert electronic surveillance on the presidential campaign of the opposition-party GOP presidential candidate raises serious Constitutional issues, as well as political and legal concerns.

We now have documentary evidence proving that key actors in the FBI and the DOJ promoted the Steele dossier despite knowing that its essential claims against Trump were unverified—evidence that should result in criminal indictments if equal justice can be obtained in a U.S. justice

---

18 Greg Miller, Ellen Nakashima, and Adam Entous, "Obama's Secret Struggle to Punish Russia for Putin's Election Assault," *Washington Post*, June 23, 2017, https://www.washingtonpost.com/graphics/2017/world/national-security/obama-putin-election-hacking/?utm_term=.db6b86198ca8. See also: Paul Sperry, "The Russia Investigation Documents Barr Seeks to Uncover," Real Clear Investigations, August 28, 2019, https://www.realclearinvestigations.com/articles/2019/08/28/the_russia_investigation_documents_barr_seeks_to_uncover_120144.html.

and intelligence system that embedded Deep State employees are still fighting to control. New evidence that the State Department under Secretary of State Kerry also promoted the Steele dossier to discredit Donald Trump raises serious questions about whether the U.S. official diplomatic community joined with the U.S. intelligence and justice communities to pull off a treasonous coup d'état against Trump that extended to the involvement of foreign intelligence and diplomatic agencies.

The mounting evidence is indisputable that in 2016, top officials of the U.S. intelligence and justice system, joined by officers in the State Department, were politically motivated, going so far as to express openly their biased support of Clinton and their hatred of Trump. These Deep State actors within the federal government were determined to prevent Trump from being elected, and if he were elected, were equally determined to remove him from office before he had served to completion his first term as president. The charge against Trump, derived from the Steele dossier, was that Trump was an agent of Putin, a Russian spy, a traitor to the United States who must be denied the presidency at all costs.

In summary, the intelligence agencies of the United States—including the CIA, the FBI, and the DOJ—with the encouragement of the State Department, conspired to develop and implement a plan to utilize lies fabricated by Christopher Steele to brand Trump as a Russian asset, with funding from Hillary Clinton's presidential campaign and the DNC, with the blessing of the Obama White House. The plan was to use information developed by foreign sources that they knew to be false to deny Trump the presidency, even if he surprisingly managed to win a duly conducted presidential election. This is the heart of my charge: that Deep State actors in 2016 conspired with Hillary Clinton and the Obama White House to conduct a coup d'état predicated on information known to be false, designed to make sure Clinton was elected president, and to deny Trump the presidency if elected. While it may take until the end of President Trump's first term in office to escape a coup d'état falsely proceeding under the premise of legitimate impeachment inquiries, the Steele dossier is shaping up to be the centerpiece of what I and others believe ultimately will backfire against these Deep State conspirators. By the time of the next national presidential election, in November 2020, I predict that the Office of the

Attorney General of the United States will have sufficient probable cause evidence of crimes committed to bring charges of treason and sedition against the Deep State traitors—including ultimately Hillary Clinton and Barack Obama, whom I believe instigated and directed the Deep State coup d'état attempt against Donald Trump.

Please also recall that the Mueller probe did not investigate the Steele dossier. Why? Because Deputy Attorney General Rod Rosenstein, in appointing Robert Mueller as special counsel, authorized him to investigate only the Trump campaign, not the Clinton campaign. This fact buttresses my conclusion here that the main purpose of the Mueller probe was to prevent, under the Trump presidency, a reopening of the criminal investigation of Secretary Clinton's email scandals or of the Clinton Foundation, as well as to block any investigation into the roles Clinton and Obama played in creating and advancing the Russia-collusion hoax against Trump. I seek to prove in subsequent chapters that the Clinton campaign and the Obama White House invented the Russian hoax during the 2016 presidential campaign and sought the appointment in 2017 of Mueller as special counsel specifically in an attempt to destroy Trump and simultaneously to make sure that Hillary Clinton or John Podesta's financial interests in Russia never surfaced. In particular, Clinton and Obama wanted to be sure their involvement in selling secret U.S. military technology to Russia under the "reset" policy or the Uranium One scandal with Russia never surfaced publicly.

Although the Steele dossier was of no interest to the Mueller probe, the dossier must be central to any honest law enforcement attempt to get to the bottom of how the FISA Court abuses occurred. As noted above, the dossier was advanced by the coup d'état coconspirators as the key evidence that Trump colluded with Russia. The Steele dossier became so important to the coup d'état that the coconspirators funded the dossier, promoted it to the State Department, leaked key details to the media, and lied to the FISA Court by swearing that it constituted credible evidence that Trump was committing treason with Russia. Without the Steele dossier, the Trump-hating coconspirators were dead in the water. All this explains why the coconspirators were desperate to hide the fact that they funded and promoted the Steele document despite knowing the document was not true and could never be verified.

A Short History of Deep State Covert Acts Creating the Steele Dossier

In the 2012 presidential election, the Democrats hired Fusion GPS to conduct opposition research on GOP presidential candidate Mitt Romney. Then, in the 2016 presidential election, Republicans anxious to block Donald Trump were the first to fund Fusion GPS.

In 2015, the Washington Free Beacon, a conservative website, hired Fusion GPS to conduct opposition research on several GOP presidential candidates, including Trump. The Washington Free Beacon is funded to a large extent by billionaire GOP donor Paul Singer, the owner of a hedge fund, Elliott Management Corporation (EMC), that specializes in acquiring distressed debt. In the 2016 presidential campaign, Singer had donated to the presidential campaigns of both Jeb Bush and Marco Rubio and was a major supporter of House speaker Paul Ryan.[19] After Trump won, Singer reportedly contributed $1 million to Trump's inauguration fund.[20]

Singer has a long history of supporting globalist causes, including amnesty for illegal immigrants and mass third-world immigration. As reported by Breitbart, he was a key backer of the Republican establishment senators sponsoring the 2013 "Gang of Eight" amnesty bill; he joined with George Soros and the Ford Foundation to fund the National Immigration Forum, an open-borders nonprofit organization.[21]

19 Joshua Caplan, "Roger Stone Says He Knows the Wall Street Billionaire Behind 'Trump Dossier,'" *The Gateway Pundit*, October 26, 2017, http://www.thegatewaypundit.com/2017/10/roger-stone-says-knows-wall-street-billionaire-behind-trump-dossier-video/. After Trump's election, Singer became a Trump supporter and contributed to Trump's inauguration.

20 Shane Goldmacher, Kenneth P. Vogel, and Darren Samuelsohn, "Trump Courts Donors with Eye on 2020," Politico, March 3, 2017, https://www.politico.com/story/2017/03/trump-donors-2020-235632.

21 Ian Mason, "5 Times Paul Singer Funded Globalist Nonsense Before the Anti-Trump Dossier," Breitbart, October 28, 2017, http://www.breitbart.com/big-government/2017/10/28/5-times-paul-singer-funded-globalist-nonsense-before-the-anti-trump-dossier/.

Singer, an advocate of same-sex marriage and LGBT rights, funded the Human Rights Campaign that led boycotts in North Carolina when the state legislature passed a law maintaining separation of bathrooms on the basis of sex.

Singer quit funding Fusion GPS on or around May 3, 2016, the date when Trump became the presumptive GOP presidential nominee by winning decisively the GOP primary in Indiana, causing Senator Ted Cruz to drop out of the race. But as the Democrats realized Trump's primary race was likely to be successful, Hillary Clinton decided to fund Fusion GPS to complete the opposition research on Trump that Singer had initiated. Clinton's presidential campaign and the Democratic National Committee instructed Marc Elias, a partner in the Seattle-based Perkins Coie law firm and the lawyer of record for both Clinton's presidential campaign and the DNC, to retain Fusion GPS to complete the opposition research on Trump.[22]

In April 2016, Perkins Coie signed the contract with Fusion GPS. The point was to launder through Perkins Coie the money that the Clinton campaign and the DNC planned to pay to Fusion GPS.[23] Clinton's campaign paid Perkins Coie $5.6 million in legal fees from June 2015 through December 2016; the DNC paid the law firm $3.6 million in "legal and compliance consulting" starting in November 2015. According to Federal Election Commission (FEC) records, the Clinton campaign and the DNC paid Perkins Coie a total of $12.4 million during the 2016 presidential election, but no payments from Perkins Coie to Fusion GPS are detailed. In the FEC records, payments from the Clinton campaign and the DNC to Perkins Coie are listed almost entirely for legal consulting,

22 Adam Entous, Devlin Barrett, and Rosalind S. Helderman, "Clinton Campaign, DNC Paid for Research that Led to Russia Dossier," *Washington Post*, October 24, 2017, https://www.washingtonpost.com/world/national-security/clinton-campaign-dnc-paid-for-research-that-led-to-russia-dossier/2017/10/24/226fabf0-b8e4-11e7-a908-a3470754bbb9_story.html?utm_term=.57eacdfe98b8.

23 "Fusion GPS Fallout: DNC, Clinton, FBI Take Heat After Bombshell That Dems Funded Trump Dossier," Fox News, October 25, 2017, http://www.foxnews.com/politics/2017/10/25/fusion-gps-fallout-dnc-clinton-fbi-take-heat-after-bombshell-that-dems-funded-trump-dossier.html.

with only one payment of $66,500 listed for "research consulting" for the DNC.[24]

Democrat-leaning Perkins Coie has a long history of working closely with the Clintons and Obama. Beginning in November 2009, Robert Bauer, a senior partner at Perkins Coie, served as White House counsel. Previously, Bauer served as Obama's personal attorney and as the general counsel for the Obama for America organization during the 2008 presidential campaign. On June 2, 2011, as the Obama birth certificate controversy was heating up, Bauer resigned as White House counsel to resume his position as a Perkins Coie partner. Bauer is married to Anita Dunn, a political operative who established a reputation in 2009 for attacking Fox News for being "an arm of the GOP." She launched the attack from her position, at the time, as President Obama's White House communications director.

When President Obama released his "long-form birth certificate" in a White House press conference on April 27, 2011, Perkins Coie partner Judith Corley was identified as the person who had traveled to Hawaii to pick up the birth certificate from Loretta Fuddy, then the director of the Hawaii Department of Health.[25] Starting January 7, 2010, Corley had worked as an attorney in the office of White House counsel responsible for representing President Obama in personal matters. In total, Corley had worked at Perkins Coie for nearly thirty years, tracing back to 1981 when she joined the firm as a law clerk.[26]

---

24 Kenneth P. Vogel and Maggie Haberman, "Conservative Website First Funded Anti-Trump Research by Firm that Later Produced Dossier," *New York Times*, October 27, 2017, https://www.nytimes.com/2017/10/27/us/politics/trump-dossier-paul-singer.html. See also: Kenneth P. Vogel, "The Trump Dossier: What We Know and Who Paid for It," *New York Times*, October 25, 2017, https://www.nytimes.com/2017/10/25/us/politics/steele-dossier-trump-expained.html.

25 "Perkins Coie Got Obama's Birth Certificate," The BLT: The Blog of Legal Times, April 27, 2011, http://legaltimes.typepad.com/blt/2011/04/perkins-coie-judith-corley-got-obamas-birth-certificate.html.

26 Martha Neil, "Meet Judith Corley, President Obama's New Personal Lawyer," *ABA Journal*, January 7, 2010, http://www.abajournal.com/news/article/meet_judith_corley_president_obamas_new_personal_lawyer.

Corley returned from Hawaii in 2011 with a computer printout of Obama's long-form birth certificate, an oddity given that Hawaii did not use computers to print birth certificates in 1961. There is no evidence that Corley was allowed by the Hawaii Department of Health to review Obama's original 1961 birth records, assuming those records exist. The only law enforcement investigation into Obama's 1961 long-form birth certificate released by the White House on April 27, 2011, was conducted by Arizona's Maricopa County Sheriff Joe Arpaio, under the direction of Mike Zullo, the head of Arpaio's "cold-case posse." On January 10, 2016, Arpaio and Zullo reported their conclusion that the long-form birth certificate document released by the White House was a forgery, as validated by two independent forensic examinations.[27] I was with Zullo and the cold-case posse in Hawaii in 2012, when the Hawaii Department of Health refused to show the Arizona law enforcement officials Obama's original 1961 birth records. In 2012, in Hawaii, I discovered the authentic long-form computer-printed birth certificate (issued to a person other than Obama) from which Obama's was forged.

In her 2017 book entitled *Hacks: The Inside Story of the Break-ins and Breakdowns That Put Donald Trump in the White House*, Donna Brazile, a former chair of the Democratic National Committee and a Clinton loyalist who is now a Fox News contributor, raised the question as to whether Clinton's campaign and the Democratic National Party relied on advice from Perkins Coie to engage in manipulating donor contributions in a manner that may have violated federal election laws. The issue involved how the Clinton campaign diverted to the DNC, at a national level, various campaign donations to the Hillary Victory Fund that were supposedly intended to be used by state Democratic Party organizations in thirty-two states. The DNC evidently used these diverted funds to pay off the massive

---

27 "Obama Birth Certificate Investigation: Sheriff Arpaio's Office Says "9 Points of Forgery' Found," ABC News 15 Arizona, December 14, 2016, last updated December 16, 2016, https://www.abc15.com/news/region-phoenix-metro/central-phoenix/sheriff-joe-arpaio-to-talk-obama-birth-certificate-investigation.

DNC debt Obama left behind.[28] Various Podesta emails on WikiLeaks appear to support the allegation that the Clinton campaign used the Hillary Victory Fund as part of a money-laundering scheme that gained Clinton's presidential campaign hundreds of millions of dollars in apparent direct violation of FEC campaign financing laws and regulations.

To understand the Clinton campaign's money-laundering scheme, we need to appreciate that the Clinton campaign knew that several top-dollar millionaire and billionaire Democratic Party donors wanted to contribute several hundred thousand dollars to Clinton's campaign, but were constrained from doing so by FEC campaign contribution limits set by law well below the amounts these millionaires and billionaires wanted to contribute. For instance, in November 2015, Podesta expressed in an email his irritation that the Clinton campaign wanted him to "hit up his clients" to contribute $33,400 per person, or $66,000 to $100,000 per couple, to attend a Hillary Victory Fund event in New York City. Attendees would join Hillary and Bill Clinton for dinner and an "intimate" evening that would feature a "memorable" performance by Sting.[29] Under FEC laws, all that the Clinton campaign could accept from an individual donor during the primaries was a maximum of $2,700, plus an additional $2,700 for the general election. But by setting up the Hillary Victory Fund as a joint venture between the Clinton campaign and the thirty-two state party committees, in a structure that appeared to many to be in violation of federal election laws,[30] the super wealthy could contribute as much as $712,220, with $356,100 going to the primary phase of the campaign and another $356,100 earmarked for the general campaign after the primaries were over.

---

28 Donna Brazile, *Hacks: The Inside Story of the Break-ins and Breakdowns That Put Donald Trump in the White House* (New York: Hachette Books, 2017), pp. 33-36 and 97-99.

29 WikiLeaks, "The Podesta File," email from John Podesta to the file, "Re: Hillary Victory Fund Dinner with Hillary & Bill Clinton and Sting," November 14, 2015, https://wikileaks.org/podesta-emails/emailid/57290.

30 Pam Martens and Russ Martens, "Are Hillary Clinton and the DNC Skirting Election Law?" Wall Street on Parade, April 25, 2016, http://wallstreetonparade.com/2016/04/are-hillary-clinton-and-the-dnc-skirting-election-law/.

After Brazile took over the DNC following the resignation of Debbie Wasserman Schultz over the WikiLeaks email scandal, Brazile realized that the Hillary Victory Fund required the thirty-two Democratic state parties to wire the money back to the DNC almost as soon as the fund had wired the states their portions. This seemed to Brazile to be a possibly illegal scheme to get around the limits placed on individual campaign donations by federal election law. What the DNC did was wire fund money to the state Democratic party organizations one day, with the agreement that the state organizations would wire the money back to the DNC at the national level the next day. In an article published on Politico on May 2, 2016, Kenneth P. Vogel and Isaac Arnsdorf concluded that the Hillary Victory Fund had "transferred $3.8 million to the state parties, but almost all of that cash ($3.3 million, or 88 percent) was quickly transferred to the DNC, usually within a day or two, by the Clinton staffer who controls the committee."[31] Vogel and Arnsdorf found that less than 1 percent of the $61 million raised by Clinton's campaign had stayed in the state parties' coffers.

When the scandal became public, Perkins Coie recommended a public relations strategy to defuse the crisis. In an email exchange in April 2016, Graham Wilson, a Perkins Coie attorney, advised officials at the DNC to be circumspect in responding to questions being asked by a Politico reporter (Vogel) who appeared to suspect the DNC was using the Hillary Victory Fund to circumvent campaign finance contribution limits.[32] Wilson's advice was for the DNC to tell Vogel that the DNC's money at the national level was "for critical investments in infrastructure, maintaining the DNC's national voter file, and bolstering our research, communications and digital capabilities, all of which will help elect Democrats up and down the ballot in November and help strengthen state parties across the

---

31 Kenneth P. Vogel and Isaac Arnsdorf, "Clinton Fundraising Leaves Little for State Parties," Politico, May 2, 2016, https://www.politico.com/story/2016/04/clinton-fundraising-leaves-little-for-state-parties-222670.

32 WikiLeaks, "The Podesta File," email chain sent by Amy Dacey, the former CEO of the DNC to Graham Wilson, a Perkins Coie partner, "Re: Hi Graham/Politico," April 30, 2016, https://wikileaks.org/dnc-emails/emailid/9799.

country." In the email exchange with the outside counsel, the DNC also made it clear that it was running the money through Amalgamated Bank, one of the largest union-owned banks in the United States. The union bank owner, the Service Employees International Union (SEIU), strongly supports the Democratic Party and supported Clinton's candidacy. To date, the DOJ has taken no legal action against Clinton or her campaign officials for this apparent violation of campaign finance laws.

The Clinton campaign and the DNC knew what they were doing when they got Perkins Coie to negotiate the contract with Fusion GPS to conduct opposition research on Trump. Given the Democrats' history with Perkins Coie, the Clintons could calculate that the law firm would do their bidding. The Perkins Coie advice in the Hillary Victory Fund scheme suggests that the law firm was more than willing to interpret the law so as to justify actions taken by the Clinton campaign and the DNC to advance Hillary's candidacy. Most importantly, the Clintons and the DNC had plausible deniability—an important element when politicians decide to bend the law—in that they hired Perkins Coie, their law firm, to get information on Trump. Perkins Coie in turn hired Fusion GPS, which in turn hired Christopher Steele. This way, the Clintons and the DNC could always deny that they had hired a foreign national to develop information from the Russian government and Russian intelligence sources about Trump's business and financial dealings—information that could be used to compromise or destroy Trump's reputation and his presidential campaign. Perkins Coie knew Fusion GPS was the right choice because Glenn Simpson had already been peddling dirt on Trump to Trump's GOP opponents. Simpson, in turn, knew he could rely upon Steele to dig up dirt on Trump in Russia, where Steele had served as an MI6 agent and where he continued to tout expertise at Orbis Business Intelligence, the London-based private intelligence firm Steele cofounded in 2009.

Steele's history with MI6 strongly suggests the plan to destroy Trump with the bogus Russia-collusion narrative originated in British intelligence, specifically within the British Government Communications Headquarters (GCHQ) unit. This helps explain why Christopher Steele, a former MI6 British intelligence officer with spying experience in Russia, was chosen by Glenn Simpson to work with Fusion GPS. Just as the

Clinton campaign and the DNC fronted their relationship with Fusion GPS through Perkins Coie, British intelligence could trust that their histories with U.S. intelligence would make it unlikely the dirty dossier would ever be traced back to GCHQ. We will develop this theme more extensively in Chapter 4.

So, in June 2016, Perkins Coie hired Fusion GPS, and Simpson in turn contracted with Orbis to get the services of Steele. From the beginning, Steele touted that the sources he used to develop the information detrimental to Trump were in Russian government and intelligence. This turned out to be an excellent cover for peddling in the Steele dossier Russian disinformation and other unverified and scurrilous information on Trump.

It is important to note that the work Simpson did for Paul Singer and the Washington Free Beacon was based entirely on public sources, with none of the information coming from Steele.[33] Neither Paul Singer nor the Washington Free Beacon had any involvement with Steele or with the Steele dossier, a document specifically developed for the Democrats after Perkins Coie contracted with Fusion GPS.

Christopher Steele's Covert Ties to U.S. Agencies

To understand the role that Christopher Steele played in the attempted coup d'état, it is important to appreciate a few key points about his background. Steele, a twenty-six-year-old married man, landed in Moscow in 1990 to work as an MI6 British intelligence spy operating under thin diplomatic cover. The Russian intelligence KGB unit evidently was onto Steele as a British spy from the beginning.[34] Despite this, Steele had remarkable longevity in Moscow. He managed to stay in Moscow through the days of General Secretary Mikhail Gorbachev's attempted *perestroika*

---

33   Vogel and Haberman, "Conservative Website First Funded Anti-Trump Research by Firm that Later Produced Dossier," *New York Times*, op. cit.

34   Howard Blum, "How Ex-Spy Christopher Steele Compiled His Explosive Trump-Russia Dossier," *Vanity Fair*, March 30, 2017, https://www.vanityfair.com/news/2017/03/how-the-explosive-russian-dossier-was-compiled-christopher-steele.

and *glasnost* reforms, through the failed August 1991 Soviet coup d'état against Gorbachev, through the fall of the Berlin Wall in November 1991, and through the beginning of Boris Yeltsin's first term as president of the newly formed Russian Federation. Back in London in 1993, Steele advanced within MI6 to the point where he held a senior position on MI6's Russian desk in 2006. That year, Steele was chosen by MI6 to be the case officer investigating the poisoning by Russia of Alexander Litvinenko, a Russian intelligence officer who at the time of his poisoning was living in London as a Russian dissident. It also turns out that Steele was Litvinenko's MI6 handler at the time he was poisoned, a less-often-repeated fact that casts doubt over Steele's effectiveness as an intelligence operative. Steele was credited with being the first to realize that Litvinenko's murder was a Russian "hit" job.[35]

After suffering the personal tragedy of his first wife's death in 2009 from cirrhosis of the liver, Steele, then forty-three years old, left MI6 to establish Orbis Business Intelligence Ltd. in London with the primary goal of providing intelligence to multinational businesses.[36] Around the time Simpson was leaving the *Wall Street Journal*, Steele was leaving MI6. The two met in London in 2009 and decided to set up a business relationship between their two firms, Fusion GPS and Orbis. Simpson and Steele "knew some of the same people and shared expertise on Russia," explained Luke Harding, a British journalist with experience working as a foreign correspondent in Russia. "The Washington-based and London-based firms worked for oligarchs litigating other oligarchs. This might involve asset tracing—identifying large sums concealed behind layers of offshore companies."[37] Orbis thus became a subcontractor of Fusion GPS. That the payment for the Steele dossier traces from Fusion GPS back to the Clinton

---

35   Nick Hopkins and Luke Harding, "Donald Trump Dossier: Intelligence Sources Vouch for Author's Credibility," *The Guardian*, January 12, 2017, https://www.theguardian.com/us-news/2017/jan/12/intelligence-sources-vouch-credibility-donald-trump-russia-dossier-author.

36   Luke Harding, "How Trump walked into Putin's Web," *The Guardian*, November 15, 2017, https://www.theguardian.com/news/2017/nov/15/how-trump-walked-into-putins-web-luke.

37   Ibid.

campaign and the DNC leaves no doubt the Steele dossier is properly characterized as "opposition research" conducted for a political candidate, not independent research.

In sum, Hillary Clinton hired a former foreign spy to use his contacts in Russia to conduct opposition research on Donald Trump, Hillary's GOP presidential opponent in 2016.

For the Clintons, Simpson and Steele were a good choice to conduct the opposition research linking Trump with Russia. Both Simpson and Steele had extensive histories with U.S. intelligence agencies, including the CIA, and with the U.S. diplomatic corps at the level of the U.S. State Department.

In 2009, Orbis was hired by England's Football Association, known as FA England, to investigate allegations of corruption within the Fédération Internationale de Football Association (FIFA) surrounding Russia's bid to host the 2018 or 2020 World Cup. In January 2017, Reuters published a bombshell report that Steele had, in the summer of 2010, met secretly in London with members of a New York-based FBI squad assigned to investigate Eurasian organized crime.[38] The FBI at that time was interested in learning what Steele had uncovered in his investigation into FIFA corruption. In May 2015, fourteen people were indicted in U.S. federal court following an investigation into FIFA corruption conducted by the FBI and the IRS Criminal Investigation Division for various offenses involving wire fraud, racketeering, and money laundering in relation to the FIFA selection of World Cup sites.[39] Among those arrested were five FIFA officials involved in a $150 million bribery kickback scheme by soccer marketing organizations *in connection with* the selection of the host country for the 2010 World Cup and the 2011 FIFA presidential

---

38 Mark Hosenball, "Former M16 Spy Known to U.S. Agencies Is Author of Reports on Trump in Russia," Reuters, January 12, 2017, https://www. reuters.com/article/us-usa-trump-steele/former-mi6-spy-known-to-u-s-agencies-is-author-of-reports-on-trump-in-russia-idUSKBN14W0HN.

39 The U.S. Attorney indictments in the 2015 FIFA case are archived by the *New York Times*. See: "FIFA Indictments," *New York Times*, May 27, 2015, https://www.nytimes.com/interactive/2015/05/27/sports/soccer/document-fifa-indictments.html.

election.[40] Steele's work in the FIFA investigation "burnished Steele's reputation inside the U.S. intelligence community and the FBI," where he was regarded as "a pro, a well-connected Brit, who understood Russian espionage and subterranean tricks."[41]

Between 2014 and 2016, Steele wrote more than one hundred reports on Russia and the Ukraine. While the reports were written for a private client, they were widely read within the U.S. Department of State, with copies sent up to then secretary of state Kerry and then assistant secretary of state for European and Eurasian affairs Victoria Nuland, who at that time was directing the State Department's response to Russia's annexation of Ukraine and Putin's covert invasion into eastern Ukraine.[42]

Glenn Simpson was widely known for his work as a correspondent for the *Wall Street Journal* who specialized in writing about post-Soviet Russia, before he left the newspaper to form Fusion GPS with Peter Fritsch, a former *Wall Street Journal* senior editor, and Thomas Catan, also a former *Wall Street Journal* journalist.

Their already-established credibility with key officials in the CIA and the State Department made Simpson and Steele the ideal tag team to peddle Clinton-funded lies to demean and defeat Donald Trump. Those lies included suggesting that Trump had unsavory financial and business ties with Russian billionaire oligarchs and a history of shady dealings in Russia with beauty pageants that allowed Russian president Vladimir Putin to compromise Trump and control Trump's presidential campaign. Clinton had candidates other than Simpson and Steele to develop the opposition research on Trump. One in particular was her longtime confidant Sidney Blumenthal. But Blumenthal was considered a Clinton loyalist and an outsider to the Washington intelligence and diplomatic communities. Blumenthal could be considered to be in the business of developing

---

40   Michael E. Miller and Fred Barbash, "U.S. Indicts World Soccer Officials in Alleged $150 Million FIFA Bribery Scandal," *Washington Post*, May 27, 2015, https://www.washingtonpost.com/news/morning-mix/wp/2015/05/27/top-fifa-officials-arrested-in-international-soccer-corruption-investigation-according-to-reports/?utm_term=.14ddd0a77550.

41   Harding, "How Trump walked into Putin's Web," op. cit.

42   Ibid.

intelligence information for private candidates, but he lacked the credibility with the Washington establishment that Simpson and Steele enjoyed.

The trust the U.S. government placed in Simpson and Steele allowed them to share with the FBI and DOJ Steele's dossier on Trump while the document was in progress. This open access permitted Simpson and Steele to share their dirt on Trump with the FBI and DOJ confidentially, knowing their explosive information was likely to prompt the Obama administration justice system to open a counterintelligence investigation into Trump. Simpson and Steele could be confident that because of their already established trust, the FBI and DOJ would buy Steele's dirt on Trump without investigating the dossier's scurrilous claims independently. Simpson and Steele calculated correctly in that the FBI and DOJ used Steele's research to establish "probable cause" to believe that Trump was a Russian agent.

At the end of this chapter, we will establish that Steele, in his hatred of Trump, also secretly promoted his dossier to various news agencies in Washington and New York. When the newspapers began publishing Steele's dirt on Trump, Simpson and Steele created the illusion with the FBI, DOJ, and the State Department that the dossier's dirt on Trump had "independent corroboration," further boosting the Obama administration's willingness to go forward and investigate Trump.

All along, Simpson and Steele knew that the anti-Trump information in his dossier lacked verification. However, should the Steele dossier blow up as a fraud, Clinton and the DNC could place blame on Perkins Coie, suggesting Perkins Coie had selected Fusion GPS to conduct the research on Trump and/or that Clinton and the DNC did not realize their payments to Perkins Coie were ending up with Simpson and Steele. In the final analysis, Clinton and the DNC had the fallback alibi that they had relied upon the legal advice of their attorneys, trusting that the opposition research developed by Fusion GPS would be accurate. Should the Steele dossier prove a fraud, as it ultimately was, the Clintons and the DNC set up Perkins Coie, not the Clintons or the Democratic Party, to take the heat as the fall guy.

The Steele Dossier Is Exposed as a Fraud

According to a report filed by Jerry Dunleavy published in the *Washington Examiner* on March 15, 2019,[43] Steele admitted in a deposition under oath, taken in London, that in developing the Trump dossier, he used unverified reports he pulled from CNN's iReport website, unaware that the submissions on that website are made by members of the public and are not checked for accuracy. Dunleavy further reported that a web archive dated July 29, 2009, shows that CNN described the iReport website as follows: "iReport.com is a user-generated site. This means the stories submitted by users are not fact-checked or screened before they post." When questioned, Steele admitted he did not understand that stories published on iReport were not generated by CNN reporters.

Dunleavy reported that Steele "was pressed on this further: 'Do you understand that CNN iReports are or were nothing more than any random individuals' assertions on the Internet?' Steele replied: 'No, I obviously presume that if it is on a CNN site that it may has [sic] some kind of CNN status. Albeit that it may be an independent person posting on the site.'" Dunleavy added: "When asked about his methodology for searching for this information, Steele described it as 'what we could call an open source search,' which he defined as 'where you go into the Internet and you access material that is available on the Internet that is of relevance or reference to the issue at hand or the person under consideration.' Steele said his dossier contained 'raw intelligence' that he admitted could contain untrue or even 'deliberately false information.'" Dunleavy also wrote: "When asked whether he warned Fusion GPS that the information in the dossier might be 'Russian disinformation,' Steele admitted that 'a general understanding existed between us and Fusion…that all material contained this risk.'"

---

43 Jerry Dunleavy, "Christopher Steele Admitted Using Posts by 'Random Individuals' on CNN Website to Back Up Trump Dossier," *Washington Examiner*, March 15, 2019, https://www.washingtonexaminer.com/news/steele-admitted-in-court-he-used-unverified-website-to-support-the-trump-dossier.

Steele Leaks the Dossier

In the London deposition under oath, Steele admitted that when the Trump dossier was finished in December 2016, he provided a copy to journalists in order to make public the information harmful to Trump's candidacy, despite being unable to verify the damaging and outright scurrilous information on Trump that the dossier contained. A Steele leak to Michael Isikoff, the chief investigative correspondent for Yahoo! News, was particularly damaging. On September 23, 2016, Isikoff published an article titled "U.S. Intel Officials Probe Ties between Trump and Kremlin."[44] Isikoff's article reported that U.S. intelligence officials were seeking to determine if Carter Page, an American businessman identified by Trump as one of his foreign policy advisors, had opened up private communications with senior Russian officials about the possibility of lifting economic sanctions if the Republican nominee became president.

The Isikoff article, based largely on leaks by Steele of material in his Trump dossier, was particularly damaging to Trump because it established the quid pro quo that Trump was willing to extend to Russia in return for help stealing the DNC emails and getting them to Julian Assange at WikiLeaks. In 2018, it became public knowledge that Isikoff's story had been cited by the DOJ as one justification in its application to the FISA Court for permission to conduct electronic surveillance on Page. Isikoff admitted that his story was based almost entirely on information from the Steele dossier, which he claimed had been passed on to him by an unnamed intermediary.[45] This is particularly damaging because the FBI and DOJ used the Isikoff article in their FISA Court warrant as independent

---

44 Michael Isikoff, "U.S. Intel Officials Probe Ties between Trump Adviser and Kremlin," Yahoo! News, September 23, 2016, https://www.yahoo.com/news/u-s-intel-officials-probe-ties-between-trump-adviser-and-kremlin-175046002.html

45 Tyler Durden, "Michael Isikoff Says He Was 'Stunned' To See His Story Cited in FISA Warrant," ZeroHedge.com, February 4, 2018, https://www.zerohedge.com/news/2018-02-04/michael-isikoff-says-he-was-stunned-see-his-story-cited-page-fisa-warrant. "Tyler Durden" is a pseudonym for the main editor of ZeroHedge.com, identified by Bloomberg Business as Daniel Ivandjiiski.

verification of the Steele dossier claims—without revealing that Steele was the source of Isikoff's article.

In his London deposition, Steele also admitted he had leaked the Trump dossier to Senator John McCain, as well as to Isikoff. McCain learned about the Russia dossier while attending the annual Halifax International Security Forum in Canada on November 18, 2016. McCain dispatched an emissary on a transatlantic flight to an undisclosed airport, where the emissary was handed the dossier. Jerry Dunleavy, in his report on the Steele deposition, noted Steele's disclosure that he also had given a copy of the Steele dossier to McCain's aide, David Kramer, who in turn shared information in the dossier with more than a dozen journalists. "'I provided copies of the December memo to Fusion GPS for onward passage to David Kramer at the request of John McCain,'" Steele said in the deposition, per Dunleavy's article. "'Senator McCain nominated him [Kramer] as the intermediary. I did not choose him as the intermediary.'" Dunleavy also reported that Steele said in the deposition that he told Kramer that he could not vouch for the truthfulness of everything in the memo and that his statement to Kramer placed "an emphasis on 'everything.'" When asked why he believed it was important to provide the dossier to McCain, Steele explained: "'Because I judged it had national security implications for the United States and the West as a whole.'"

Steele had reason to believe that Kramer would give his dossier added credibility. David Kramer had served as the U.S. assistant secretary of state for democracy, human rights, and labor from 2008 to 2009. He was in attendance at the Halifax meeting with McCain, after which he agreed to go to London to meet Steele in person.

In a deposition given in a U.S. District Court in Florida on December 13, 2017, Kramer described his conversation with Steele in London, noting that Steele admitted to him that the Trump dossier had not been verified.[46] "He [Steele] explained that what was produced [in the Trump

---

46   Transcript of videotaped deposition of David Kramer in the U.S. District Court for the Southern District of Florida, in the case *Aleksej Gubarev, et al., vs. BuzzFeed, Inc, et al.,* December 13, 2017, https://media.washtimes.com/media/misc/2019/03/16/BOOK_Kramer_trans..pdf.

dossier] needed to be corroborated and verified," Kramer said in the deposition. Kramer continued to note that Steele admitted that he himself did not feel he was in a position to vouch for everything in the dossier. "But he [Steele] felt that based on the sources and based on his own company's track record, he felt that at least he had the best sources possible to produce information," Kramer added, noting that Steele also admitted that some of his information in the dossier was raw intelligence, which Kramer understood to mean "human intelligence which has not been corroborated or verified by other sources."

Kramer also noted that Steele explained to him in London that he had decided to leak the Trump dossier because "he was rather alarmed by what he had found, and felt that it was, while he was not an American citizen, felt it was his duty to continue to pursue what he had uncovered." Steele did not hand over a copy of the dossier to Kramer in London, but he arranged for Glenn Simpson to get him a copy on Kramer's return to the United States. Kramer affirmed that both Steele and Simpson knew that Kramer was going to give a copy of the dossier to Senator McCain. When asked why Steele wanted McCain to bring the dossier to the FBI, when Steele had already met with the FBI to discuss it, Kramer answered that "having Senator McCain provide it [the Steele dossier] to the FBI would give it a little more oomph than it had had up until that point." When asked why Steele and Simpson preferred McCain to take the Steele dossier to the FBI, rather than Senator Chuck Schumer, a Democrat, Kramer answered, "I think they [Simpson and Steele] felt a senior Republican was better to be the recipient of this rather than a Democrat because if it were a Democrat, I think the view was that it would have been a political attack." These answers further confirm that Steele and Simpson were pursuing a strategy to legitimate the Trump dossier by having it brought to the FBI, DOJ, and State Department through trusted top-level agency personnel or trusted sources such as John McCain, a GOP senator widely known to dislike Donald Trump.

Kramer testified that he handed over the Steele dossier on November 30, 2016. On December 10, 2016, McCain arranged a private meeting with then FBI director James Comey to hand over the dossier.

Kramer admitted that after December 10, 2016, though he could not recall exact dates, he shared the Steele dossier with the news media, including reporter David Corn at *Mother Jones*; World Affairs Editor Julian Borger at the *Guardian* in London; reporters Matthew Mosk and Brian Ross at ABC News; Moscow reporter Alan Cullison with the *Wall Street Journal*; reporter Peter Stone at McClatchy, investigative reporter Bob Little at NPR (National Public Radio); reporters Tom Hamburger and Rosalind S. Helderman at *Washington Post*; reporter Ken Bensinger at BuzzFeed; and, at Steele's specific request, investigative reporter Carl Bernstein of Watergate fame. On January 10, 2017, ten days before Trump's inauguration as president, as Kramer was meeting with Borger from the *Guardian*, he learned that CNN and BuzzFeed had broken the story, with BuzzFeed publishing an unredacted version of the document on its website. BuzzFeed reported in an article published on January 10, 2017, that the Trump dossier contained allegations that the Russian government had been "cultivating, supporting, and assisting" then president-elect Donald Trump for years.[47] In his deposition, Kramer affirmed that Steele provided hard copies of the Steele dossier to many of the journalists with whom he met.[48]

After Clinton lost the 2016 election, Simpson and Steele decided they would make the Steele dossier the centerpiece of the Democrats' effort to impeach Trump. After the November 2016 election, the tag team of Simpson and Steele devised a strategy to leak the Steele dossier to the mainstream media to stimulate widespread public acceptance of

---

47 Ken Bensinger, Miriam Elder, and Mark Schoofs, "These Reports Allege Trump Has Deep Ties to Russia," BuzzFeed, January 10, 2017, https://www.buzzfeed.com/kenbensinger/these-reports-allege-trump-has-deep-ties-to-russia?utm_term=.clnE9oeA73#.ikvEvq4lyw. The same day, BuzzFeed published Christopher Steele's Fusion GPS "Russia dossier" on Trump on the internet. See https://www.documentcloud.org/documents/3259984-Trump-Intelligence-Allegations.html.

48 Adam Shaw, "Court Files Reveal Role of McCain, Associate in Spreading Anti-Trump Dossier," Fox News, March 15, 2019, https://www.foxnews.com/politics/court-files-reveal-role-of-mccain-aide-in-spreading-anti-trump-dossier.

the lies at the heart of their unverified and salacious opposition research against Trump.

In summary, before the election, Steele leaked the dossier to Michael Isikoff at Yahoo! News, trusting that Isikoff would publish information from it as if the information had been independently corroborated. This assisted the FBI and the DOJ in their efforts to open a counterintelligence investigation against Trump, and also gave them the ammunition to pad their FISA court application with a published news source that gave the information in the Steele dossier the patina of independent media corroboration and verification. Then, in December 2016, after Clinton lost the election, Simpson peddled the Steele dossier through the offices of Senator John McCain to a large number of mainstream media known to dislike Trump. The goal then was to plant the Russia-collusion narrative firmly in the mainstream media, setting up the premise after the election that Trump was a Russian asset—a Russian spy—who needed to be impeached before he had served out his first term in office as president of the United States in order to preserve the national security of the United States.

In December 2016, McCain handed then FBI director Comey a copy of the Steele dossier, evidently not knowing that Comey already had various drafts of Steele's work, provided by Steele through FBI and DOJ channels as the dossier was being written.

Chapter Three

THE STEELE DOSSIER
AT CENTER STAGE

Selecting British foreign intelligence agent Christopher Steele to write the dossier was only the first part of the task before Hillary Clinton. Her goal was not finished until Glenn Simpson and Steele worked together to peddle the dossier to the FBI and DOJ, giving them "proof" of Trump's treachery and justification to conduct electronic surveillance on his presidential campaign.

Simpson and Steele's other mission was to leak the contents of the Steele dossier to the mainstream media, paying particular attention to journalists known to be Clinton partisans. Here, the goal was to get before the American public the narrative that Trump had been working with Russia to steal the 2016 election from Clinton. Given their blind determination that Clinton was heir apparent to the 2016 presidency, those working on the Clinton campaign had confidence that the public would accept the narrative the mainstream media fed them—whether it was true or not.

Simpson and Steele Prepare to Peddle Their Anti-Trump Dossier

According to closed-door testimony before the House Judiciary Committee in joint session with the House Oversight and Government Reform Committee, Bruce Ohr, a senior officer within Obama's DOJ, admitted that he and Steele first met in 2007, when Steele was still with MI6. At that time, Ohr had traveled to London to talk with British government officials about Russian organized crime; the FBI office at the U.S. embassy in London set up the meeting. Ohr next saw Steele in 2008, at an international conference in London on the subject of Russian organized crime. Subsequent to 2008, Ohr stayed in touch with Steele; they had lunch together when possible and otherwise communicated by telephone and email.[49]

As we shall see in the next few paragraphs, Bruce Ohr and his wife, Nellie, played a major role in the DOJ's clandestine involvement in the Steele dossier scandal. Until Ohr's multiple secret meetings with Steele in 2016 started becoming public knowledge in 2017, Ohr did his best to remain silent about the role he played in promoting the Steele dossier to the FBI and DOJ. What we now know is that Ohr parlayed his experience in racketeering prosecutions into a senior position within the DOJ. In 2016, he held one of the top positions within the DOJ; he was the associate deputy attorney general. When the role Ohr played with Steele—and the fact that Nellie was an employee of Fusion GPS—became publicly known, Ohr was demoted. In December 2017, Ohr lost his position as associate deputy attorney general but retained an important position at the DOJ, serving as director of the Organized Crime Drug Enforcement Task Force (OCDEFT).[50] Finally, in January 2018, Ohr lost his job as head of that task force because he had concealed his direct involvement with Steele.[51] As of this writing, Ohr is still employed by the DOJ.

---

49 "Interview of Bruce Ohr," Executive Session, Committee on the Judiciary, Joint with the Committee on Government Reform and Oversight, U.S. House of Representatives, Washington, D.C., August 28, 2018. Transcript made public by GOP Representative Doug Collins of Georgia.

50 Jake Gibson, "Top DOJ Official Demoted amid Probe of Contacts with Trump Dossier Firm," Fox News, December 7, 2017, https://www.foxnews.com/politics/top-doj-official-demoted-amid-probe-of-contacts-with-trump-dossier-firm.

51 Jake Gibson, "DOJ Official Who Concealed Meetings with Trump Dossier Figures Loses Another Job Title," Fox News, January 8, 2018, https://www.foxnews.com/politics/doj-official-who-concealed-meetings-with-trump-dossier-figures-loses-another-job-title.

On June 20, 2016, Steele submitted his first report—alleging that the Russians had compromising material on Trump—to Fusion GPS. On July 5, 2016, ironically the same day FBI Director James Comey made his public statement announcing Hillary Clinton would not be prosecuted for using a private email server, Michael Gaeta, the FBI agent who headed the FBI's Eurasian crime squad, traveled to London to meet with Steele in the Orbis offices. Gaeta also served as an assistant legal attaché at the U.S. embassy in Rome, where he had met previously with Steele in 2010, during Steele's investigation into FIFA corruption.[52] Steele sought the London meeting in July 2016 to share with the FBI his concocted misinformation designed to "prove" that Putin owned Trump. Simpson and Steele strategized to launder the Trump dossier to the FBI through their contacts at the State Department (such as Victoria Nuland, as we will see in a moment) and the DOJ (through Bruce Ohr). But the meeting with Gaeta in Rome also shows that Simpson and Steele were keen to establish a relationship with Gaeta as Steele's FBI "handler." Gaeta played a peripheral but important role in the Simpson-Steele plan to legitimate their unverified dossier.

Gaeta worked closely with Victoria Nuland, who in 2016 was assistant secretary of state for European and Eurasian affairs. Though she ultimately became a Clinton loyalist, Nuland had served as the principal foreign policy advisor to Vice President Dick Cheney, a position that gave her credentials with Republicans in Washington. Knowing they would attract Nuland's attention by meeting in Rome with Gaeta, Simpson and Steele advanced their plan for their dossier to gain credibility by advancing it through career officials in both the DOJ and the State Department.[53] Nuland is married to Robert Kagan, a foreign policy expert who is a senior fellow at the Brookings Institute and a member of the Council of Foreign

---

52 Rowan Scarborough, "Obama Aide Started Christopher Steele-FBI Alliance," *Washington Times*, March 13, 2018, https://www.washingtontimes.com/news/2018/mar/13/obama-aide-started-christopher-steele-fbi-alliance/.

53 Jeff Carlson, "Little-Known FBI Unit Played Major Role Disseminating Steele Dossier," *The Epoch Times*, August 31, 2018, https://www.theepochtimes.com/how-a-little-known-fbi-unit-helped-to-disseminate-the-steele-dossier_2638330.html.

Relations. Kagan disassociated himself from the GOP and became a Clinton supporter in 2016, largely in reaction to the political rise of Trump whom he characterized as a Frankenstein monster and compared to Napoleon for his embrace of nationalism.[54] Kagan supported Hillary Clinton for president in 2016. He celebrated his change of allegiance in an opinion piece he wrote in the *Washington Post* in which he characterized Donald Trump as a "fascist."[55]

Well versed in the bureaucratic machinations of Washington, Simpson and Steele must have known that Gaeta (FBI) was required to get Nuland's permission (State Department) to attend the Rome meeting. Sworn in as assistant secretary of state for European and Eurasian affairs on September 18, 2013, Nuland had a history of working closely with Secretary of State Kerry. Nuland gave Gaeta permission, familiar and comfortable with Steele because of the many Steele reports she had previously read. Appearing on CBS News's *Face the Nation* on February 4, 2018, Nuland explained that after debriefing Gaeta on his meeting with Steele in London in July 2016, she made sure the information was passed onto the FBI. "He [Steele] passed two to four pages of short points of what he was finding, and our immediate reaction to that was, 'This is not in our purview. This needs to go to the FBI, if there is concern here that one candidate or the election as a whole might be influenced by the Russian Federation. That is something for the FBI to investigate.'"[56] This advanced the Simpson-Steele strategy by having information from the scurrilous

---

54 Robert Kagan, "Trump Is the GOP's Frankenstein Monster. Now He's Strong Enough to Destroy the Party," *Washington Post*, op-ed, February 25, 2016, https://www.washingtonpost.com/opinions/trump-is-the-gops-frankenstein-monster-now-hes-strong-enough-to-destroy-the-party/2016/02/25/3e443f28-dbc1-11e5-925f-1d10062cc82d_story.html.

55 Robert Kagan, "This is How Fascism Comes to America," *Washington Post*, May 18, 2016, https://www.washingtonpost.com/opinions/this-is-how-fascism-comes-to-america/2016/05/17/c4e32c58-1c47-11e6-8c7b-6931e66333e7_story.html.

56 Emily Tillett, "Victoria Nuland Says Obama State Dept. Informed FBI of Reporting from Steele Dossier," CBS News, February 4, 2018, https://www.cbsnews.com/news/victoria-nuland-says-obama-state-dept-informed-fbi-of-reporting-from-steele-dossier/.

dossier passed to the FBI through Ohr, a top-ranking official in the Justice Department, and through Nuland, a top-ranking career official in the State Department. In September 2016, Gaeta returned to Rome, where Steele handed him an unfinished but more complete dossier to deliver to the FBI's Eurasian crime squad, with another copy going to Nuland at the State Department. Among the additions to the Steele dossier were allegations that Trump was complicit in Russia stealing the DNC emails that Julian Assange and WikiLeaks began making public on July 22, 2016.[57]

On June 10, 2019, the conservative nonprofit Judicial Watch released forty-three pages of documents obtained under a Freedom of Information Act (FOIA) request. These documents show how Jonathan Winer, the State Department's special envoy for Libya, also played a key role in facilitating Steele's access to top State Department officials, as well as to prominent business executives. For some ten years, from 1985 to 1994, Winer, educated as a lawyer, served as legal counsel and principal legislative assistant to Kerry in the Senate. From 1994 to 2000, Winer was at the State Department serving as deputy assistant secretary for law enforcement and crime. Leaving the State Department, Winer worked from 2000 to 2008 in the Washington office of Alston & Bird LLP, an international law firm with offices in London, Brussels, and Beijing. From 2008 to 2013, Winer worked for APCO Worldwide, a global public affairs and strategic communications consulting firm. Brought back to the State Department in September 2013, after Kerry became secretary of state, Winer assumed his position as special envoy to Libya in the State Department's Bureau of Near Eastern Affairs.[58] Please also file away the interesting detail that Winer in his private law practice took on as a client Bill Browder, an investor whose activities in Russia we will discuss at length in Chapter 9. Winer, it turns out, was one of the key early architects of what became known as the Magnitsky Act, a U.S. law that forms the centerpiece of the intrigue surrounding the now-famous Trump Tower meeting between various Russians and Trump campaign officials including Donald Trump,

---

57   Andrew C. McCarthy, *Ball of Collusion: Rig an Election and Destroy a Presidency* (New York: Encounter Books, 2019), Chapter Nine.

58   "John Winer: Biography," State Department Website, no date, https://2009-2017.state.gov/r/pa/ei/biog/bureau/240474.htm.

Jr., Trump's son-in-law Jared Kushner, and Trump campaign manager Paul Manafort, a meeting that we shall discuss at length in Chapter 9.[59]

Winer also had a history with Steele. Winer and Steele had known each other since 2009 when each was in private international affairs consulting trade. When Winer returned to the State Department in 2013, Steele offered to circulate to him reports he was writing on Russia. In 2014 and 2015, Steele's reports were a hot commodity (especially to Winer who was getting the reports from Steele at no cost), given Steele's intelligence background with Russia and the crisis brewing at that time between Russia and Ukraine, a subject upon which Steele could claim international expertise.[60]

In September 2016, Winer and Steele met in Washington to discuss the information Steele had developed on Trump. This meeting was nothing out of the ordinary given that from 2013 to 2015, Winer had widely circulated some one hundred of Steele's previous reports within the State Department. In particular, he made sure that Steele's reports on Russia and Ukraine were sent to the desks of both Nuland and Secretary of State Kerry. "In a series of emails on November 20, 2014, Winer openly acts as a liaison for Steele, attempting to set up meetings for 'Chris' and referencing 'Three Orbis Reports' in the subject line of the email," Judicial Watch noted. "These documents show that Fusion GPS and Clinton spy Christopher Steele had a close relationship with the Obama State Department."[61] Nuland has admitted to receiving an early version of the Steele dossier in July 2016, which would coincide with Ohr's first in-person meeting with

---

59 Jonathan M. Winer, "Putin's Proposed Deal with Trump: An Offer America Can Only Refuse," *The Daily Beast*, July 19, 2018, https://www.thedailybeast.com/putins-proposed-deal-with-trump-an-offer-america-can-only-refuse.

60 Eric Felten, "Was Christopher Steele Disseminating Russian Disinformation to the State Department?" *Washington Examiner*, September 14, 2018, https://www.washingtonexaminer.com/weekly-standard/was-christopher-steele-disseminating-russian-disinformation-to-the-fbi.

61 "Judicial Watch Releases State Department Emails Showing Dossier Author Christopher Steele's Close Relationship with State Department," Judicial Watch, June 10, 2019, https://www.judicialwatch.org/press-room/press-releases/judicial-watch-releases-state-department-emails-showing-dossier-author-christopher-steeles-close-relationship-with-state-department/.

Steele over breakfast at the Mayflower Hotel in Washington, D.C., on July 30, 2016. This meeting was also attended by Ohr's wife, Nellie, at that time an unnamed employee of Fusion GPS and through that employment relationship a Steele associate.

Steele had to know his dossier was not the only opposition research being circulated by Clinton partisans to damage Trump. This was proved by the op-ed that Winer wrote in February 2018, affirming that long-time Clinton confidant Sidney Blumenthal and former journalist Cody Shearer had approached Winer with separate dossiers. Ultimately, Steele incorporated into his evolving dossier material developed by Blumenthal and Shearer. Note that Steele was not "the author" of his dossier in that as the dossier evolved in its many different versions, Steele was willing to incorporate without independent verification material developed by others, including Blumenthal and Shearer.

Blumenthal had served as an aide to President Bill Clinton from 1997 to 2001, but was blocked from joining Hillary Clinton at the State Department because Obama administration officials were still bristling over the role Blumenthal played in the 2008 presidential campaign starting the rumors Obama was not born in the United States. Though he had no official position with the Clintons, records show Blumenthal was paid at least $320,000 per year by the Clinton political machine. Known among the Clintons as a hatchet man, Blumenthal won the nickname "Vicious Sid" for the role he played smearing Monica Lewinsky. During Hillary's years as secretary of state, Blumenthal wrote some three hundred pages of emails to her, with a particularly controversial set of the emails dealing with Libya during the years Hillary participated in the internal conflict that ended with the murder of Muammar Gaddafi. Blumenthal also achieved distinction when Marcel Lazar, the original Guccifer, hacked his emails only to discover that Secretary Clinton was communicating over a private email server.[62]

---

62   Lisa Lerer and Matthew Lee, "A Man Blocked from Working at the State Department is at the Center of Hillary Clinton's Latest Controversy," Associated Press, May 22, 2015, https://www.businessinsider.com/sidney-blumenthal-is-at-the-center-of-hillary-clintons-latest-controversy-2015-5. See also: Micah Morrison, "Hillary Clinton's Rogue Agenda: Why Sid Blumenthal Matters," *New York Post*, October 31, 2015, https://nypost.com/2015/10/31/hillary-clintons-rogue-agenda-why-sid-blumenthal-matters/.

Cody Shearer's brother-in-law was Strobe Talbott, the Bill Clinton friend from Oxford who served during the Clinton administration in the State Department as an ambassador-at-large and special advisor to Secretary of State Warren Christopher on new independent states. During the Clinton administration, Nuland was chief of staff to Deputy Secretary of State Talbott. Described as an "unsanctioned diplomat, private eye, and Clinton flunky," Shearer entered the Clinton White House in 1992, introduced by Talbott. During his time at the White House, Shearer allegedly worked with Clinton enforcers to intimidate women who had accused Clinton of sexual harassment. Shearer has a history of the mysterious involvement in foreign affairs, including an effort in the 1990s to negotiate with Radovan Karadžić, the Bosnian-Serb president reputed to have orchestrated the mass killings—including the Srebrenica genocide—of Bosnian Muslims during the Yugoslavia wars. Shearer was in Libya with Blumenthal during the 2011 revolution, when Blumenthal was sending Hillary self-serving "intelligence" emails about Libya that left little disguised of Blumenthal's interest in capturing oil interests in the troubled country as a result of the internal turmoil that deposed Gaddafi.[63]

In his 2018 op-ed, Winer wrote: "In the summer of 2016, Steele told me that he had learned of disturbing information regarding possible ties between Donald Trump, his campaign, and senior Russian officials." Then, in late September 2016, Steele met in Washington with his "old friend," Sidney Blumenthal, whom Winer met some thirty years earlier, when Winer was reporting on the Iran-Contra affair for Senator Kerry and Blumenthal was a reporter at the *Washington Post*. Winer noted that at the time he met with Blumenthal in September 2016, the subject of Russian hacking was front and center in the 2016 presidential campaign. Recalling that meeting, Winer continued: "While talking about that hacking, Blumenthal and I discussed Steele's reports. He showed me notes gathered by a journalist I did not know, Cody Shearer, that alleged the Russians

63 Brendan Bordelon, "Meet Cody Shearer, the Strangest Character in Hillary's Vast Left-Wing Conspiracy," *National Review*, June 1, 2015, https://www.nationalreview.com/2015/06/meet-cody-shearer-strangest-character-hillarys-vast-left-wing-conspiracy-brendan/.

had comprising information on Trump of a sexual and financial nature."[64] After meeting with Blumenthal, Winer shared with Steele the dossier developed by Blumenthal and Shearer. In turn, Steele submitted part of the Blumenthal-Shearer dossier to the FBI to further substantiate his own investigation into the Trump campaign.[65]

By now, it should be apparent that Steele was adept at manipulating to his advantage a cozy network of interconnected Clinton loyalists with a long and complicated history of benefiting from their Clinton ties that has characterized much of Washington, D.C., since the 1990s. Steele played his extensive associations with this complicated network of Clinton cronies with the skill of a professional con man selling snake oil to marks too anxious for a cure—in this case, a cure for Donald Trump, whose startling political rise was viewed as loathsome for Clinton leftists prone to see Trump as an "America First" Nazi—a shifting view that Trump Derangement Syndrome made easily interchangeable with an accusation that Trump was a Russian spy. By now, it should be clear that Steele's play in this con game was his certainty that he could leverage his previous history with the FBI and the State Department to make credible to Trump-haters within the justice and foreign policy establishment his deceitful opposition research. Steele could be confident adding dirt from these Clinton operatives would only enhance his credibility to Trump-haters. Remarkably, Steele managed to peddle as true his dossier with an aura of credibility that would obviate the need for independent verification, despite the dossier's difficult-to-read accumulation of lies amounting to nothing more than deceitful opposition and hateful fabrications aimed at destroying Trump

---

64 Jonathan M. Winer, "Devin Nunes Is Investigating Me. Here's the Truth," *Washington Post*, February 8, 2018, https://www.washingtonpost.com/ opinions/devin-nunes-is-investigating-me-heres-the-truth/2018/02/08/ cc621170-0cf4-11e8-8b0d-891602206fb7_story.html?utm_term=. e7121f862a7d. See also: "Second Trump-Russia Dossier Being Assessed by FBI," *The Guardian*, January 30, 2018, https://www.theguardian.com/ us-news/2018/jan/30/trump-russia-collusion-fbi-cody-shearer-memo.

65 Lee Smith, "Unpacking the Other Clinton-Linked Russia Dossier," Real Clear Investigations, April 26, 2018, https://www.realclearinvestigations. com/articles/2018/04/25/test.html.

with outright calumny and innuendos suggesting sexual perversion and loyalty to Russia architected by Putin through "kompromat."

Please note that a key part of Simpson and Steele's desire to target Gaeta and Winer to launder their Trump dossier to the Obama administration was to give a diplomatic corps air of authenticity to it, a strategy Simpson and Steele had correctly calculated would reassure the DOJ and the FBI and get them to take the dossier seriously. Winer, as I will show later in this chapter, developed reasons to suspect the dossier was largely unverifiable. Yet, given the interest the Steele dossier piqued in Nuland, Winer chose to downplay his concerns. That the State Department and the DOJ seriously considered relying upon the Steele dossier without demanding independent corroboration shows just how anxious the Obama-controlled State Department and DOJ were to obtain dirt that could be used to block Trump from the presidency. With the State Department and the DOJ positioned to push the Steele dossier to the FBI, Simpson and Steele knew the FBI would be sufficiently reassured so as to be interested in looking at it, or at least to have an excuse for seriously considering the otherwise disgraceful dossier. The strategy was carefully designed to reassure the FBI to buy into the Steele dossier without feeling the need to undertake serious independent corroboration.

Beginning with the first memo dated June 20, 2016, through the completion of the Steele dossier dated December 13, 2016, Steele filed with Glenn Simpson at Fusion GPS a series of seventeen reports from various, often unspecified sources, totaling thirty-five pages. Steele's accusations against Trump included openly salacious claims, with one memo describing Trump's "personal obsessions and sexual perversion" during his 2013 stay at Moscow's Ritz-Carlton hotel for the Miss Universe pageant, which involved an incident with prostitutes. Steele reported that Trump booked the presidential suite at the hotel, "where he knew President and Mrs. Obama (whom he hated) had stayed on one of their official trips to Russia." The memo continued to report that Trump had "defiled" the Obamas' bed by getting a number of prostitutes to urinate on him, performing "a 'golden showers' show in front of him." The memo also claimed: "The hotel was known to be under FSB [Russia's main security agency responsible for counterintelligence operations] control with microphones and concealed cameras in all the main rooms to record anything they wanted to."

Steele's reports led readers to conclude that Trump had been colluding with Russia, with both sides trading favors, in a series of lucrative real estate and development business deals in Russia, especially in connection with the 2018 World Cup, which was hosted by Russia. This, plus various claims Trump had worked with Russian oligarchs to convince Putin to allow Trump to build a Trump Tower in Moscow, set up the basis for arguing that Putin had "compromised" Trump. The suggestion was that Putin could control and blackmail Trump by threatening to disclose intimate details of Trump's dealings over many years in Russia. The reports concluded by alleging that Trump had coordinated with Russia on the hacking operation against the Clinton campaign, with Trump secretly paying for it.[66]

In an interview with Bloomberg Politics in January 2017, Putin ridiculed the "golden pee" allegations against Trump. "[Trump] is a grown man, and secondly he's someone who has been involved with beauty contests for many years and has met the most beautiful women in the world," Putin said. "I find it hard to believe that he rushed to some hotel to meet girls of loose morals, although ours are undoubtedly the best in the world."[67]

Bruce Ohr Is Conflicted Over His Wife's Work for Fusion GPS

As noted previously, in his closed-door testimony before the House Judiciary Committee in joint session with the House Oversight and Government

---

66   Luke Harding, "How Trump Walked into Putin's Web," op. cit.

67   Olga Tanas, Henry Meyer, and Ilya Arkhipov, "Putin Says He Doesn't Believe Trump Met Prostitutes in Russia," Bloomberg Politics, January 17, 2017, https://www.bloomberg.com/news/articles/2017-01-17/putin-says-he-doesn-t-believe-trump-met-prostitutes-in-russia. See also: Zack Beauchamp, "Vladimir Putin Thinks Russian Prostitutes Are 'Undoubtedly the Best in the World,'" *Vox*, January 17, 2017, https://www.vox.com/world/2017/1/17/14296414/putin-trump-russian-prostitutes-yes-really.

Reform Committee on August 28, 2018, Bruce Ohr detailed a relationship with Christopher Steele that went back to their first meeting in 2007 at a London conference on Russian organized crime, while Steele was still an MI6 spy. In the transcript of Ohr's testimony, it appears that Ohr tried to pass off his conversations in 2016 with Simpson and Steele as just being part of his job. "Well, my job, for a long time, included responsibility for the organized crime program at the Department of Justice," Ohr explained. "And so, for many years, I had been overseeing investigations and meeting with people, talking about organized crime." Ohr commented that it was in this context that he first met Steele, Simpson, and other unspecified people.

"And from time to time, these people would give me information about Russian oligarchs and other Russian organized crime figures, and I would then pass that on to the FBI or introduce people to the FBI so they could continue," Ohr testified. He went on to admit that in 2016, he received information from both Simpson and Steele on the Fusion GPS investigation into Donald Trump.

Emails document that as early as January 12, 2016, when Steele sent Ohr a New Year's greeting, he brought up the case of Oleg Deripaska—the Russian billionaire aluminum magnate and close associate of Vladimir Putin—who at that time was trying to get a visa to visit the United States to attend an Asia-Pacific economic meeting. As reported by Byron York, the chief political correspondent for the *Washington Examiner*, the United States had revoked Deripaska's visa on suspicion of his involvement with organized crime.[68] Deripaska had ties with former senator John McCain and Paul Manafort, the former Trump campaign manager who Mueller prosecuted for tax evasion regarding offshore banking accounts that Manafort maintained from his work overseas, including his work in Ukraine.

The complicated Deripaska saga includes a particularly sordid chapter featuring former Senator Robert Dole, a distinguished GOP statesman who

---

68 Byron York, "Emails Show 2016 Links among Steele, Ohr, Simpson—with Russian Oligarch in Background," *Washington Examiner*, August 8, 2018, https://www.washingtonexaminer.com/news/emails-show-2016-links-among-steele-ohr-simpson-with-russian-oligarch-in-background.

was the Republican candidate for president in 1996 and the candidate for vice president in 1976. At one time, Deripaska hired Dole to lobby for his ability to return to the United States. For the purposes of this book, it is sufficient to note that Christopher Steele's political sympathies were not so determinedly anti-Putin as we might believe from his hatred of Trump, as evidenced by his willingness to do Deripaska's bidding as a hired gun.

The Steele-Ohr emails dated July 1, 2016, contain the first mention of Donald Trump. "I am seeing [redacted] in London next week to discuss ongoing business," Steele wrote to Ohr, "but there is something separate I wanted to discuss with you informally and separately. It concerns our favorite business tycoon!" Ohr testified that he presumed "our favorite business tycoon" was Oleg Deripaska because Steele had never talked to him about Trump before the breakfast meeting subsequently arranged at the Mayflower Hotel. In September 2015, Ohr and some FBI agents met with Deripaska in New York to seek the Russian oligarch's help on organized crime investigations. Steele facilitated that meeting through his Orbis Business Intelligence firm that a law firm hired as a subcontractor in the law firm's defense of a lawsuit filed by a Deripaska business rival. From 2009 to 2011, Deripaska cooperated with the FBI, spending a reported $25 million of his own money on an FBI-supervised operation to rescue FBI agent Robert Levinson, who was captured in Iran while working as a CIA contractor.[69] Deripaska tried to dissuade the FBI from thinking that Trump and Russia were colluding during the 2016 election. Deripaska gained visa entry to the United States from 2009 to 2017, when he was cooperating with the FBI. He was banned again in April 2018 as one of several Russians sanctioned by President Trump for meddling in the 2016 election in the United States.[70]

On Saturday, July 30, 2016, Ohr and Nellie met with Steele for breakfast at the Mayflower Hotel in Washington. This date is important because it is the day before the FBI initiated Operation Crossfire Hurricane, a

---

69 John Solomon, "Russian Oligarch, Justice Department, and a Clear Case of Collusion," *The Hill*, August 28, 2018, https://thehill.com/hilltv/rising/404061-russian-oligarch-justice-department-and-a-clear-case-of-collusion.

70 Ibid.

counterintelligence investigation into the links between the Russian government and the Trump campaign.[71] The date is also important because Donald Trump had received the GOP nomination for president only a few days prior, on July 19, 2016, at the Republican National Convention in Cleveland, Ohio. On the date Steele met with the Ohrs at the Mayflower, Steele had no doubt that his mission was to use the dossier to derail Trump's candidacy.

Until Bruce Ohr's testimony to the House committees, it was not known publicly that his wife worked for Fusion GPS. Glenn Simpson hired Nellie Ohr in 2015, before Simpson contracted with Perkins Coie and before Fusion GPS hired Steele. Nellie Ohr continued working with Fusion GPS after Steele was hired. Subsequently, in her own testimony before the House Judiciary Committee in joint session with the House Oversight and Government Reform Committee, she confirmed that when Simpson hired her at Fusion GPS, he knew that her husband worked at the DOJ.[72] In response to questions by House committee members, Bruce Ohr admitted that he had not been open with his supervisors at the DOJ about the fact that his wife was working at Fusion GPS, nor did he go out of his way to share this information openly with the FBI. Deputy Attorney General Rod Rosenstein did not know until October 2017 that Ohr's wife worked for Fusion GPS. Two months later, Ohr was demoted.[73]

---

71 Jerry Dunleavy, "Nellie Ohr Met Christopher Steele at Mayflower Hotel the Day Before FBI's Trump-Russia Investigation Began," *Washington Examiner*, March 28, 2019, https://www.washingtonexaminer.com/news/nellie-ohr-transcript-reveals-details-from-steele-meeting-one-day-before-trump-russia-investigation-began.

72 Testimony of Nellie Ohr, Executive Session, Committee on the Judiciary, Joint with the Committee on Government Reform, U.S. House of Representatives, Washington, D.C., October 19, 2018.

73 Margot Cleveland, "11 Key Things Inside The House Interview with Spygate Figure Bruce Ohr," *The Federalist*, March 11, 2019, https://thefederalist.com/2019/03/11/11-key-things-inside-house-interview-spygate-figure-bruce-ohr/.

Also important, Ohr testified that at the Mayflower Hotel breakfast Steele told him that a former head of the Russian Foreign Intelligence Service, Russia's external intelligence agency known as the SVR, had Donald Trump "over a barrel." Ohr also said at the breakfast meeting Steele told him that Carter Page had met with high-level Russian officials when he was in Moscow. While a detailed discussion of Page is reserved for the next chapter, it is important to note here that Steele was dropping information on Page in this first meeting on July 30, 2016, at the Mayflower Hotel with the DOJ's Bruce Ohr, a meeting Steele had set up in order to get the dossier information to the FBI in a credible fashion. Ohr should have realized the importance of this information in that Trump had announced in a meeting with the *Washington Post* editorial board on March 21, 2016 that Page was a foreign policy advisor to his campaign.

Ohr claimed that the meeting at the Mayflower Hotel was the first time he learned that Steele was working for Fusion GPS to dig up dirt on Russia to discredit Trump. During the discussion at breakfast, Ohr claimed he and Nellie both realized she was working on some of the same Russian figures as Steele. "At some point, I became aware that some of the people she [Nellie Ohr] was invest— [investigating] she was researching were some of the same people that I heard about from Chris Steele and Glenn Simpson," Ohr told Congress. Ohr insisted that Nellie was not hired by Fusion GPS specifically to research Trump's ties to Russia. "She was a Russia analyst, and she would research people and companies that Fusion GPS asked her to look into," Ohr testified. "She would do her research on the internet, open sources; and she would report her findings to Fusion GPS."

Ohr testified that Nellie Ohr, sometime in 2016 after the meeting with Steele at the Mayflower Hotel, gave her husband a thumb drive to hand over to the FBI that contained the research she had been doing for Fusion GPS on various Russian individuals. Ohr said he could not remember the exact date Nellie gave him the thumb drive. Ohr testified he handed the thumb drive over to the FBI without loading it on his own computer. He explained that he never opened any thumb drive someone gave him on his computer at work, deciding always to hand the thumb drive over to the FBI. "Nellie was present with me in the end of July, when I first heard Russian information—information relating to the Russian investigation from Chris Steele," Ohr told the House committees, referring to Nellie having attended his meeting with Steele at the Mayflower Hotel. "So she was present for some of that conversation. So she was certainly aware at that point that Chris Steele was giving me information about Russia."

Ohr's answers were evasive in that he claimed to not know precisely what assignments regarding Russia his wife was working on for Fusion GPS. "At some point, I don't remember when, I became aware that she was looking at some of the same figures as part of her work for Fusion GPS. And so it came up—again, I don't remember the exact date—where basically she was concerned that maybe the FBI might want her information as well, and so provided the information to me." Ohr also claimed that even though he did not open the thumb drive on his computer at work, he assumed it contained information on Russia that Nellie had developed in her work for Fusion GPS.

Documents obtained by Judicial Watch revealed that on December 5, 2016, approximately one month after the 2016 election, Ohr turned over to the FBI a spreadsheet prepared by his wife that listed eighty different people and groups, many affiliated with Russia, whom Nellie was tracking for Fusion GPS. The spreadsheet showed linkages between some forty of those listed on the spreadsheet and Trump and his family. Those scrutinized by Nellie for their "linkages" to Trump included global businessmen, lobbyists, and other figures alleged to have ties to Russian organized crime and Russian intelligence agencies.[74] Clearly, Ohr's attempts in his congressional testimony to distance himself from his wife's Trump-Russia investigation for Fusion GPS were fabrications designed to protect himself. After Hillary lost, Ohr appears to have lost all restraint, evidently determined to make sure the FBI had access to his

---

74 Jerry Dunleavy, "Hundreds of Pages of Emails Show Nellie Ohr Researched Trump-Russia Connections," *Washington Examiner*, August 25, 2019, https://www.washingtonexaminer.com/news/hundreds-of-pages-of-emails-show-nellie-ohr-researched-trump-russia-connections.

wife's extensive research into possible Russian collusion to use in their counterintelligence investigation aimed at removing Trump from office.

When pressed to give a more complete list of people at the FBI whom he had contacted, Ohr testified that, on July 30, 2016, following that morning's breakfast meeting with Steele, he debriefed the FBI's Andrew McCabe, Peter Strzok, and Lisa Page—key figures in the "Spygate" aspect of the coup d'état attempt that we will examine in detail in the next chapter. Ohr also mentioned that he shared this information with Andrew Weissmann, who was then heading the criminal fraud section of the DOJ. In the first chapter, I mentioned Weissmann as the prosecutor I believe prompted Mueller to give his press conference on May 29, 2019—most likely because Weissmann was disappointed that President Trump claimed to have been "exonerated" by the Mueller report. Weissmann, regarded by many as "Mueller's pit bull," is a prosecutor whom former Assistant U.S. Attorney Sidney Powell has charged with misconduct in litigating the Enron case. Ohr also disclosed that he referred the material to Bruce Swartz, the counselor for international affairs in the Criminal Division of the FBI. In the final analysis, Ohr must have understood that the information he was getting from Simpson and Steele, supplemented by information developed by his wife, was aimed at destroying Trump. That he turned over his wife's Fusion GPS spreadsheet after Hillary lost—information Nellie designed to suggest Russia was trying to influence the Trump campaign in order to make sure Clinton lost the U.S. election—is another indication of Ohr's animus against Trump.

Ohr testified that in addition to his various meetings with Steele, he had two in-person meetings with Simpson, the first on August 22, 2016, and the second on December 10, 2016, after the election. In the second meeting, Simpson handed Ohr a thumb drive containing more information about the contacts between Russia and the Trump campaign. (This was a second thumb drive, different from the one Ohr testified that his wife Nellie had given him.) The second thumb drive is important because it documents DOJ interest in the Steele dossier even after the November 2016 election. Also important is that Ohr's December 2016 meeting with Simpson occurred the month after Steele had been fired by the FBI. As we shall see later in this chapter, Steele had entered into a contract with the FBI in February 2016, agreeing to be a confidential human source for the FBI during the 2016 presidential election cycle. This was several months prior to Simpson subcontracting with Steele's firm Orbis in order to retain Steele to write what became known as the "Steele dossier."

Ohr claimed he turned this second thumb drive Simpson gave him in the December 2016 meeting over to the FBI, again not opening it first on his computer at work to examine the contents. Ohr also testified that he suspected Simpson's thumb drive contained the completed dossier on Donald Trump. "This was in December," Ohr testified. "The rest of the conversation had to do with additional information that he [Simpson] had gathered about the possible connections between the Russian Government and the Trump campaign, and he gives me a thumb drive." Ohr continued: "I think the natural assumption at that point—I had not seen the dossier. I had heard there was such a thing as a dossier, but I hadn't seen it. So he gives me a thumb drive. I assumed this was the dossier." Again, Ohr insisting he did not see the "completed" Steele dossier until after the election might be the case, but the implication that he did not see until after the election any versions of the Steele dossier in progress is not credible.

Ohr's testimony that he met with Simpson on August 22, 2016, conflicts with Simpson's sworn testimony to the House Intelligence Committee on November 14, 2017, that he first met with Ohr after the 2016 election, around Thanksgiving.[75] This caused Republican Representative John Ratcliffe of Texas to assert that Simpson was in "real legal jeopardy" over this inconsistency.[76] On October 16, 2018, Simpson pleaded the Fifth Amendment when he appeared before the House Judiciary Committee in response to a subpoena, a move that disappointed

75 Interview with Glenn Simpson, Executive Session, Permanent Select Committee on Intelligence, U.S. House of Representatives, Washington, D.C., November 14, 2017.

76 Daniel Chaitin, "Fusion GPS Co-Founder Glenn Simpson in 'Real Legal Jeopardy,' GOP Investigator Says," *Washington Examiner*, October 14, 2018, https://www.washingtonexaminer.com/news/fusion-gps-co-founder-glenn-simpson-in-real-legal-jeopardy-gop-investigator-says.

Republicans on the committee who wanted to question him after he had given a deposition in the U.K. on the case.[77]

Although Ohr in his testimony to Congress repeatedly claimed that his memory was vague, he remembered learning from either Simpson or Steele that somebody associated with the Trump campaign had advance knowledge of when Julian Assange and WikiLeaks planned to release hacked or stolen information from the Clinton campaign.

This is important because from my forty hours with Mueller's prosecutors, I can attest that this was a key issue. The Mueller prosecutors believed that Roger Stone's cryptic tweet on August 21, 2016, "It will soon [be John] Podesta's time in the barrel," reflected that Stone had advance knowledge that Assange would make public Podesta's emails—and that Stone got that information from me.

As I explained in the first chapter discussing the forty grueling hours of "voluntary interviews" I spent with Mueller's prosecutors in September and October 2018, the prosecutors were convinced that in July and August 2016, I had been in contact with Assange and had learned in advance Assange's plans regarding the DNC emails he yet had to make public. As I explained earlier, I have never had any contact with Assange or with WikiLeaks, either directly or indirectly. But Ohr's comment is interesting in that he must have gotten information from somewhere, possibly from either Simpson or Steele. Clearly, Ohr wanted to get on the record that he had information suggesting the Trump campaign knew in advance that WikiLeaks would make public Podesta's stolen emails in October. Ohr may also have told this to the Mueller prosecutors, giving them corroboration for their suspicion that Roger Stone also had the same advance knowledge—information that the Mueller prosecutors believed came from me. As far as I know, prior to October 2016, no one except for Assange and WikiLeaks had any advance knowledge of precisely what remaining emails Assange possessed, or of when he planned to make them

---

77 Kelly Cohen, "GPS Founder Glenn Simpson Pleads the Fifth before House Committees," *Washington Examiner*, October 16, 2018, https://www.washingtonexaminer.com/news/gps-founder-glenn-simpson-pleads-the-fifth-before-house-committees.

public. Unless Simpson and Steele passed onto Ohr advance knowledge from sources in touch directly with Assange, we were all just speculating. What is not speculation is that in order to make their case for Russian collusion, the Mueller prosecutors needed the argument that the Trump campaign had advance knowledge Assange was going to make public Podesta's emails in October. If they could not prove the advance knowledge argument, Mueller prosecutors were dead in the water on their Russia-collusion suppositions.

When various members of the House committees asked Ohr why he had chosen to act as an intermediary with Simpson and Steele, instead of directing them to the FBI, Ohr responded that his impression was that they were more comfortable talking to him than to the FBI. In the congressional questioning, Ohr presented himself as remarkably naïve in refusing to acknowledge that Simpson and Steele may have been using him to give the Steele dossier credibility to the FBI. Ohr clearly did not want to acknowledge to Congress the obvious: namely, that Simpson and Steele had used him to launder their anti-Trump disinformation to the FBI. But it remains the case that information from Simpson and Steele, passed to the DOJ and FBI through Ohr, appeared credible precisely because of Ohr's expertise on Russian organized crime and his prior relationship with Steele in dealing with Deripaska.

Ohr denied having any role in Fusion GPS's Russia investigation besides acting as a middleman. He insisted that his only role consisted of passing Simpson and Steele's information on to the contact agent the FBI had assigned to him, and as indicated above, to additional FBI officials as he felt was required. "My job as I saw it was to get the information over there [to the FBI] and let them figure it out," he said. But Ohr also appeared unbelievably naïve when asked if he had ever inquired of Simpson or Steele who was paying for the Fusion GPS research.

In an apparent effort to cover his role sanitizing the Steele dossier, Ohr insisted that when handing over to the FBI the information he had gathered from Simpson and/or Steele, he had warned the FBI that the information might not be reliable. "These guys [Simpson and Steele] were hired by somebody relating to—who's related to the Clinton campaign, and be aware—" Ohr said before being cut off by Representative Trey

Gowdy, who asked if Ohr had passed that information to the FBI. Ohr testified that he had done so. "I wanted them [the FBI] to be aware of any possible bias or, you know, as they evaluate the information, they need to know the circumstances," Ohr explained to Gowdy. Ohr testified that in 2016, he may have known that Simpson and Steele were paid by someone related to the Clinton campaign, but he did not know the DNC and the Clinton campaign had paid Perkins Coie, the law firm that then paid Fusion GPS, who in turn hired Christopher Steele.

In Ohr's testimony to Congress, his discomfort is obvious. Ohr had to know that he was deeply involved in a serious conflict of interest. What was clear was that Ohr was worried about the negative consequences to his DOJ career that could result once Congress and the public knew his wife was working for Fusion GPS to develop information that became part of the Steele dossier. Why else would he be less than forthcoming in his answers? Ohr was a career prosecutor who specialized in organized crime cases involving Russia and Eurasia. He had advanced through the ranks to head the Justice Department's Organized Crime and Racketeering Section. Prosecuting those cases successfully demanded skill in following the money. Ohr knew that Simpson and Steele did not work for nothing, and he could easily have figured out that if Steele was researching dirt about Russian involvement in the Trump campaign, it was likely that Hillary Clinton was paying for it, directly or indirectly.

Simpson was clever enough to appreciate the hold he had over Ohr, given that Fusion GPS was his wife's employer. Simpson had plausible deniability that he hired Nellie Ohr to get control over Bruce Ohr because he had hired Nellie well before Fusion GPS got the Perkins Coie contract. Simpson could argue that he kept her at the company after the contract only because she is a legitimate Russian expert who speaks fluent Russian. In interviewing Nellie for employment, Fusion GPS had to have confirmed that her husband held a top position in the DOJ. Clearly, that had to be a plus in the Fusion GPS decision to hire her.

Nellie Ohr: An Expert on Russia

The record confirms that the professional connections among Glenn Simpson, Bruce Ohr, and Nellie Ohr go deep. A report from the DOJ's

National Institute for Justice documents that in 2010, Simpson, Bruce, and Nellie attended an expert forum on international organized crime. The final report lists as participants Glenn Simpson, a senior fellow at the International Assessment and Strategy Center, a think tank in Alexandria, Virginia; Nellie Ohr, a researcher for Open Source Works in Washington, D.C., the CIA's in-house center devoted to the intelligence analysis of unclassified, open-source information; and Bruce Ohr, the chief of the organized crime and racketeering section in the Criminal Division of the Justice Department.[78]

Ohr organized that working group as part of his job at that time, when he was head of the organized crime and racketeering section of the U.S. Department of Justice's Criminal Division. Nellie identified herself as a researcher with the CIA's Open Source Works in Washington. Diana West, an expert on the subject of Russian infiltration into the United States going back to the Russian Revolution in 1917, noted that Open Source Works is "the in-house, open-source, analysis shop of the CIA." West has pointed out that Nellie's family background makes her a "daughter of the academic left." Nellie is the daughter of Dr. Kathleen Armstrong Hauke, a writer known for popularizing the works of African American journalist Ted Poston, who traveled to the Soviet Union with poet Langston Hughes in 1932.

The record also confirms that Nellie Ohr is indeed a Russia expert. In 1983, she earned a bachelor's degree in Russian history and literature from Harvard, where she met Bruce, who graduated from Harvard Law School in 1987. But after Fusion GPS got the Perkins Coie contract, Simpson clearly understood that Ohr was a particularly good choice to be his middleman in laundering the Steele dirt to the FBI. Ohr had to know his continued cooperation with Simpson and Steele would likely keep Nellie employed by Simpson's firm. Ohr obviously played along, hoping his

---

78 John T. Picarelli, "Expert Working Group Report on International Organized Crime," Document No. 230846, National Institute of Justice Discussion Paper, U.S. Department of Justice, June 2010, https://www.ncjrs.gov/pdffiles1/nij/230846.pdf.

conflict of interest over Nellie's employment situation (and his passing information from Nellie to Steele) would never be made public.

Nellie had the credentials not only to be a Russian expert, but also to hate Trump on ideological grounds. After her studies at Harvard, she received a doctorate in Russian history from Stanford after completing her 1990 thesis on collective farms under Stalin in the period from 1933 to 1937. Nellie's credentials include being a Russia scholar at the Wilson Center and a professor at Vassar College. Diana West, an expert on Russian penetration into the United States since the 1917 Russian Revolution, has concluded that Nellie is a "Stalin apologist."[79] West has documented that Nellie's "academic mission" was to get U.S. students to move past the terrorism of the Stalin era, during which Stalin is estimated to have murdered twenty to twenty-five million people, to appreciate "the excitement" of the Stalin experiment with Bolshevik agriculture. In 1989, Nellie spent time in Moscow at the Russian State Library doing research for her doctoral dissertation.

As noted earlier, in his testimony to the House committees, Ohr was reluctant to acknowledge to Congress that his wife was working on the Steele dossier. When asked directly if he had told the FBI that his wife was working on the Steele dossier and providing information, Ohr said he did not recall specifically what he had told the FBI. "I think she [Nellie] was working on the same topic, so you could say in a broader sense maybe. But the dossier itself, as far as I know, and I could be wrong, but those appear to be Chris Steele's reports, not Fusion GPS." The answer was clearly evasive because Ohr knew both Chris Steele and his wife Nellie worked for Fusion GPS and that information Nellie had developed on Trump for Fusion GPS had been passed onto Steele. "I don't know what information from my wife was given to Christopher Steele," Ohr testified. "I knew she was giving it to Fusion GPS, obviously." The distinction was tenuous at best.

---

79   Diana West, *The Red Thread: A Search for Ideological Drivers Inside the An-ti-Trump Conspiracy* (Washington, D.C.: Center for Security Policy Press, 2019), pp. 3-10.

In his testimony to Congress, Bruce Ohr was also careful not to disclose his personal political feelings, but it is hard to believe that he married Nellie without realizing her leftist leanings, or that he lived with Nellie while she was employed by Fusion GPS and was unaware that she was also involved in the project of digging up dirt in Russia about Trump. He acknowledged in his testimony that when he turned over to the FBI the thumb drive Nellie had given him, and again when he turned over the spreadsheet Nellie had given him after the election, he realized he was handing over information about Trump's contacts in Russia. Looked at objectively, Simpson and Steele both manipulated their past credentials in anti-Russian intelligence brilliantly, picking Ohr to broker to the FBI their unverified Russian disinformation and outright filthy lies.

Nellie Ohr was also quite evasive in her testimony to Congress. Republican Representative John Ratcliffe asked Nellie directly whether she realized at the Mayflower Hotel meeting with Steele that the work she was doing for Simpson at Fusion GPS was ultimately directed toward Steele. "In that moment, when you realized that [she and Steele were both working for Fusion GPS] at the breakfast, did it cross your mind that maybe the work you were doing for Fusion GPS, as it pertained to Donald Trump in your reports, had been communicated to Christopher Steele." Nellie in her answer tried unsuccessfully to dodge the question. "I probably didn't think that through," Nellie answered Radcliff. "I mean, I didn't think about it." Radcliff asked a follow-up question: "At some point in time, based on your husband's prior testimony, did it dawn on you that the work you had been doing maybe had been part of the information upon which Mr. Steele was relying or using in preparation of the dossier." Nellie again attempted to dodge the question. "Judging from the content of the dossier, it seems to be quite separate, but I don't know for sure," she responded. Ratcliffe pressed: "But at some point didn't you come to the conclusion that the research that you had been doing should be made known to the FBI because it had a connection to Christopher Steele?" Nellie insisted she did not know the content of the Steele dossier until after it was made public.

Under questioning by Republican representative Mark Meadows, Nellie reluctantly acknowledged there had been an "aha" moment during the

Mayflower Hotel breakfast meeting when she realized she and Steele were both working for Glenn Simpson and Fusion GPS. But when pressed with various of the claims in the Steele dossier, Nellie continued to deny the claims came from her research. She did, however, acknowledge that she understood that the fact that she was investigating for Fusion GPS various Trump ties to Russian crime figures suggested it was possible Trump had committed crimes in cahoots with Russian mobsters. Nellie Ohr hesitatingly admitted to the House Judiciary Committee in joint session with the House Committee on Oversight and Government Reform that she would have been reluctant to conduct opposition research on Hillary Clinton because she favored Hillary Clinton as a presidential candidate.

On May 1, 2019, Representative Mark Meadows submitted a criminal referral to the U.S. Justice Department, charging that Nellie Ohr had lied under oath in her testimony to the House Committee on the Judiciary and the House Committee on Oversight and Government Reform on October 19, 2018. Meadows noted that during her transcribed interview, Ms. Ohr had testified she did not have knowledge of the Department of Justice's investigations on Russia. She also denied that she shared her research on Russian organized crime and Donald Trump with individuals outside of Fusion GPS. Yet, Meadows insisted, documents reviewed by Congress raised concerns she shared her research on Trump and Russia with various DOJ officials.[80] In May 2019, Judicial Watch released 339 pages of "Hi Honey" emails from Nellie Ohr to her high-ranking DOJ husband, proving that Nellie Ohr sent "reams" of open-source intelligence

---

80 Mark Meadows, "Final Criminal Referral – Nellie Ohr 5.1.19," uploaded by John Solomon on May 2, 2019, Scribd.com, https://www. scribd.com/document/408347748/Final-Criminal-Referral-Nellie-Ohr-5-1-19. See also: Chaitin and Jerry Dunleavy, "Mark Meadows sends criminal referral targeting Nellie Ohr to DOJ," *Washington Examiner*, May 1, 2019, https://www.washingtonexaminer.com/news/ mark-meadows-sends-criminal-referral-targeting-nellie-ohr-to-doj.

to her husband and on various occasions to three DOJ prosecutors: Lisa Holtyn, Ivana Nizich, and Joseph Wheatley.[81]

Investigative reporter John Solomon singled out one Nellie Ohr email for comment. "Hi Honey, if you ever get a moment you might find the penultimate article interesting – especially the summary in the final paragraph," Nellie Ohr emailed to her husband on July 6, 2016, in what Solomon characterized as a typical communication. Solomon pointed out that the article and the paragraph Mrs. Ohr flagged suggested that Trump was "a Putin stooge." Nellie Ohr's email to her husband continued as follows: "If Putin wanted to concoct the ideal candidate to service his purposes, his laboratory creation would look like Donald Trump." Solomon concluded the following: "Such overt political content flowing into the emails of a DOJ charged with the nonpartisan mission of prosecuting crimes is jarring enough. It raises additional questions about potential conflict of interest when it is being injected by a spouse working as a Democratic contractor trying to defeat Trump, and she is forwarding her own research to her husband's department and co-workers."[82]

Everyone working with Simpson and Steele had to realize that the information being developed on Trump's ties to Russia was designed, despite its unverified nature, to destroy Trump's candidacy. What Simpson and Steele had correctly calculated was that Ohr and a top level of the DOJ were so biased against Trump that their lies would be received by him with open eyes. By sanitizing their information through Victoria Nuland at the State Department and Bruce Ohr at the DOJ, Simpson and Steele correctly calculated that Nuland and Ohr's credibility would obviate the need

---

81 "Judicial Watch: Nellie Ohr Deleted Emails Exchanged with DOJ Husband Bruce Ohr," Judicial Watch, May 16, 2019, https://www.judicialwatch.org/press-releases/judicial-watch-nellie-ohr-deleted-emails-exchanged-with-doj-husband-bruce-ohr/. Judicial Watch has archived the 399 Nellie Ohr emails at https://www.judicialwatch.org/wp-content/uploads/2019/03/JW-v-DOJ-Ohr-Steele-Fusion-GPS-00490.pdf.

82 John Solomon, "Nellie Ohr's 'Hi Honey' Emails to DOJ about Russia Collusion Should Alarm Us All," *The Hill*, May 1, 2019, https://thehill.com/opinion/white-house/441580-nellie-ohrs-hi-honey-emails-to-doj-about-russia-collusion-should-alarm-us.

for the anti-Trump biased FBI higher-ups to engage in a serious effort to corroborate and verify Steele's information independently. Put simply, Simpson and Steele sold their lying dossier to the Justice Department precisely because top officials in the DOJ, the FBI, and the State Department were Clinton partisans determined to deny Trump the presidency.

The FBI and DOJ Ignored Warnings Not to Trust the Steele Dossier

On May 7, 2019, investigative reporter John Solomon published a bombshell report in *The Hill*.[83] Solomon revealed that on October 11, 2016, Deputy Assistant Secretary of State for European and Eurasian Affairs Kathleen Kavalec had written a contemporaneous account of her meeting with Christopher Steele and Tatyana Duran, a colleague from Steele's Orbis firm, in which Kavalec raised questions about the veracity of the dossier's claims. Kavalec's notes documented that in the meeting, Steele admitted that his research for the Trump dossier was political, funded by Hillary Clinton's campaign, and that he had been given an Election Day deadline to get the information out.

The meeting between Kavalec and Steele happened just ten days before the FBI and DOJ used the discredited Steele dossier to secure a FISA Court warrant on October 11, 2016, authorizing electronic surveillance of Trump campaign advisor Carter Page to explore Trump campaign ties to Russia. Solomon noted that in their application to the FISA Court, the FBI swore that Steele's "reporting has been corroborated and used in criminal proceedings" and that the FBI has determined him to be "reliable" and was "unaware of any derogatory information pertaining" to their informant, who simultaneously worked for Fusion GPS, the firm

---

83 John Solomon, "Steele's Stunning Pre-FISA Confession: Informant Needed to Air Trump Dirt Before Election," *The Hill*, May 7, 2019, https://thehill. com/opinion/white-house/442592-steeles-stunning-pre-fisa-confession-informant-needed-to-air-trump-dirt#.XNIAVvr8PT0.twitter. See also: John Solomon, "FBI's Steele Story Falls Apart: False Intel and Media Contacts Were Flagged Before FISA," *The Hill*, May 9, 2019, https://thehill.com/ opinion/white-house/442944-fbis-steele-story-falls-apart-false-intel-and-media-contacts-were-flagged.

paid by the DNC and the Clinton campaign to find Russian dirt on Trump. Yet, Solomon notes, Kavalec needed just a single encounter with Steele to find one of his key claims about Trump-Russia collusion was blatantly false.

In her typed summary of the meeting with Steele, Kavalec wrote that Steele told her the Russians had constructed a "technical/human operation run out of Moscow targeting the election." The notes suggest this technical/human operation run out of Moscow had recruited émigrés in the United States to "do hacking and recruiting." She further quoted Steele as saying, "Payments to those recruited are made out of the Russian Consulate in Miami." Solomon commented that Kavalec bluntly debunked that claim by commenting: "It is important to note that there is no Russian consulate in Miami." Solomon concluded that alone should have been a flashing red alert notifying the State Department, the DOJ, and the FBI that Steele had fabricated claims in his anti-Trump dossier.

Also in the typed summary of the meeting with Steele, Kavalec wrote that Steele's client (the Clinton campaign) was anxious to see this information come to light before November 8, the date of the 2016 presidential election. As we have noted, the fact that the Steele dossier was opposition research funded by Clinton's campaign and the DNC was kept secret by the FBI and the DOJ, not disclosed in their application to the FISA Court. Solomon reported that Kavalec's October 11, 2016 meeting with Steele was most likely brokered by Jonathan Winer. The next day, Kavalec thanked Winer in an email that was released as part of a Citizens United FOIA request. "Thanks for bringing your friend by yesterday—it was very helpful," Kavalec emailed to Winer.[84]

---

84 John Solomon, "Steele's Stunning Pre-FISA Confession: Informant Needed to Air Trump Dirt Before Election," *The Hill*, May 7, 2019, https://thehill.com/opinion/white-house/442592-steeles-stunning-pre-fisa-confession-informant-needed-to-air-trump-dirt. See also: Jeff Carlson, "Steele's Meeting With US Official Casts Doubt on FBI's Official Story," *The Epoch Times*, June 14, 2019, https://www.theepochtimes.com/memo-shows-steele-revealed-bias-ahead-of-fisa-warrant_2922391.html.

Yet Solomon further reported that, according to the former chairman of the House Intelligence Committee, Republican Representative Devin Nunes of California, the Democrats did not supply the committee with a copy of the Kavalec memo. "They [the Democrats] tried to hide a lot of documents from us during our investigation, and it usually turns out there's a reason," Nunes told Solomon. Investigators with the Senate and House judiciary committees also affirmed to Solomon that they knew nothing about the Kavalec memo, even though they had investigated Steele's activities during and after the 2016 presidential election. The Kavalec memo is perhaps the one piece of documentary evidence establishing most clearly that the DOJ and FBI obtained the four FISA Court warrants illegally to conduct electronic surveillance on Carter Page. The Kavalec memo came to light only as a result of open-records litigation undertaken by Citizens United.[85]

Solomon reported that State Department officials had received a copy of the Steele dossier in July 2016 and a more detailed briefing in October 2016, presumably through the efforts of Winer. The State Department referred to the FBI the information obtained from Steele without mentioning Kavalec's reservations. Solomon noted that sources told him in 2018 that Kavalec had the most important (and memorialized) interaction with Steele before the FISA warrant was issued, but FBI and State Department officials refused to discuss the meeting, or even to confirm that the meeting had happened. The Kavalec memo constitutes proof that the government knew yet hid from the FISA Court not only that the harmful claims about Trump made in the Steele dossier were unverified and unlikely true, but also that the Clinton campaign and the DNC had paid for the Steele dossier through the contract Perkins Coie had negotiated with Fusion GPS.

"Orbis undertook the Russia/Trump connection at the behest of an institution he declined to identify that had been hacked," Kavalec wrote.

---

85 Daniel Chaitin, "DOJ Inspector General Found All Four Carter Page FISA Warrants Were Illegally Obtained, Joe diGenova Says," *Washington Examiner*, August 28, 2019, https://www.washingtonexaminer.com/news/doj-inspector-general-found-all-four-carter-page-fisa-warrants-were-illegally-obtained-joe-digenova-says.

But Solomon noted that the DNC was the highest-profile victim of election-year hacking, suggesting that Kavalec must have had a very good idea that Steele's client involved Hillary Clinton. "The institution approached them [Orbis and Steele] based on the recommendation of Glenn Simpson and Peter Fritsch [Orbis cofounder] and is keen to see this information come to light before November 8," Kavalec wrote. "Orbis undertook the investigation in June of 2016."

Solomon noted that everything else in the memo was redacted and that the FBI under Director Christopher Wray had classified the document as "secret" just a few days before Solomon published it, with a note from the FBI that the document was not scheduled to be declassified until 2041, twenty-five years after the 2016 election. "You may already have this information but wanted to pass it on just in case," Kavalec wrote as the lone sentence in an email sent two days after her meeting with Steele to alert others. But the names of the recipients, the subject line, and the attachments to that memo are all redacted. Solomon correctly concluded that the Kavalec memo and email, despite being heavily redacted, were the first written proof that the U.S. government knew well before the FBI secured the FISA warrant that Steele had a political motive and an election deadline to make the dossier public. Solomon also concluded that before the Carter Page FISA warrant was issued, Kavalec had transmitted her meeting memorandum to one or more people within the Obama administration whose jobs were so sensitive that their identity had to be protected.

Despite Kavalec's documenting that the Steele dossier lacked verification, evidence makes clear that even after Trump was elected president, Kavalec at the State Department and Bruce Ohr at the DOJ were both still very receptive to receiving dirt from Steele about Trump and Russia. This evidence was obtained in emails that Judicial Watch released on May 15, 2019. As reported by Judicial Watch, in a November 21, 2016 email exchange, Kavalec thanked Ohr for "coming by" to discuss the work of the Organized Crime Drug Enforcement Task Force. Kavalec provided Ohr with links to *Mother Jones* and OpenSecrets.org articles suggesting that a Russian American oil magnate gave money to Trump's campaign. Ohr responded, "I really hope we can get something going here....We will take another look at this."[86] This alone should make Bruce Ohr's anti-Trump bias obvious, suggesting as well that Kavalec was receptive to dirt on Trump, providing it could be validated.

Bruce Ohr's testimony before the House Judiciary Committee in joint session with the House Committee on Oversight and Government Reform on August 28, 2018, nearly two years after Trump was elected president, suggests he too wanted to present himself as having warned the FBI not to trust Steele. In response to questioning by GOP Representative Gowdy of South Carolina, Ohr admitted that he knew Steele was a hard Hillary Clinton partisan, determined to make sure Trump was defeated. "As I told you, I don't recall the exact words," Ohr explained to Gowdy. "I definitely had a very strong impression that he [Steele] did not want Donald Trump to win, because he believed his information he was giving me was accurate, and that he was, as I said, very concerned, or he was very desperate, which is what I then told the FBI."

In response to questioning by GOP representative Jim Jordan of Ohio, Ohr was vague about when he told this to the FBI. Jordan asked Ohr, "Earlier you said that you told the FBI that Mr. Steele, when you were conveying to them where you were getting this information, Mr. Steele was desperate to stop Trump from winning. When did you convey that to the FBI?" Ohr answered: "I don't think it was after the July 30 [2016] meeting, although I am not entirely sure. It may have been after the September meeting." As Jordan continued to press, Ohr equivocated that he may have told the FBI that Steele was "desperate" to see Trump defeated after either the August or the September meeting he had had with Steele in 2016. This is an important point. The FBI initiated the counterintelligence investigation into the links between the Russian government and the Trump campaign on July 31, 2016, the day after Bruce and Nellie Ohr met with Christopher Steele at the Mayflower Hotel. The timing would suggest Ohr's briefing of the FBI on his meeting with Steele played

---

86 "Judicial Watch Releases Email Exchange Between State Department Official and Bruce Ohr Targeting Trump with Steele Dossier Material," Judicial Watch, May 15, 2019, https://www.judicialwatch.org/press-room/press-releases/judicial-watch-releases-email-exchange-between-state-department-official-and-bruce-ohr-targeting-trump-with-steele-dossier-material/.

a role in the FBI's decision the next day to open the counterintelligence investigation against Trump. But if Ohr can be believed, it also means the FBI opened the counterintelligence investigation after having been warned that their main source of information about Trump and Russia came from Christopher Steele, a person Ohr realized was "desperate" to see Trump defeated.

Yet, when pressed by GOP representative Mark Meadows of North Carolina, then the chairman of the House Freedom Caucus, Ohr rationalized Steele's motivation for conducting the anti-Trump research. "Chris Steele has, for a long time, been very concerned about Russian crime and corruption and what he sees as Russian malign acts around the world, in the U.S., U.K., and elsewhere," Ohr testified. "And if he had information that he believed showed that the Russian government was acting in a hostile way to the United States, he wanted to get that information to me." Even in August 2018, Ohr still had sympathy for Steele, apparently without appreciating the extent to which Simpson and Steele had used him to promote their unverifiable lies about Trump to the FBI. As noted earlier, in his testimony to the House committees, Ohr insisted he did not know the Clinton campaign and the DNC were behind Perkins Coie hiring Fusion GPS to produce the Steele dossier until nearly a year after the election, in October 2017 when the *Washington Post* broke the news.

Steele Terminated by the FBI

Also noted earlier, in February 2016, the FBI hired Steele, agreeing to pay him as a confidential human source to the FBI. Heavily redacted documents released by the FBI indicate that the FBI paid Steele at least eleven times during 2016, although the amounts of the payments were not disclosed.[87] So, by June 2016, the FBI was paying Steele as a confidential human source while the Clinton campaign and the DNC were also paying

---

87   Tyler Durden, "New FBI Docs Reveal Agency Paid Steele, Admonished Him, and Strzok Sat on Weiner Probe," ZeroHedge.com, August 4, 2018, https://www.zerohedge.com/news/2018-08-04/new-fbi-docs-reveal-agency-paid-steele-admonished-him-and-strzok-sat-weiner-probe.

Steele indirectly through the Perkins Coie payments to Fusion GPS to dig up dirt on Trump.

The FBI deal to use Steele as a confidential source terminated in November 2016, when the FBI first suspended and then terminated Steele for "an unauthorized disclosure to the media of his relationship with the FBI."[88] The precipitating incident involved information Steele leaked to journalist David Corn that Corn subsequently wrote about in a *Mother Jones* article published on October 31, 2016. That article revealed that an "unidentified spy" (namely, Steele) had begun working with the FBI.[89] The FBI considered this an unauthorized disclosure to the media by Steele of his relationship with the FBI, an unpardonable sin that obviously broke the FBI's trust in Steele. In his testimony to the House committees, Ohr also acknowledged that he knew the FBI had begun paying Steele, but he claimed not to know the specific nature of the work Steele was doing for the FBI. So, it was no secret within the FBI that Steele was working for the FBI and getting paid for the effort, while he was also being paid by Fusion GPS through Orbis, and by the DNC and Clinton campaign through the Perkins Coie contract with Fusion GPS. But in talking to Corn, Steele broke the FBI's unwritten rules (and possibly even his contract with the FBI) that required Steele to keep his working relationship with the FBI secret, unless the FBI authorized disclosure.

In his article, Corn gave enough details about the unidentified spy for experts to quickly identify the spy as Christopher Steele. He disclosed that the "veteran spy" was giving the FBI information on a Russian operation

---

88 Brooke Singman, "FISA Memo: Steele Fired as an FBI Source for Breaking 'Cardinal Rule'—Leaking to the Media," Fox News, February 2, 2018, https://www.foxnews.com/politics/fisa-memo-steele-fired-as-an-fbi-source-for-breaking-cardinal-rule-leaking-to-the-media. See also: Morgan Chalfant, "FBI Releases Heavily Redacted Documents on Christopher Steele," *The Hill*, August 3, 2018, https://thehill.com/policy/national-security/400318-fbi-releases-heavily-redacted-documents-on-christopher-steele.

89 David Corn, "A Veteran Spy Has Given the FBI Information Alleging a Russian Operation to Cultivate Donald Trump," *Mother Jones*, October 31, 2016, https://www.motherjones.com/politics/2016/10/veteran-spy-gave-fbi-info-alleging-russian-operation-cultivate-donald-trump/.

to cultivate Donald Trump. "He [the unidentified spy] regularly consults with U.S. government agencies on Russian matters, and near the start of July on his own initiative—without the permission of the U.S. company that hired him—he sent a report that he had written for that firm to a contact at the FBI, according to the former intelligence officer and his American associates, who asked not to be identified," Corn wrote. "The former spy says he concluded that the information he had collected on Trump was 'sufficiently serious' to share with the FBI."

Although the time frame of "the start of July" does not jibe with Bruce Ohr's testimony, Corn appeared to be describing Steele's meeting with Ohr at the Mayflower Hotel. Another mistake Corn made was to claim he was an employee of the FBI when at most Steele was an independent contractor. But Corn's article gave credence to the Russia-collusion narrative the Clinton campaign was feeding to the mainstream media. If an unidentified spy who regularly consulted with the U.S. government on Russia was giving the FBI information adverse to Trump, that buttressed the otherwise unsubstantiated assertion. Corn stressed that the unidentified former spy had been assigned the task of researching Trump's dealings in Russia, and that this was "for an opposition research project originally financed by a Republican client critical of the celebrity mogul [Trump]."

Corn went on to state that "before the former spy was retained, the project's financing switched to a client allied with the Democrats." Corn cleverly made this reference vague, avoiding any effort he may have made to discover the Clinton campaign or the DNC as the project's funders. Finally, Corn wrote that he had reviewed reports the former spy [Steele] wrote in his first memo, based supposedly on the former intelligence officer's conversations with Russian sources, that noted the "Russian regime has been cultivating, supporting and assisting TRUMP for at least five years." This suggests that in leaking the article to Corn, Steele had shared with Corn his anti-Trump dossier.

Steele may have thought he was advancing the dossier's lies by getting Corn to publish this story clearly accusing Trump of collusion with Russia. In leaking the story to Corn, Steele was repeating the pattern of previously leaking information from the Steele dossier to Michael Isikoff. By Corn and Isikoff publishing Steele's leaked information as if that information had been dug up by investigations Corn and Isikoff were conducting independently from Steele, the FBI was able to use as "corroboration" what in truth is known as "circular reporting." That Corn and Isikoff are both hard-left Democrat partisans was evidenced by the book they co-authored in 2018 titled *Russian Roulette: The Inside Story of Putin's War on America and the Election of Donald Trump.*[90] What Steele appears to have forgotten is that the FBI expects contract agents like Steele to talk with nobody except the FBI. The FBI evidently reserves to itself the right to leak information to the press.

Steele Tries to Worm into the Mueller Investigation

Even after Steele was terminated as a confidential FBI source, Ohr continued to meet with him and to pass Steele's information on to the FBI. In his testimony to the House committees, Ohr affirmed that Steele continued to call him after he had been terminated. Ohr also volunteered that the FBI had given him an agent "handler" to whom he would forward the information that Steele offered after his termination. Remarkably, Ohr also testified that after Steele had been terminated, the FBI wanted Ohr to ask Steele the next time he called whether he would be willing to meet with the FBI again. Ohr also affirmed that after Steele was terminated, Deputy Attorney General Rod Rosenstein was interested in retaining him to work with Special Counsel Mueller. This was despite the fact that the FBI had specifically informed Steele in his termination memo that he could no longer operate to obtain any intelligence whatsoever on behalf of the FBI.

Remarkably, after his own termination for misconduct and after the appointment of Robert Mueller as special counsel, Steele approached Ohr to see if he might be able to work with Ohr to assist Mueller's investigation. "Whenever convenient, I would like a chat, there's a lot going on and we are frustrated with how long this re-engagement with the Bureau [the FBI] and Mueller is taking," Steele texted Ohr on August 6, 2017.

---

90 Michael Isikoff and David Corn, *Russian Roulette: The Inside Story of Putin's War on America and the Election of Donald Trump* (New York: Twelve, Hachette Book Group, 2018).

"Anything you could do to accelerate the process would be much appreciated."[91] Ohr texted back enthusiastically, "Chris, good to hear from you." Ohr proposed times when the two could discuss the idea.

Investigative reporter John Solomon noted that spokespeople for Rosenstein and Mueller declined to tell him whether their bosses knew about Steele's overtures or if Steele provided any further assistance to the FBI or the DOJ after Mueller took over. Yet, Solomon noted that in a private letter to Congress that was shared with him, Rosenstein declared he was unaware that Ohr was again thinking of working with Steele, this time to put Steele in a position "to assist" Mueller. Steele never gave up promoting his fraudulent information on Trump, thinking that he might repeat the performance, this time getting Ohr to worm Steele into the Mueller investigation.

When Solomon began questioning him about this, Rosenstein became extremely defensive, denying strongly that he had entertained Ohr's suggestion that Steele might work with Mueller. Rosenstein wrote that Ohr was "not assigned to the Russia investigation and he was not in the chain of command. Any involvement Mr. Ohr had in this matter was without [Rosenstein's] knowledge."[92] However, Solomon reported that FBI agents interviewed Ohr more than a half-dozen times in late 2016 and 2017 to learn what Steele was saying.[93] From early November 1, 2016, until November 2017, one year after the election, Ohr received and passed on more than a dozen communications from Steele.

On June 7, 2019, in response to a FOIA request, Judicial Watch released documents from the DOJ showing that on November 13, 2016,

---

91 John Solomon, "Opinion: Top DOJ Official Discussed Getting Steele Back into FBI, Mueller Probe," *The Hill*, August 8, 2018, https://thehill.com/hilltv/rising/401007-opinion-top-doj-official-discussed-getting-steele-back-into-fbi-mueller-probe.

92 Margot Cleveland, "11 Key Things inside the House Interview with Spygate Figure Bruce Ohr," op. cit.

93 John Solomon, "Opinion: How a Senior DOJ Official Helped Dem Researchers on Trump-Russia Case," *The Hill*, August 7, 2018, https://thehill.com/hilltv/rising/400810-opinion-how-a-senior-justice-official-helped-dems-on-trump-russia-case.

Ohr was given a performance award of $28,000 for his work for the DOJ coordinating with Steele in the controversial FBI surveillance of the Trump campaign during the 2016 election. The bonus was nearly double the $14,250 performance award he was given on November 29, 2015. The documents show that Ohr was removed from his position as associate deputy attorney general on December 6, 2017. Then, on January 7, 2018, Ohr was reassigned from his position as director of the OCDEFT to counselor for international affairs in the DOJ's Criminal Division, receiving a $2,600 pay increase in the process.[94]

The Nunes Memo: Proof the Steele Dossier Formed "an Essential Part" of the Carter Page FISA Application

The "Nunes memo," a four-page memo written by Representative Devin Nunes and released to the public by the then-GOP-controlled House Intelligence Committee on February 2, 2018, leaves no doubt that the Steele dossier played a crucial role in the FBI/DOJ FISA Court application first made on October 11, 2016.[95] "The 'dossier' compiled by Christopher Steele (Steele dossier) on behalf of the Democratic National Committee (DNC) and the Hillary Clinton campaign formed an essential part of the Carter Page FISA application," Nunes wrote. "Steele was a longtime FBI source who was paid over $160,000 by the DNC and the Clinton campaign, via the law firm Perkins Coie and research firm Fusion GPS, to obtain derogatory information on Donald Trump's ties to Russia."

Nunes noted that neither the initial application in October 2016 nor any of the three subsequent renewals "disclose[s] or reference[s] the role of

---

94 "Judicial Watch: DOJ Documents Show Bruce Ohr Was Given a $28,000 Bonus During Russiagate Investigation Plus a Raise," Judicial Watch Press Release, June 7, 2019, https://www.judicialwatch.org/press-room/press-releases/judicial-watch-doj-documents-show-bruce-ohr-was-given-a-28000-bonus-during-russiagate-investigation-plus-a-raise/.

95 Memo from HPSCI Majority Staff to HPSCI Majority Staff, "Foreign Intelligence Surveillance Act Abuses at the Department of Justice and the Federal Bureau of Investigation," January 18, 2018, declassified by order of President Trump on February 2, 2018.

the DNC, Clinton campaign, or any party/campaign in funding Steele's efforts, even though the political origins of the Steele dossier were then known to senior DOJ and FBI officials." Nunes's unstated conclusion appeared to be that had the political origins of the Steele dossier been fully disclosed by the government to the FISA Court, the court may well have denied approval.

The Nunes memo also took exception to the fact that the government's FISA Court applications extensively cited Michael Isikoff's article published by Yahoo! News on September 23, 2016, without referencing Steele as the source of that article. Clearly, Nunes was objecting to the obvious fraud of using Yahoo! News as independent corroboration of the damaging evidence against Trump contained in the Steele dossier, when Steele was the source of both. Nunes also discussed Steele's termination as an FBI source "for what the FBI defines as the most serious of violations— an unauthorized disclosure to the media of his relationship with the FBI," related to the article published by David Corn in *Mother Jones* on October 31, 2016. "While the FISA application relied upon Steele's past record of credible reporting on other unrelated matters, it ignored or concealed his anti-Trump financial and ideological motivations," Nunes stressed.

Nunes concluded with a point that is impossible to dismiss: Namely, that Deputy FBI Director Andrew McCabe had testified before the House Intelligence Committee in December 2017 that no surveillance warrant would have been sought from the FISA Court without the Steele dossier information.

Conclusion

This is an extremely perilous moment in the history of our constitutional republic. Never before has one political party, namely the Democrats under the leadership of Hillary Clinton, sought to weaponize the U.S. justice system with the goal of investigating the presidential candidate of the opposing political party. Clinton funded opposition research that branded her presidential race opponent, Donald Trump, as a traitor. Clinton's continuing effort after losing the election was to bring Trump to trial for treason while imprisoning many of his key political advisors and campaign officials. Never before in our history has a political party—in this case the

Democrats with their increasing determination to transform the United States fundamentally into a socialist state—allowed its ideological zeal to justify criminalizing politics in order to win the presidency and to steal the highest political elected office in the land.

What this chapter proves is that Hillary Clinton hired a British foreign agent to produce Russian disinformation and unverified lies, including the basest form of calumny regarding sexual matters, to attack Trump. Despite failing to obtain independent corroboration, the FBI and the DOJ utilized Steele's dossier as a "verified" basis to obtain federal court permission to conduct electronic surveillance on Trump. In other words, the evidence strongly suggests that Clinton and her political operatives, including Deep State operatives within the government, committed the very crimes they accused Trump of committing, in that they were the ones conspiring to make sure Trump lost.

In my own case, I can attest personally that Mueller's prosecutors hated my politics, my books and other political writings, and my belief in God. When they could find no other crime for which to imprison me, Mueller's prosecutors sought to enlist the cooperation of the FBI to develop a "process crime"—accusing me of lying—simply because I could not give them the evidence against Donald Trump that they wanted. My problem was that Mueller's operating premise that I had linked Roger Stone to Julian Assange was untrue. Furious to find that their key premise in the Russia-collusion case against Donald Trump was false, Mueller's team handed me a plea deal that itself was criminal in nature. In an effort to save his failing "Russia collusion" case against Trump, Mueller required me to plead guilty to a crime I did not commit in order not to be put in federal prison for the rest of my life.

In the final analysis, I decided that at seventy-two years old, with a clean personal record, I would rather die in the worst federal prison in the land than to lie under oath before a federal judge and before God.

Chapter Four

THE STRANGE CASE
OF CARTER PAGE

The Deep State decision to implement what amounted to a coup d'état after Trump's surprise election victory can be traced back to June 16, 2015, when Trump descended the golden escalator into the atrium of Trump Tower to declare his presidential candidacy. The Deep State further resolved to block Trump on June 23, 2016, when the United Kingdom defied its Westminster party leaders by voting in a historic referendum to leave the European Union—a move known as Brexit (a word formed from "British exit"). The U.K. is likely to be only the first of the EU's member states seeking to escape the totalitarian rule of the unelected bureaucrats who set the rules for the EU from Brussels. Deep State officials in the U.K. were also upset over Trump's claims in 2015 that the cost of stationing U.S. troops is enormous and that pulling back from Europe would save millions.[96] With regard to Syria, Trump insisted in 2015 that while Bashar al-Assad was "bad," the United States "must stop in nation-building."[97]

---

96 Tim Hains, "MTP's Todd to Donald Trump: It Sounds Like You're Not a Fan of NATO," Real Clear Politics, August 17, 2015, https://www.realclear-politics.com/video/2015/08/17/mtps_todd_to_donald_trump_it_sounds_like_youre_not_a_fan_of_nato.html.

97 Ben Jacobs, "The Donald Trump Doctrine: 'Assad Is Bad' But US Must Stop 'Nation-Building,'" *The Guardian*, October 13, 2015, https://www.the guardian.com/us-news/2015/oct/13/donald-trump-foreign-policy-doctrine-nation-building.

These views were frightening to a Deep State Eurocentric establishment across the Atlantic that wanted the U.S. to continue a strong Cold War antagonism toward Russia. Deep State intelligence agencies in the U.K. feared that Trump, if elected, would seek better relations with Russia—a policy Trump as candidate ultimately espoused.[98]

June 23, 2016, the dramatic night during which the U.K. votes on the referendum were being tallied, delivered one of the most dramatic shocks that establishment leaders in Great Britain and throughout Europe had felt in decades.[99] In the aftermath of the Brexit vote, fear rocked the British government's intelligence apparatus with the possibility that Donald Trump would pull off a second election miracle, giving the U.S. presidency to a populist determined to run on the theme "Make America Great Again."

The Brexit phenomenon, championed by British politician Nigel Farage, and what developed into the #MAGA internet phenomenon, which helped get Trump elected in the United States, had the effect of threatening to kill the one-world-government dream that globalists had nurtured since the founding of the United Nations at the end of World War II. One has to look no further for proof of this than Jean Monnet, known as "The Father of Europe," who chronicled dreams that a united Europe would lead to one-world government in his 1978 book *Mémoires*, published the year before he died. Just like Hillary Clinton on Election Day 2016, the British globalist establishment felt on June 24, 2016, "so close but yet so far away," as then British prime minister David Cameron resigned in defeat.

A key point of this chapter is to expand on the theme that the plan to destroy Trump with the bogus Russia-collusion narrative originated in British intelligence, specifically within the British Government

---

98 Carl Schreck, "Trump Vows To Seek Better Relations With Russia If Elected," Radio Free Europe, Radio Liberty, April 27, 2016, https://www.rferl.org/a/us-trump-foreign-policy-speech-russia/27702091.html.

99 Anushka Asthana, Ben Quinn, and Rowena Mason, "UK Votes to Leave EU after Dramatic Night Divides Nation," *The Guardian*, June 24, 2016, https://www.theguardian.com/politics/2016/jun/24/britain-votes-for-brexit-eu-referendum-david-cameron.

Communications Headquarters (GCHQ) unit. Recall that Christopher Steele, a former MI6 British intelligence agent, had experience spying for Great Britain in Russia. Glenn Simpson chose Steele to work with Fusion GPS in part because Steele's experience as a spy in Russia would give credence to the assumption that Steele was digging up his dirt on Trump from Russian sources. As we saw in the last chapter, the Steele dossier also had information the State Department's Jonathan Winer provided from the anti-Trump dossiers being developed by Sidney Blumenthal and Cory Shearer, as well as the information Nellie Steele was developing on Trump for Fusion GPS. Just as the Clinton campaign and the DNC fronted their relationship with Fusion GPS through Perkins Coie, British intelligence could trust that their histories with U.S. intelligence would make it unlikely the dirty dossier would ever be publicly traced back to GCHQ.

British intelligence trusted Steele to do the job he was assigned to do, knowing that when his dossier reached the desks of John Brennan, then the head of the CIA in the United States, and James Clapper, then U.S. director of national intelligence, his credentials would lend credibility to Steele's work product, just as it did with the FBI. The globalist-oriented British intelligence elite running GCHQ had abundant reasons to believe that U.S. intelligence agents were a ready audience looking for dirt on Trump and likely to be excited to find in the Steele dossier just what they were looking for—especially since the dirt would be discovered by a former head of the MI6 Russia desk.

Deep State Spying Goes International

This chapter and Chapter 6 will demonstrate that British intelligence, with the enthusiastic cooperation of the CIA and the NSA, in 2015 began activating an international spy network that included operatives in Great Britain, Italy, and Australia. The goal of the covert international operation was to entrap various Trump foreign policy advisors in what would appear to be suspicious schemes to collude with Russia to the detriment of Hillary Clinton. In January 2016, John Brennan organized a secret "Donald Trump Task Force" in the CIA, with the blessing of James Clapper, director of national intelligence.[100] Brennan organized the Donald Trump Task Force on the premise that Trump was a spy, an asset of Putin running for president in the United States. The Task Force members, including officials from the FBI and NSA, were handpicked, with no posting of jobs. As a counterintelligence operation, Brennan's Task Force could recruit foreign intelligence agencies including MI6 in the U.K., as well as Italian and Australian intelligence agencies. The Task Force spent CIA money to fund travel overseas and to pay cooperating assets to set up entrapment schemes of Trump campaign officials including Carter Page and George Papadopoulos. Out of Brennan's clandestine Donald Trump Task Force, the Justice Department officially commenced Operation Crossfire Hurricane. On July 31, 2016, when the FBI officially commenced Crossfire Hurricane as a counterintelligence operation, the DOJ could send FBI officials overseas on FBI official business to work hand-in-hand with their CIA, U.K., Italian, and Australian intelligence counterparts recruited into the international "Stop Trump" movement.

There was a definite progression of Justice Department involvement in the "Stop Trump" movement. The DOJ and FBI had begun investigating Trump early in the 2016 election campaign, long before, with various FBI agents recruited to join Brennan's CIA secret Donald Trump Task Force. As we will see in this chapter and the next two, the U.S. intelligence and justice agencies worked in conjunction with foreign intelligence agents to plant evidence that Carter Page was coordinating with Russian intelligence to establish channels for Trump to collude with Putin in the 2016 election. At the same time, the "Stop Trump" international conspiracy plotted to plant evidence George Papadopoulos had advance knowledge in May 2016 that the Russians had damaging material on Hillary Clinton in the form of stolen emails. When Trump was elected, the Deep State conspirators merely shifted gears. Operation Crossfire Hurricane continued with FISA Court-approved electronic surveillance into

---

100   Larry C. Johnson, "Exposing John Brennan's Secret CIA Trump Task Force?" Turcopolier.typepad.com, October 26, 2019, https://turcopolier.ty-pepad.com/sic_semper_tyrannis/2019/10/john-brennans-secret-cia-trump-task-force-by-larry-c-johnson.html.

2017, after Trump was inaugurated president. But Trump's decision to fire James Comey as FBI director on May 9, 2017, set off a chain reaction that changed the nature of the Russia investigation. Acting Attorney General Rod Rosenstein, who began directing the Russia investigation after Attorney General Jeff Sessions recused himself, held a series of secret meetings with former FBI director Robert Mueller probing whether Mueller would be willing to serve as special counsel should Rosenstein feel the need to appoint one.

On May 12, 2017, Rosenstein emailed Mueller, saying, "The boss and his staff do not know about our discussions." This cryptic email affirms that Rosenstein had kept his discussions with Mueller private from Jeff Sessions or President Trump, most probably from both. On May 16, 2017, Mueller met at the White House with President Trump about returning to head the Justice Department. Mueller in his congressional testimony on July 24, 2019, said under oath, "My understanding was that I was not applying for the job [of FBI director]. I was asked to give my input on what it would take to do the job." But John Dowd, Trump's attorney during much of the Russia investigation, had a different view of the Mueller-Trump meeting. Dowd called the meeting the "most dishonorable conduct I have ever witnessed," adding, "Captain Robert Mueller, U.S. Marine Corps, sits in front of his commander-in-chief being interviewed for FBI director, knowing he is going to investigate the president and never says a word." The day after Trump turned down Mueller to replace Comey in the May 17, 2017, meeting, Rosenstein appointed Mueller as special counsel.[101] As of this writing, questions have been raised regarding whether Mueller should face perjury charges for denying in his congressional testimony that he was applying for the job of FBI director in his private meeting with Trump after Comey's firing.

But there is more. When Trump fired Comey, Andrew McCabe became the acting FBI director. That same month, May 2017, in the wake

---

101   Bret Baier and Jake Gibson, "Mueller Was Pursuing FBI Director
      When He Met with Trump in 2017, Administration Officials Say,"
      Fox News, October 9, 2019, https://www.foxnews.com/politics/
      robert-mueller-fbi-director-job-trump-meeting.

of Comey's firing, McCabe joined Rosenstein in their one-two punch hit on Trump. Almost immediately after being named FBI acting director, McCabe opened an FBI criminal investigation into whether Trump had obstructed justice.[102] So, the FBI's counterintelligence investigation that opened on July 31, 2016, with Operation Crossfire Hurricane was supplemented with an FBI criminal investigation aimed at investigating criminal charges that Trump had obstructed justice by firing Comey.

Moving from 2015 to today, the Deep State's purpose shifted from defeating Trump at the polls in the November 2016 election to impeaching him for whatever high crimes or misdemeanors could be found or, failing that, manufactured. After Comey was fired in May 2017, the Deep State had four ongoing investigations of Trump: (1) the Donald Trump Task Force operating in the CIA under the auspices of Brennan with the blessing of Clapper; (2) the FBI counterintelligence mission known as Operation Crossfire Hurricane; (3) the Mueller Special Counsel probe into Russian interference in the 2016 election; and (4) the FBI criminal investigation focusing on developing probable cause evidence Trump had obstructed justice by attempting to block investigations into the alleged Russian collusion.

Everywhere we look in this sordid melodrama aimed at destroying Trump, the Steele dossier surfaces as the evidentiary centerpiece despite the salacious and unverifiable nature of the allegations Fusion GPS launched at Trump, funded by Hillary Clinton and the DNC. As shown in the previous two chapters, the Steele dossier, despite its known flaws, was the centerpiece of the FBI/DOJ application to the FISA Court on October 21, 2016, to get permission to conduct electronic surveillance on Trump's presidential campaign.

In this chapter, I shall show why it was critical for the DOJ and FBI coconspirators to get these electronic surveillance powers in their plan to destroy Trump. A key date in development in Operation Crossfire Hurricane was October 21, 2016, the date the DOJ applied to the FISA Court

---

102 Caitlin Oprysko, "McCabe Says He Opened Investigations into Trump to Put Russia Probe on Solid Ground," Politico, February 14, 2019, https://www. politico.com/story/2019/02/14/fbi-investigation-trump-russia-1169846.

to obtain a warrant authorizing electronic surveillance of Carter Page. This date was less than three weeks before Election Day. Truthfully, Page and Papadopoulos were low-level foreign policy advisors to Trump's campaign. But the DOJ and FBI coconspirators were determined to transform Page and Papadopoulos from being minor actors in the Trump campaign to being at center stage in the Deep State's allegations that Trump was a Russian agent. In Mueller's final report, despite finding no evidence of Russian collusion, both Page and Papadopoulos are featured as having had contacts with Russians the Deep State still considers suspicious.

Starting during the campaign and continuing after the election, the mainstream media relied on CNN and MSNBC to hype the theme 24/7 that Donald Trump was a Russian spy. The Trump-hating media continued to broadcast this lie right up until March 2019, when Mueller presented his final report, which admitted to the nation that his Trump-hating investigators had found no evidence that the Trump campaign colluded with Russia.

Yet, in their partisan political enthusiasm to elect Clinton by destroying Trump, the "Three Amigos"—John Brennan, James Clapper, and James Comey—violated FBI and DOJ procedures and most likely committed crimes. Among their likely crimes was their support of the DOJ and FBI decision to provide the unverified Steele dossier to the FISA Court as the key evidence in their FISA Court application to place Trump under electronic surveillance—without notifying the FISA Court that the Steele dossier was opposition research funded by Clinton's campaign and the DNC.

Those in the mainstream media, having compromised what was left of their credibility by serving as virtual spokespersons for the Obama regime, eagerly published the leaks coming from Simpson and Steele, from the FBI, from the DOJ, and from the CIA. The goal was to defeat Trump by forcing his campaign to spend most of its time rebutting Deep State assaults. When that did not work, the Deep State coconspirators shifted gears, deciding to use the Steele dossier as "Exhibit A" in their determined plan to impeach Trump.

The Mueller Investigation Final Report Crashes and Burns

Once the Mueller report was publicly known not to have produced the evidence much anticipated by the Trump-hating mainstream media, the Deep State coconspirators began running in fear. The Deep State actors participating in the failed 2016 coup d'état began to realize their plot would be exposed. The end to the Deep State coup d'état was brutally simple: once Mueller's "witch hunt" crashed and burned, the Deep State cover-up of the 2016 coup d'état was seriously at risk. To keep the move to impeach Trump going, Mueller handed off his failed special counsel investigation to the House of Representatives, where charges against Trump could morph into a purely political matter.

Reading his statement in fewer than ten minutes to a national television audience on May 29, 2019, Robert Mueller was left standing metaphorically naked, hiding behind a podium on the stage alone, admitting that his investigation had failed. In his statement, Mueller made clear that his 448-page report of dead-end investigations could yet have another life, serving as the lead document in a handoff to the House of Representatives to pursue impeachment. In other words, having failed miserably to establish a criminal case, Mueller was now admitting to the nation that the real purpose of the fraudulent investigation had been politically motivated from the beginning. In his demeanor, as he read aloud words that could have been read silently as a press release, Mueller displayed himself as a failed man. He was just another "empty suit" about to be abandoned at the end of a long, worn-out career in which he spent decades doing double duty as a senior Department of Justice and FBI official with decades of public service, who quietly worked behind the scenes as a big-time Deep State law enforcement fixer with a political fondness for the Clintons and the Obamas.[103]

---

103 Thomas Lipscomb, email to the author, dated June 6, 2018. Thomas Lipscomb is a brilliant media executive and CEO who funded Times Books at the *New York Times* to enjoy a legacy of having published numerous bestselling books. The FBI assigned to Mueller's Office of Special Counsel in their exhaustive surveillance of my emails found, among other things, Lipscomb's email on GCHQ involvement. The FBI's discovery of this email prompted the FBI to send agents to visit Mr. Lipscomb in person to see if he knew whether I had any contact with Julian Assange or WikiLeaks.

The day Attorney General William Barr shut down Mueller's "fishing expedition" because he lacked probable cause regarding a crime having been committed, the Deep State traitors—including Brennan, Clapper, Comey, and the other Clinton-partisan players in the coup d'état—began scattering and blaming one another. GCHQ also predictably denied any involvement in an international conspiracy by globalist-driven intelligence agencies to destroy Trump. Going on the attack, GCHQ derided any mention of their involvement in the coup d'état as a "conspiracy theory." The purpose of this chapter is to make sure that the traitors in the intelligence communities around the world, including in the United States, are held responsible for the failed coup d'état, so that they do not avoid criminal charges, but instead are brought to justice.

Carter Page: Framed as a Traitor by the Steele Dossier

In language designed to suggest that Christopher Steele had a Russian source for his information, the Steele dossier names Carter Page as the main intermediary between the Trump campaign and Russians close to Vladimir Putin. Page is introduced into the Steele dossier in the following paragraph:

> Speaking in confidence to a compatriot in late July 2016, Source E, an ethnic Russian close associate of Republican U.S. presidential candidate Donald TRUMP, admitted that there was a well-developed conspiracy of co-operation between them and the Russian leadership. This was managed on the TRUMP side by the Republican candidate's campaign manager, Paul MANAFORT, who was using foreign policy advisor, Carter PAGE, and others as intermediaries. The two sides had a mutual interest in defeating Democratic presidential candidate Hillary CLINTON, whom President PUTIN apparently both hated and feared.

Page is a U.S. entrepreneur working in the energy sector, not a Russian spy. The flimsy evidence Steele assembled to make the case that Page used his position as a named foreign policy advisor to the Trump campaign to act as an agent of Russia, collaborating and conspiring with the Russians at the direction of Donald Trump, centers on a keynote speech that Page gave based on his past scholarly work. He gave the speech to an academic conference at the New Economic School, a prestigious Moscow educational institute, in his private capacity as a petroleum industry consultant during a five-day trip to Moscow in July 2016.[104]

Page's résumé shows that he served as a U.S. Naval officer in Europe and the Middle East, spending a brief time in Navy intelligence. After leaving the Navy, Page completed a fellowship at the Council on Foreign Relations. He is a graduate of the U.S. Naval Academy at Annapolis (1993). He received a master's degree from Georgetown University in 1994, a master's in business administration from New York University's Stern School of Business in 2001, and a doctorate from the School of Oriental and African Studies (SOAS) at the University of London in 2012. Early in his professional career, Page worked as an investment banker at Merrill Lynch, where he served as the chief operating officer of the energy and power group in New York. From 2004 to 2007, Page was the deputy branch manager of the Merrill Lynch office in Moscow, where he advised on strategic and financial transactions in the energy and power section. After leaving Merrill Lynch in 2008, he formed his own consulting and investment fund, Global Energy Capital.

Despite his credentials, Page was one of many Trump campaign "advisors" who served as an unpaid volunteer on the Trump campaign's foreign policy committee and never played a central role in Trump's campaign. The foreign policy committee had only one official meeting with then candidate Trump, a meeting Page recalls as having happened early in the campaign, on March 31, 2016. Because of previous commitments, Page was unable to attend. In an interview with investigative journalist Sharyl Attkisson, Page insisted he had never met Donald Trump one-on-one in

---

104 Scott Shane, Mark Mazzetti, and Adam Goldman, "Trump Adviser's Visit to Moscow Got the FBI's Attention," *New York Times*, April 19, 2017, https://www.nytimes.com/2017/04/19/us/politics/carter-page-russia-trump.html.

person and had never spoken with him by telephone.[105] Attkisson was astonished to hear this. "Remarkably, the FBI's supposedly most solid link to their Trump-Russia collusion theory says he'd never even spoken to Donald Trump," she stated on air. Various reports suggest that until he was named as a foreign policy advisor to Trump, Page had a relatively low profile in the energy industry in Russia.[106] In New York City, Global Energy Capital operated out of a corporate coworking space, with Page its only employee. In fairness, Page expressed to me in an email his frustration that this description was a "fake news talking point." Page insists all his colleagues fled "when the false allegations from the Democrats and resultant terror threats began." Page noted that many of his colleagues and associates "are still feeling the damage done by the Witch Hunt."[107]

But by the time the FBI recirculated the Steele dossier into the first FISA Court application on October 21, 2016, Page was being portrayed as the central player orchestrating Trump's collusion with Russia. The Steele dossier notes that during his speaking engagement in Russia in July 2016, Page held "secret meetings" with two prominent Russians linked to Putin: Igor Sechin, a counselor to Putin who served as CEO and chairman of the management board of Rosneft, a major energy company headquartered in Moscow, and Igor Diveykin, a close Putin associate. Diveykin, who served until 2016 as Putin's deputy chief for internal policy in what U.S. intelligence has termed "The Moscow Project," is credited as being responsible for the collection of intelligence by Russian agencies related to

105   Tim Hains, "Carter Page: I Experienced the Trump-Russia Witch Hunt First Hand, Now We're Getting the Real Truth," *Real Clear Politics*, March 31, 2019, https://www.realclearpolitics.com/video/2019/03/31/carter_page_i_experienced_the_trump-russia_witch_hunt_first_hand_now_were_getting_the_real_truth.html.

106   Julia Ioffe, "The Mystery of Trump's Man in Moscow," *Politico Magazine*, September 23, 2016, https://web.archive.org/web/20160924010026/http://www.politico.com/magazine/story/2016/09/the-mystery-of-trumps-man-in-moscow-214283.

107   Jason Zengerle, "What (if Anything) Does Carter Page Know?" *The New York Times Magazine*, December 18, 2017, https://www.nytimes.com/2017/12/18/magazine/what-if-anything-does-carter-page-know.html.

the U.S. 2016 presidential campaign.[108] The Steele dossier notes that in 2016, Sechin was under sanction by the U.S. government over his involvement in Ukraine. According to the dossier, Sechin told Page that Trump could receive a "large stake" in Rosneft in exchange for lifting the sanction on Sechin once Trump was president. Here is the exact language from the Steele dossier:

> Speaking to a trusted compatriot in mid-October 2016, a close associate of Rosneft President and PUTIN ally Igor SECHIN elaborated on the reported secret meeting between the latter and Carter PAGE, of U.S. Republican presidential candidate's foreign policy team, in Moscow in July 2016. The secret meeting had been confirmed to him/her by a senior member of SECHIN's staff, in addition to by the Rosneft President himself. It took place on either 7 or 8 July, the same day or the day after Carter PAGE made a public speech to the Higher Economic School in Moscow.
>
> In terms of substance of their discussion, SECHIN's associate said that the Rosneft President was keen to lift personal and corporate western sanctions imposed on the company, that he offered PAGE/TRUMP's associates the brokerage of up to a 19 percent (privatized) stake in Rosneft in return. PAGE had expressed interest and confirmed that were TRUMP elected U.S. president, then the sanctions on Russia would be lifted.

The first FISA Court application (on October 21, 2016) targeted Page for electronic surveillance. "This application targets Carter Page," the Justice Department's FISA Court application states. "The FBI believes Page

---

108 "Until Late 2016, Igor Divicine Served as Vladimir Putin's Deputy Chief for Internal Policy," Center for American Progress, "The Moscow Project," no date, https://themoscowproject.org/players/igordiveykin/. The Center for American Progress is a left-oriented think-tank headquartered in Washington, D.C. and founded by John Podesta.

has been the subject of targeted recruitment by the Russian Government [redacted] undermine and influence the outcome of the 2016 U.S. Presidential election in violation of U.S. criminal law."

The Grassley-Graham Memo

In a January 4, 2018, memo that was declassified and made public despite the objections of the FBI, Senator Chuck Grassley, then chairman of the Committee on the Judiciary and Senator Lindsey Graham, then chairman of the Judiciary Committee's Subcommittee on Crime and Terror, expressed their dismay over the way the DOJ relied upon the Steele dossier without independent verification to frame the charges against Carter Page in its four FISA Court applications. "The bulk of the application consists of allegations against Page that were disclosed to the FBI by Mr. Steele and are also outlined in the Steele Dossier," Grassley and Graham wrote. "The application appears to contain no information corroborating the dossier allegations against Mr. Page, although it does cite to a news article that appears to be sourced to Mr. Steele's dossier as well."[109]

The news article cited in the Grassley-Graham memo was the article discussed in Chapter 3 that Michael Isikoff published via Yahoo! News on September 23, 2016, reporting without attribution the information from the Steele dossier that Steele had leaked to him.[110] Isikoff reported that unnamed sources had briefed then Senate minority leader Harry Reid and unnamed senior members of Congress on Carter Page's activities in Moscow—information obviously leaked from the Steele dossier. As a result of the unspecified briefing, Reid wrote to then FBI director James Comey, citing reports of meetings between a Trump advisor (a reference to Page)

---

109   Senators Charles E. Grassley and Lindsey O. Graham, "The Grassley-Graham Memo," date redacted, submitted to Deputy Attorney General Rosenstein and FBI Director Wray, dated January 4, 2018, referring Christopher Steele for criminal investigation for lying to Congress about the Steele Dossier.

110   Michael Isikoff, "U.S. Intel Officials Probe Ties between Trump Adviser and Kremlin," Yahoo! News, September 23, 2016, https://www.yahoo.com/news/u-s-intel-officials-probe-ties-between-trump-adviser-and-kremlin-175046002.html.

and "high ranking sanctioned individuals" in Moscow (a reference to Igor Sechin and Diveykin). According to Isikoff, Reid cited these meetings "as evidence of 'significant and disturbing ties' between the Trump campaign and the Kremlin that needed to be investigated by the bureau." Isikoff further detailed that some of the members of Congress who had been briefed were "taken aback" when they learned about Page's contacts in Moscow, "viewing them as a possible back channel to the Russians that could undercut U.S. foreign policy."

The Grassley-Graham memo also said that Comey, in sworn testimony before the Senate Select Committee on Intelligence in June 2017, disclosed that he had briefed President-Elect Trump on the Steele dossier in January 2017, the contents of which Comey described as "salacious" and "unverified." Shocked by these disclosures, Grassley and Graham noted the following:

> When asked at the March 2017 briefing [following the release of two FISA applications to the chairman and ranking member of the Senate Judiciary Committee] why the FBI relied on the dossier in the FISA applications absent meaningful corroboration—and in light of the highly political motives surrounding its creation—then-Director Comey stated that the FBI included the dossier allegations about Carter Page in the FISA applications because Mr. Steele was considered reliable due to his past work with the Bureau.

The Grassley-Graham memo continues, noting that documents reviewed by the Senate Intelligence Committee show the FBI took important investigative steps based largely on Steele's information, relying upon Steele's credibility with the FBI in his previous investigative efforts regarding the FIFA international soccer scandal and the reporting Steele did subsequently on Ukraine. Yet, Grassley and Graham note the FISA application failed to disclose that the identities of Simpson's ultimate clients at Fusion GPS were the Clinton campaign and the DNC.

Grassley and Graham's conclusions were highly critical of the FBI:

The FBI stated to the FISC that "based on [Steele's] previous reporting history with the FBI, whereby [Steele] provided reliable information to the FBI, the FBI believes [Steele's] reporting to be credible." In short, it appears the FBI relied on admittedly uncorroborated information, funded by and obtained for Secretary Clinton's presidential campaign, in order to conduct surveillance of the opposing presidential candidate. It did so based on Mr. Steele's personal credibility and presumably having faith in his process of obtaining the information.

By leaking to the press derogatory information on Carter Page drawn entirely from the dossier Steele knew to be unverifiable because it was untrue, Steele callously sought to make the public think Page was presumed guilty of treason. This was all part of his strategy to gain credibility for the lies he told in the dossier with the intent to destroy Donald Trump's presidential candidacy. In their memo, Grassley and Graham express their astonishment that in the January 2017 FISA application, the FBI continued to vouch for Steele's credibility despite admitting that Steele had been fired by the FBI for making "unauthorized disclosure of information to the press." Grassley and Graham noted that lying to the FBI is a crime, yet the FBI never stopped relying on the Steele dossier, even after learning that Steele had leaked information from the dossier as early as "late summer/autumn 2016," to a large number of press reporters.

Not surprisingly, Grassley and Graham ended their memo by recommending Steele to the DOJ for criminal investigation for violating Title 18, United States Code, Section 1001, which prohibits a person from making materially false, fictitious, or fraudulent statements to any department or agency of the United States, including Congress. Andrew McCarthy has also noted there is no "vicarious credibility" in criminal investigations. "When the government seeks a warrant, it is supposed to show the court that the actual sources of information are reliable—i.e., they were in a position to see or hear the relevant facts, and are worthy of belief," McCarthy writes. "It is not sufficient to show that the agent who assembles the source information is credible."[111]

Steele's Leak to Michael Isikoff at Yahoo! News

The rumors about Carter Page preceded by several months the publication of Isikoff's article in September 2016. Page explained on Tucker Carlson's Fox News television show that as early as July 2016, he started getting phone calls from various news reporters, including those at the *Wall Street Journal*, the *New York Times*, the *Washington Post*, and CNN, "all asking me about these same two names of people I've never even heard of.[112] I'd heard of Sechin, but I never even heard of Diveykin." When Page asked where they had gotten this information, various reporters told him the information about Sechin and Diveykin had come from the Clinton campaign.

In my own experience with Mueller's prosecutors and the FBI, I can attest that I got frequent calls from the media, including the same media outlets Page mentioned, when the media had inside information about the Mueller investigation that had not yet become public. When I asked these reporters where they had gotten their information, they typically told me they had gotten it from "sources close to Mueller's investigators." I came to the conclusion that the assertion that no leaks were coming from the Mueller prosecution team was just another Deep State lie.

In a telephone conversation I had with Page on June 17, 2018, Page explained that "for decades" he had worked as an informant for both the FBI and the CIA.[113] This developed out of the contacts he had made

---

111   Andrew C. McCarthy, "FISA Applications Confirm: The FBI Relied on the Unverified Steele Dossier," *National Review*, July 23, 2018, https://www.nationalreview.com/2018/07/carter-page-fisa-applications-fbi-steele-dossier/.

112   "Carter Page: Russian Spy Allegations 'Ridiculous,'" Fox News, July 23, 2018, https://video.foxnews.com/v/5812919351001/#sp=show-clips.

113   Daniel Chaitin, "Carter Page Says He Consulted State Department, FBI, and CIA for Years," *Washington Examiner*, June 9, 2019, https://www.washingtonexaminer.com/news/carter-page-says-he-consulted-state-fbi-and-cia-for-years.

working as a Navy intelligence officer. Evidence has surfaced suggesting that Page worked as an undercover employee (UCE) for the FBI.[114] The 2013 case involved Preet Bharara, the U.S. attorney for the Southern District of New York, prosecuting Evgeny Buryakov as a Russian spy operating in the United States. In a press release dated March 11, 2016, Bharara's office announced that Buryakov had pled guilty. Buryakov had worked in New York with two other Russian agents, Igor Sporyshev and Victor Podobnyy. In his press release, Bharara noted that Sporyshev had "attempted to recruit an FBI undercover employee ('UCE-1'), who was posing as an analyst from a New York-based energy company."[115] The *New York Times*, in an article published on April 4, 2017, identified the New York-based energy analyst who had played a role as an undercover employee for the FBI in the Buryakov case (UCE-1) as none other than Carter Page.[116]

It is hard to believe that between March 2016, when Buryakov plead guilty in a case where Page played a role as an undercover employee for the FBI, and October 2016, when the DOJ made the first FISA Court application, Page somehow became a Russian spy. Certainly, Bharara's office could have explained to the FBI and DOJ in Washington that there was no reason to believe that Page had become a traitor overnight.

This also struck Sharyl Attkisson as preposterous. "So the theory was, at the time, that a guy who had helped the FBI and the CIA in the

---

114 Blogger known as "sundance," "In March 2016 Carter Page Was an FBI Employee—In October 2016 FBI Told FISA Court He's a Spy," The Conservative Treehouse, February 5, 2018, https://theconservativetreehouse.com/2018/02/05/in-march-2016-carter-page-was-an-fbi-employee-in-october-2016-fbi-told-fisa-court-hes-a-spy/.

115 U.S. Attorney's Office, Southern District of New York, Department of Justice, "Evgeny Buryakov Pleads Guilty in Manhattan Federal Court in Connection with Conspiracy to Work for Russian Intelligence," March 11, 2016, https://www.justice.gov/usao-sdny/pr/evgeny-buryakov-pleads-guilty-manhattan-federal-court-connection-conspiracy-work.

116 Adam Goldman, "Russian Spies Tried to Recruit Carter Page Before He Advised Trump," *New York Times*, April 4, 2017, https://www.nytimes.com/2017/04/04/us/politics/carter-page-trump-russia.html.

past, including with potential spy cases, himself became a spy while being watched by the FBI?" Attkisson asked Page in her interview with him.

"It's just so outrageous, preposterous," Page answered. "Where do you even begin?"

In his testimony before the House Intelligence Committee on November 2, 2017, Page denied ever having met Sechin or Diveykin, claiming without hesitation that they were two people "I had never even heard of in my life"; he went on to say that "each of these people [Sechin and Diveykin] I've never met in my life." Page testified that the first time he heard Diveykin's name was on July 26, 2016, when a reporter from the *Wall Street Journal* telephoned him and said, "We're told you met with Igor Sechin during your Moscow trip. We are also told you recently met with a senior Kremlin official [Diveykin]." Page told the House Intelligence Committee that he has never had a relationship with the Russian government, though he admitted he may have talked with certain Russian government officials over the years, just as he had interacted with certain Russian businesspeople in the energy and power sector. Page insisted that his trip to Russia in July 2016 to give his speech to the New Economic School in Moscow was the only trip he made to Russia during the entire time of Trump's candidacy. He also insisted that he made it "perfectly clear" that he had not been representing Trump or the Trump campaign on that trip.

Enter Intelligence Agent Stefan Halper

Carter Page first met Stefan Halper, a professor at Cambridge University in the U.K., in July 2016, when, after delivering his speech at the New Economic School in Moscow, Page stopped off in London to attend a conference hosted by the Centre for Research in the Arts, Social Sciences and Humanities (CRASSH), a Cambridge research institute. Page has stated for the record that the organizers of the conference paid his round-trip airfare from New York. The event was sponsored by Halper's department at Cambridge, the Department of Politics and International Studies, with that department sharing space in the building where the symposium was held. The conference was titled "2016's Race to Change the World."

Attending the conference was Sir Richard Dearlove, a Cambridge alumnus with a forty-year career with the British intelligence service, MI6, where he rose to serve as its head from 1999 to 2004. The *Wall Street Journal* editorial board observed that Dearlove overlapped at MI6 with Steele, who was recruited by MI6 after graduating from Cambridge in the 1980s. Dearlove reputedly became Steele's mentor during their years together at MI6. Dearlove has described Steele's reputation at MI6 as "superb." In 2008, when visiting the U.K., President Obama was briefed on a paper Steele had written on Russia.[117] Dearlove, along with Halper, was part of a small group that ran the Cambridge Intelligence Seminar, an academic forum that in 2014 was attended by General Michael Flynn, President Obama's Defense Intelligence Agency director at the time. The conference Page attended, "2016's Race to Change the World," was billed by Cambridge University's Department of Politics and International Studies as a Halper/Dearlove forum held under the auspices of the Cambridge Intelligence Seminar series.

The *Wall Street Journal* editorial board confirmed in print on May 22, 2018, that Stefan Halper was the "top secret" informant the FBI had asked to get close to Trump campaign officials. Why? The obvious answer is that the FBI wanted someone to get inside the Trump campaign organization in order to spy on Trump campaign officials.[118] Halper had the right credentials for the job. As reported by Jerry Dunleavy in the *Washington Examiner* on April 10, 2019,[119] Halper graduated from Stanford University in 1967 and received doctorates from Oxford University in 1971 and Cambridge University in 2004. At Cambridge,

---

117 Jane Mayer, "Christopher Steele, the Man Behind the Steele Dossier," *The New Yorker*, March 5, 2018, https://www.newyorker.com/magazine/2018/03/12/christopher-steele-the-man-behind-the-trump-dossier.

118 The Editorial Board, "When Carter Page Met Stefan Halper," *Wall Street Journal*, Opinion Piece, May 22, 2018, https://www.wsj.com/articles/when-carter-page-met-stefan-halper-1527029988.

119 Jerry Dunleavy, "Stefan Halper: The Cambridge Don the FBI Sent to Spy on Trump," *Washington Examiner*, April 10, 2019, https://www.washingtonexaminer.com/news/stefan-halper-the-cambridge-professor-the-fbi-sent-to-spy-on-trump.

he was the director of American studies in the Department of Politics and International Studies; he taught classes and delivered papers at institutions around the world, including Chatham House in London, the Center for Strategic and International Studies in Washington, and the U.S. Naval War College.

Halper also held positions in the administrations of Presidents Richard Nixon, Gerald Ford, and Ronald Reagan. He served on the U.S. Domestic Policy Council, part of the Executive Office of the President, from 1971 to 1973. Following that, he was transferred to the Office of Management and Budget (OMB), where he worked as an assistant director of the Management and Evaluation Division until 1974. After Nixon's resignation, Halper worked as assistant to the White House's chief of staff from 1974 until January 20, 1977 (the day Jimmy Carter was inaugurated president). In 1979 and 1980, Halper worked as the national director for policy development for George H. W. Bush's presidential campaign. In 1980, he held the same position for the Reagan-Bush presidential campaign. Then, from 1981 to 1984, he held the position of deputy assistant secretary of state for politico-military affairs. In this position, Halper served under Secretaries of Defense Alexander Haig, Walter J. Stoessel Jr., and George P. Shultz. From 1984 to 2001, he also served as senior advisor in the Department of Defense and the DOJ.[120] At some point during his career in Washington, Halper also became an informant for the CIA.[121]

Halper's ties to the CIA go back to his father-in-law Ray Cline, the key CIA analyst on Korea from 1949–1953. Cline played an important role by evaluating U-2 intelligence flights over Cuba. Cline's findings on these flights established in an October 20, 1962, meeting of the National Security Council that Cuba had sixteen operational Russian SS-4

---

120 Stefan Halper, Biography for Faculty, Scholars and Research Professors, Institute of World Politics, no date, https://www.iwp.edu/faculty/stefan-halper/.

121 Adam Goldman, Michael S. Schmidt, and Mark Mazzetti, "FBI Sent Investigator Posing as Assistant to Meet with Trump Aide in 2016," *New York Times*, May 2, 2019, https://www.nytimes.com/2019/05/02/us/politics/fbi-government-investigator-trump.html.

missiles, each with a range of 1020 nautical miles, that could be fired approximately eighteen hours after a decision to fire was made.[122]Cline rose to being a deputy director of the CIA and director of intelligence and research at the State Department. Cline later played a strategy role for George H. W. Bush in his 1979–1980 primary race for the presidency, organizing for Bush what Cline characterized as "something like one of my old CIA staffs." Cline recommended to George H. W. Bush that he should hire Halper as director of policy development and research.[123]

Halper, it turns out, played a controversial role heading the 1980 Reagan presidential campaign "research staff" that was subsequently disclosed to be tied to a CIA spying operation on the presidential campaign of the then governor Jimmy Carter, the Democratic nominee facing Ronald Reagan. In 1983, news sources identified Halper as connected to the CIA's successful effort to obtain a copy of Jimmy Carter's briefing book, which was leaked to the Reagan campaign in advance of the only Carter-Reagan debate held in 1980. Throughout the 1980 presidential campaign operation, Halper was reported to have provided twenty-four-hour news updates and policy ideas to the traveling Reagan campaign. Harper's connection to CIA spying on the Carter campaign was allegedly directed by George H. W. Bush, who had served as CIA director under President Gerald Ford from January 30, 1976, to January 20, 1977, and was Ronald Reagan's vice-presidential candidate

122 "Minutes of the 505th Meeting of the National Security Council, Washington, October 20, 1962," Office of the Historian, U.S. Department of State, in the study "Foreign Relations of the United States 1961–1963, Volume XI, Cuban Missile Crisis and Aftermath," https://history.state.gov/historicaldocuments/frus1961-63v11/d34.

123 Bill Peterson, with contributions from Ronald White, "Coming in from the Cold, Going Out to the Bush Campaign," *Washington Post*, March 1, 1980, https://www.washingtonpost.com/archive/politics/1980/03/01/coming-in-from-the-cold-going-out-to-the-bush-campaign/3758ff60-0d13-43a6-9a6f-c692e20d5378/.

in 1980.[124] Given Halper's long-time association with the Bush family and his willingness to work in a counterintelligence capacity with U.S. intelligence to undermine Trump, we have additional confirmation the Bush family refused to support Trump in 2016, especially after Trump eliminated Jeb Bush in the 2016 presidential GOP primaries.

On Saturday, August 20, 2016, Carter Page, an avid bike rider, rode his mountain bike to Halper's Northern Virginia farm for a visit. "By the time Page arrived at Halper's farm, he had been rattled by media calls during the prior week in which reporters alleged having information that Page met with two senior Russian intelligence figures in Moscow," investigative reporter John Solomon wrote in *The Hill*.[125] "The reporters suggested his trip [to Moscow] might have been part of a larger plot to coordinate with Russia to benefit Trump's election as president." Solomon noted that this allegation was one of the many in the uncorroborated Steele dossier charges guiding the FBI's Russia-collusion probe.

"I'm certain that nothing I said that day at the professor's farm could be deemed as anything other than exculpatory," Page told *The Hill*. "And once again, in September, I explained reality to the FBI. Contrary to the DNC's false reports, I have never met those Russians, and I did not know of any effort to coordinate, collude or conspire with Russia. Period." But the timing of the trip to see Halper at his Northern Virginia farm suggests that Halper's mission was identical to his mission with George Papadopoulos: namely, to induce his visitor to make incriminating statements that Halper could record on tape.

---

124 Kyle Cheney, "Warner: Identifying FBI Source to Undermine Russia Probe Could Be a Crime," TheIntercept.com, May 18, 2018, https://theintercept.com/2018/05/19/the-fbi-informant-who-monitored-the-trump-campaign-stefan-halper-oversaw-a-cia-spying-operation-in-the-1980-presidential-election/. See also: Leslie H. Gelb, "Reagan Aides Describe Operation to Gather Inside Data on Carter," *New York Times*, July 7, 1983, https://www.nytimes.com/1983/07/07/us/reagan-aides-describe-operation-to-gather-inside-data-on-carter.html.

125 John Solomon, "The Damning Proof of Innocence That FBI Likely Withheld in Russian Probe," *The Hill*, March 14, 2019, https://thehill.com/opinion/white-house/434054-the-damning-proof-of-innocence-that-fbi-likely-withheld-in-russian-probe.

Page has gone public, claiming his contact with Halper "intensified" in the days leading up to the FBI/DOJ's application to the FISA Court on October 21, 2016. "I had a longstanding relationship with Professor Halper," Page told host Maria Bartiromo in a Fox News televised interview. "I always believe in 'innocent until proven guilty,' but my conversations with him [Halper] intensified right in the month before my illegitimate FISA warrant in September 2016, when all these defamatory articles are being placed by the [Democratic National Committee]."[126]

On August 18, 2018, investigative reporter Sara Carter revealed that whistleblower Adam Lovinger, a former Defense Department analyst in the Pentagon's Office of Net Assessment, had information that he claimed could prove that a key player in the FBI's Russia-collusion probe, Professor Stefan Halper, was a setup.[127] The Pentagon suspended Lovinger's top-secret clearance on May 1, 2017, when he exposed through an internal review that Halper had received an extravagant payment of roughly $1 million in taxpayer money to write a few Defense Department foreign policy reports. Lovinger also expressed concerns about Halper's role in conducting what appeared to be diplomatic meetings with foreigners on behalf of the U.S. government—a role, Carter noted, that Halper was forbidden to have under federal law, given his employment by the Defense Department as a contractor.

At her article's conclusion, Carter noted that Halper appeared to have significant ties to the Russian government, as well as sources connected with Russian president Vladimir Putin. Carter had obtained documents suggesting that Halper had invited senior Russian intelligence officials to coteach his courses at the Cambridge Intelligence Seminar and had also accepted money to finance the course from a top Russian oligarch, the billionaire Andrey Cheglakov, who had known ties to Putin. In December

126   Gregg Re, "Carter Page Says FBI Informant 'Intensified' Communications Just Prior to FISA Warrant," Fox News, June 9, 2019, https://www.foxnews.com/politics/fbi-informant-intensified-communications-just-prior-to-fisa-warrant-carter-page-says.

127   Sara Carter, "Whistleblower Exposes Key Player in FBI Russia Probe: 'It Was All a Set-Up,'" Sara-Carter.com, August 27, 2018, https://saraacarter.com/whistleblower-exposes-key-player-in-fbi-russia-probe-it-was-all-a-set-up/.

2016, when Cheglakov's funding became public knowledge, Dearlove and Halper resigned from the Cambridge Intelligence Seminar, with Halper telling the *Financial Times* of London that the reason he stepped down was "unacceptable Russian influence on this group."[128] Former assistant U.S. attorney Andrew McCarthy has commented that Halper's comment was odd, given that Halper is an old friend of former Kremlin spy chief Vyacheslav Trubnikov.[129] According to the notes State Department official Kathleen Kavalec made on her meeting with Steele on October 11, 2016, at State Department headquarters in Washington, Christopher Steele claimed Trubnikov was one of the two key Russian sources for his dossier, along with Putin aide Vladislav Surkov. While the Steele dossier does not mention Trubnikov or Surkov by name, Kavalec's notes indicate that according to Steele, these two were involved with the Steele dossiers most salacious allegations—those involving prostitutes and the "golden showers" incident.[130] Given the unverified nature of the salacious claim, there is no reason to believe Steele ever interviewed either Trubnikov or Surkov.

As we shall see again in the next two chapters regarding George Papadopoulos, Halper's assignment was apparently to get Page in a relaxed setting, where Halper could induce Page to make incriminating statements that Halper was surreptitiously recording.

Carter Page Is Exonerated but Slurred by Mueller's Final Report

The final Mueller report exonerated Page of any wrongdoing. Still, the report cast his involvement in the Buryakov case in a suspicious light. The Mueller report commented, "After returning to the United States [from his assignment for Merrill Lynch in Moscow], Page became acquainted

---

128 Sam Jones, Defense and Security Editor, "Intelligence Experts Accuse Cambridge Forum of Kremlin Links," *Financial Times*, December 16, 2016, https://www.ft.com/content/d43cd586-c396-11e6-9bca-2b93a6856354.

129 McCarthy, *Ball of Collusion*, op. cit. p. 208.

130 Chuck Ross, "Steele Identified Russia Dossier Sources, Notes Reveal," *Daily Caller*, May 16, 2019, https://dailycaller.com/2019/05/16/steele-dossier-sources-state-department/.

with at least two Russian intelligence officers [associates of Buryakov], one of whom was later charged in 2015 with conspiracy to act as an unregistered agent of Russia." This comment, on page six, volume one of the report, failed to note that Page had worked as an undercover agent for the FBI in its investigation and prosecution of Buryakov. Then, on page 183 in volume one, Mueller's final report delivered the only conclusion about Carter Page that should have been contained in the report: namely that the Office of Special Counsel "did not find evidence likely to prove beyond a reasonable doubt that Campaign officials such as Paul Manafort, George Papadopoulos, and Carter Page acted as agents of the Russian government—or at its direction, control, or request—during the relevant time period."[131] Page was an innocent man, wrongly accused of treason simply because he paid his own expenses to give a speech to a Moscow educational institute while he was listed as a Trump foreign policy advisor.

In my telephone interview with Page, I asked him why those involved in the Mueller investigation chose to believe Steele's lies about him and Russia instead of having the FBI interview him before seeking FISA Court approval to conduct electronic surveillance on him. After all, the State Department, the CIA, and the FBI had had decades of experience trusting Page as an informant and an undercover operative for the U.S. government. "I will tell you why," Page answered. "It's because the Mueller investigation was a fraud. Mueller was more interested in buying a Clinton-funded effort to attack my character to destroy me, rather than simply coming to me and learning the truth. Mueller attacked me for exercising my First Amendment rights in giving a speech to an educational institute in Moscow."

According to published reports, the FBI interviewed Page for approximately ten hours over a series of five meetings in March 2017, long after the FBI and DOJ used the Steele dossier to begin electronic surveillance on him—and on the Trump campaign, through the FISA Court warrant issued for him. According to the *Washington Post*, in this series of interviews, "Page repeatedly denied wrongdoing when asked about allegations

---

131 Special Counsel Robert S. Mueller, III, *Report on the Investigation into Russian Interference in the 2016 Presidential Election*, Volume I of II, Washington, D.C., March 2019.

that he may have acted as a kind of go-between for Russia and the Trump campaign, according to a person familiar with Page's account."[132]

Why Mueller Did Not Seek to Prosecute Carter Page

That Mueller did not seek to obtain from Page a plea deal on an FBI "perjury trap" process crime strongly suggests that Mueller was concerned that Page would bring forward as a defense the decades of extensive work he had done as an informant and an undercover operative working with the FBI and CIA. What Mueller wanted from Page was not to prosecute him, but to secretly target him for electronic surveillance. The FBI sought to prosecute Page in the press by leaking to Michael Isikoff at Yahoo! News the lies in the Steele dossier accusing Page of colluding with Russian agents in Moscow.

The key premise of a FISA Court warrant for electronic surveillance is that a U.S. citizen is spying for a foreign country. In this case, the target of the investigation was Carter Page, but the FBI and DOJ were in effect given permission to extend the electronic surveillance to everyone with whom the target, Page, was in communication. These "collateral" persons of interest allowed the FBI and DOJ to extend the surveillance web to include a yet unknown number of persons, including possibly Donald Trump himself.

The initial FISA Court application on October 21, 2016, was not the last application for electronic surveillance over Donald Trump's campaign or advisors that the Obama administration made. Subsequently, the Obama FBI and DOJ made three renewal applications (in January, April, and June 2017) to the FISA Court, obtaining permission to continue electronic surveillance of the White House during the first year of Trump's presidency. As we shall also see in subsequent chapters, the Obama

---

132 Devlin Barrett, "FBI Has Questioned Trump Campaign Adviser Carter Page at Length in Russia Probe," *Washington Post*, June 26, 2017, https://www.washingtonpost.com/world/national-security/fbi-has-questioned-trump-campaign-adviser-carter-page-at-length-in-russia-probe/2017/06/26/1a271dcc-5aa5-11e7-a9f6-7c3296387341_story.html?utm_term=.8f2b1d0729ec.

administration engaged in the practice of "unmasking" to the mainstream media the names of those captured by FISA surveillance, thereby using the clandestine approval for FISA surveillance to violate the rights of innocent Americans whose only "crime" was to be involved in the Trump campaign, the Trump transition, or the Trump presidency.

Chapter Five

THE GEORGE
PAPADOPOULOS SETUP

G eorge Papadopoulos's case provides indisputable proof that the 2016 coup d'état involved several international intelligence agencies conspiring to destroy Donald Trump's political career.

I seek to establish in this chapter that U.S. and British intelligence agencies were assisted by Italian and Australian intelligence agencies in the scheme to entrap Papadopoulos. The purpose of the entrapment scheme was to get evidence that could be used in the FBI's Operation Crossfire Hurricane, and later by Mueller's special counsel investigation, to "prove" that the Trump campaign had conspired with Russia to defeat Hillary Clinton in 2016. Appearing on Judge Jeanine's show on Fox News on June 15, 2019, Papadopoulos made this exact accusation, saying:

> This was a global effort to take Trump down.... Absolutely, I think all these foreign governments were being prodded by the State Department to essentially weaponize their intelligence agencies against us. That's why you saw many Trump associates who were abroad being spied on. And, I believe, hopefully the president did bring this up during his

last visit to the U.K., because the U.K. was heavily involved in this and should be called out to the light right now.[133]

In particular, Papadopoulos has alleged correctly that British intelligence was at the heart of the conspiracy.

All Roads Lead to London

In his book, *Deep State Target: How I Got Caught in the Crosshairs of the Plot to Bring Down President Trump*,[134] Papadopoulos describes how he was "horrified and enraged" when he first heard news of the 9/11 attack as a fourteen-year-old sitting in a ninth-grade biology class at Hinsdale Central High School in a suburb of Chicago. Papadopoulos recalls realizing that day what it meant for him, the son of Greek immigrants, to be an American. He decided he did not want to follow in the footsteps of his grandfather, his father, and later his brother to take "the family medical school path." Instead, he decided to go into politics. He graduated from DePaul University with a bachelor's degree in political science. From there, he headed overseas, enrolling at University College in London, where he earned an MS in security studies. There, he fell in love with London, a city he describes as "the most cosmopolitan, international city on the planet."

Deciding not to pursue a law degree, Papadopoulos took an unpaid position as an intern at the Hudson Institute from 2011 to 2015. Like Carter Page, he developed an expertise in energy policy, sensing he could make money working internationally in the oil and natural gas businesses. In 2015, he sent his résumé to Ben Carson's presidential campaign and got a job as a foreign policy advisor for three months, from December 2015 to February 2016. But he felt out of his element among the evangelical Christians who began and ended every Carson meeting with a prayer.

After his stint with the Carson campaign, Papadopoulos returned to London, where he signed on with the London Centre of International

---

133 "George Papadopoulos: Obama State Department Prodded Foreign Governments to Spy on Trump," YouTube video, 3:52, "james hoft," June 15, 2019, https://www.youtube.com/watch?v=mjsOwIpB1Ro.

134 George Papadopoulos, *Deep State Target: How I Got Caught in the Crosshairs of the Plot to Bring Down President Trump* (New York: Diversion Books, 2019).

Law Practice (LCILP), an organization that he describes as "a strange operation," noting that he is not entirely sure why the LCILP exists.

"There is still no actual law practice going on [at the LCILP]," he observes. "There are a lot of young, intelligent experts on staff, and there seem to be a number of clients from the Arab world coming into the office," he says. "But as far as actual work, it all seems pretty hazy." As noted above, Papadopoulos had studied in London; he had spent four months with Energy Stream, a British consulting firm. At the LCILP, he was head of the Centre for International Energy and Natural Resources Law and Security, a position that appears to have been largely in name only.[135]

What Papadopoulos was about to realize was that at the LCILP, he had dropped into an international intelligence maze that recognized in him the perfect candidate to be entrapped in the Russia-collusion narrative that British intelligence was in the process of developing, with the enthusiastic cooperation of John Brennan at the helm of the CIA, to destroy Trump's political future.

While he was in London in early March 2016, overtures that Papadopoulos had been making back home paid off with Sam Clovis, the head of efforts to assemble a board of experts in various fields of public policy to advise the Trump campaign. In a Skype interview with Papadopoulos in London, Clovis agreed to add Papadopoulos to the list of unpaid advisors to the Trump campaign.

The appointment of Papadopoulos and Carter Page to Trump's foreign policy team became public knowledge when then candidate Trump, in his March 21, 2016, meeting with the editorial board of the *Washington Post*, answered a question posed by Frederick Ryan Jr., the newspaper's publisher: "We've heard you're going to be announcing your foreign policy team shortly. Any you can share with us?" Trump responded, "Well, I hadn't thought of doing it, but if you want I can give you some of the names." Trump proceeded to name both Papadopoulos and Page as members of

---

135 Brian Whitaker, "The Trump-Russia Affair and an Odd Company in London," Medium.com, November 6, 2017, https://medium.com/@Brian_Whit/the-trump-russia-affair-and-an-odd-company-in-london-9437e0343db2.

his newly appointed campaign foreign policy advisors.[136] In announcing Carter Page, Trump pointed out that Page was a PhD, stressing his academic credentials. Then, in the next breath, Trump named Papadopoulos by saying, "George Papadopoulos, he's an energy and oil consultant, excellent guy."

At that time, Trump apparently had only the information Clovis gave him about the named campaign foreign policy advisors. Clovis had "hired" both Papadopoulos and Page as foreign policy advisors to the campaign without having first met either one of them. Papadopoulos only attended one meeting that Trump attended in person and Page never met Trump. Throughout their limited tenure as Trump campaign advisors, Papadopoulos and Page typically communicated with the campaign through Clovis, not with Trump directly. Truthfully, Trump gave very little, if any, attention to any of the various policy advisors Clovis picked.

Enter Joseph Mifsud, the Master Spy in the Papadopoulos Saga

At the LCILP, Papadopoulos quickly hooked up with another LCILP associate, Joseph Mifsud, a Maltese-born academic who was associated with Link Campus University, a school established in 1999 to be the Rome branch of the University of Malta. In 2016, Link Campus University was billing itself as the "International University of Rome." According to reports published in Italian newspapers, Mifsud owns 35 percent of Link International, of which Link Campus University in Rome owns 55 percent.[137]

---

136 Post Opinions Staff, "A Transcript of Donald Trump's Meeting with the *Washington Post* Editorial Board," *Washington Post*, March 21, 2016, https://www.washingtonpost.com/blogs/post-partisan/wp/2016/03/21/a-transcript-of-donald-trumps-meeting-with-the-washington-post-editorial-board/.

137 Luciano Capone, "*L'introvabile Mifsud? Nascosto a Roma*," *Il Foglio*, April 18, 2019, https://www.ilfoglio.it/cronache/2019/04/18/news/lintrovabile-mifsud-nascosto-a-roma-250313/. In English: Luciano Capone, "Missing Mifsud was Hidden in Rome," *Il Foglio*, April 18, 2019, https://www.ilfoglio.it/esteri/2019/04/18/news/missing-mifsud-was-hidden-in-rome-250522/.

The Democrats on the House Permanent Select Committee on Intelligence have asserted that the Russians, in their approach to Papadopoulos, "used common tradecraft and employed a cutout—a Maltese professor named Joseph Mifsud."[138] But the evidence is that while Mifsud is an academic by training and profession, he has many close ties with British, Italian, and U.S. intelligence. Tagging Mifsud as the "Maltese Phantom of Russiagate," Real Clear Investigations reporter Lee Smith agrees, noting that although Mifsud has traveled many times to Russia and has contacts with Russian academics, his closest ties are to Western government, politicians, and institutions, including the CIA. After receiving his bachelor's degree from the University of Malta in 1982, he received a master's degree from the University of Padua (Italy) in 1989 and a doctorate from Queen's University in Belfast (Ireland). Working at the Ministry of Foreign Affairs in Malta in 2004, Mifsud played a role in Malta's entry into the European Union. In 2008, he was named president of the European-Mediterranean University of Slovenia.

Mifsud's background might have been academic, but Smith has properly observed that one of Mifsud's main jobs "has been to train diplomats, police officers, and intelligence officers at schools in London and Rome, where he has lived and worked over the last dozen years."[139] In the 2016 presidential election, Mifsud importantly had ties to the Democratic Party and to CrowdStrike, the cybersecurity firm funded by Google's Clinton-supporting Eric Schmidt. In subsequent chapters, I will show how the Clinton campaign, after realizing that John Podesta's emails had been hacked in March 2016, called in CrowdStrike to establish "proof" that the Russians were responsible for hacking emails from the DNC servers. Andrew Bagley, CrowdStrike's privacy counsel, attended Link Campus in Rome in 2010. In a tweet that Papadopoulos posted on April 3, 2019, he

---

138   "Minority View," House Permanent Select Committee on Intelligence, March 28, 2018, https://intelligence.house.gov/uploadedfiles/20180411_-_final_-_hpsci_minority_views_on_majority_report.pdf.

139   Lee Smith, "The Maltese Phantom of Russiagate," Real Clear Investigations, May 30, 2018, https://www.realclearinvestigations.com/articles/2018/05/26/the_maltese_phantom_of_russiagate_.html.

claimed the founder of CrowdStrike attended Link Campus for events, commenting that this was the same place he met Mifsud.

Before he departed London to fly back to the United States to hook up with the Trump campaign, Papadopoulos accepted an invitation from a woman he identified as the FBI's legal attaché in the U.K. to fly to Rome to attend an international conference organized by Mifsud at Link Campus University. Papadopoulos eventually concluded that his entire association with Mifsud, that began with the invitation from the FBI legal attaché to meet Mifsud in Rome, was an "FBI setup," suggesting that, with the encouragement of the FBI, foreign governments were interfering in the 2016 election.[140]

As experts who have studied the coup d'état against Donald Trump launched by British and U.S. intelligence have come to realize, "all roads in Russia-gate lead to London."[141] In his book, Papadopoulos describes Link Campus University in Rome as "Spook University." After arriving in Rome for the conference on March 12, 2016, he met Mifsud for the first time. At the time of their first meeting, on or about March 14, 2016, Papadopoulos understood that Mifsud was an academic with a doctorate in education from Queen's University in Belfast and a specialty in foreign affairs and important contacts around the world. In the evening Papadopoulos dined with Mifsud at an expensive restaurant near the Trevi Fountain in Rome. During dinner, Mifsud offered to introduce Papadopoulos to his international connections and "set up a meeting between Trump and Putin." That the FBI in London and Mifsud in Italy were interested in Papadopoulos a week before Trump made a public announcement Papadopoulos was joining the campaign as a foreign policy advisor raises interesting questions of whether Clovis (and possibly other Trump campaign

---

140 Margot Cleveland, "Papadopoulos Hints Conversation that Launched Trump-Russia Probe Was FBI Setup," *The Federalist*, April 1, 2019, https://thefederalist.com/2019/04/01/papadopoulos-hints-conversation-launched-trump-russia-probe-fbi-setup/.

141 Elizabeth Vos, "All Russiagate Roads Lead to London as Evidence Emerges of Joseph Mifsud's Links to UK Intelligence," *Disobedient Media*, April 4, 2018, https://disobedientmedia.com/2018/04/all-russiagate-roads-lead-to-london-as-evidence-emerges-of-joseph-mifsuds-links-to-uk-intelligence/.

senior officials) were under FBI and/or NSA electronic surveillance as early as March 2016—some seven months before October 21, 2016, the date the DOJ and FBI first obtained FISA Court approval to conduct electronic surveillance on Carter Page.

Then, on March 24, 2016, with Papadopoulos back in London, Mifsud invited him to lunch at the Grange Holborn Hotel, which Papadopoulos described as "a luxe London establishment located not far from the British Museum and Russell Square." At the lunch, Mifsud introduced Papadopoulos to Olga Polonskaya, a woman Papadopoulos understood to be Putin's niece (a woman whose real name is Olga Vinogradova, a thirty-year-old Russian from St. Petersburg and the former manager of a wine distribution company who may have had a romantic relationship with Mifsud).[142] "I can't believe my good fortune," Papadopoulos wrote after this lunch. "It's like I'm living a dream. In less than two weeks, I've joined a campaign, I've glided through a conference of power brokers in Rome, met a super-connected professor who seems to know everyone in Europe, and now I'm meeting a gorgeous Russian woman—the niece of Vladimir Putin, no less—with a hotline to the Kremlin. Everything is elegant, everything is posh and catered. It's so easy. It's like a dream, a movie. Everything is out of central casting." In a sense, Papadopoulos was right, except it was not Hollywood doing the casting, it was GCHQ and the CIA, with the likely assistance of Italian intelligence and the willing cooperation of the DOJ and the FBI.

On April 18, 2016, Mifsud, who then was supposedly in Russia, introduced Papadopoulos by email to Ivan Timofeev, a Russian who was the program director at the Russia International Affairs Council. Timofeev apparently is in charge of the conference Mifsud was then attending in Russia. Timofeev explained to Papadopoulos that he had contacts at the Russian Ministry of Foreign Affairs (MFA) and suggested that he and Papadopoulos should meet in London or Moscow. Papadopoulos writes in

---

142 Sharon LaFraniere, David D. Kirkpatrick, Andrew Higgins, and Michael Schwartz, "A London Meeting of an Unlikely Group: How a Trump Advisor Came to Learn of Clinton 'Dirt,'" *New York Times*, November 10, 2017, https://www.nytimes.com/2017/11/10/us/russia-inquiry-trump.html. See also: McCarthy, *Ball of Collusion*, op. cit, p. 130.

his book the following about his meeting Olga and Timofeev: "The back and forth with Timofeev is encouraging to me. He's the first, really the only, Russian I've ever been in contact with besides the enigmatic Olga. I emailed my contacts at campaign headquarters: "The Russian government has an open invitation by Putin for Mr. Trump to meet him when he is ready."

On April 26, 2016, after Mifsud returned from Russia, Papadopoulos met him for breakfast in London at the Andaz hotel, near the Liverpool Street station. This turned out to be the key meeting in the intelligence agency entrapment scheme. The setup for the breakfast meeting was that Mifsud had just returned from a conference in Russia. While he was there, Olga had emailed to Papadopoulos the following message: "The Russian government has an open invitation for Mr. Trump to meet with him [Putin] when he is ready. The advantage of being in London is that these governments tend to speak a bit more openly in 'neutral cities.'"

But at the breakfast meeting, Mifsud surprised Papadopoulos. He leaned across the table in a conspiratorial manner and whispered to Papadopoulos that "the Russians have 'dirt' on Hillary Clinton—emails of Clinton. They have thousands of them." In his book, Papadopoulos says he was shocked to hear this, but he really didn't know what to do with the information. "My mission is to make a meeting [between Trump and Putin] happen," Papadopoulos writes. "End of story. Hacking, security breaches, potential blackmail—that is illegal and treasonous." Papadopoulos insists he did not want to pursue the subject, but instead returned to the theme of arranging the proposed Putin-Trump meeting. "But when we said goodbye, I have a feeling he's still just spinning me," Papadopoulos concludes about Mifsud.

The Fateful May 10 Meeting

Next, a series of intelligence-connected operatives intervened to set up Papadopoulos to meet with Alexander Downer, a leftist Australian politician who served as Australian high commissioner to the U.K. from 2014 to 2018.

On the rainy London evening of May 10, 2016, Papadopoulos got together with Downer and his assistant, the Australian intelligence officer Erika Thompson, for drinks at the Kensington Wine Rooms, a swanky joint that boasts of having some 150 different wines available by the glass. This turns out to be the coup de grâce meeting of the entrapment scheme. Passing on the wine and ordering gin and tonics, Downer told Papadopoulos that he was a big fan of Hillary Clinton and a board member of Hakluyt, a private British security firm with close ties to the Obama administration. Downer flattered Papadopoulos by indicating that he was familiar with Papadopoulos's various writings on the Middle East and energy policy. What happened next is described by Papadopoulos in his book:

> And then something happens.
>
> Or, more accurately, Downer later claims something happens.
>
> In his version of events, he asks me a question about Russia and Trump.
>
> I then tell him that the Russians have a surprise, or some damaging material related to Hillary Clinton.
>
> I have no memory of this. None. Zero. Nada.
>
> In my version of events, Downer brusquely leaves me and Erika at the table, and we go our separate ways. I remember feeling completely disappointed by the meeting and pissed off about being treated so rudely.
>
> Downer's version, however, is the one that matters.

A day or two after the meeting at the wine bar, Downer, who appears also to be an informant to the Australian Secret Intelligence Service, the equivalent of the CIA, claims to have reported by cable to his diplomatic superiors in Canberra about his conversation with Papadopoulos at the wine bar.[143]

---

143 AAP and Melanie Sun, "Declassified Mueller Report Would Reveal UK, Australian Intelligence Involved in Anti-Trump 'Witch Hunt,' Says Former Trump Aide," *The Epoch Times*, March 25, 2019, https://www. theepochtimes.com/former-trump-aide-says-declassified-mueller-report-would-reveal-uk-australian-intelligence-involved-in-anti-trump-witch-hunt_2852129.html.

This information appears to have been buried somewhere within the Australian government until July 22, 2016, when Julian Assange and WikiLeaks began, over two days, making public some forty thousand stolen DNC emails that forced Debbie Wasserman Schultz to resign as DNC chair. Various reports indicate that Joe Hockey, Australia's ambassador to the United States in Washington, an initial suspect for the leak of Mifsud's remarks, was the person who told his American counterparts about the Papadopoulos conversation.[144] Others, including Papadopoulos, suggest—apparently correctly—that Downer himself shared the information with Chargé d'Affaires Elizabeth Dibble, the U.S. deputy chief of mission at the U.S. embassy in London. Dibble, a career diplomat who from 2008 to 2010 was the deputy chief of mission and chargé d'affaires at the U.S. Embassy in Rome, apparently conveyed Downer's information to the State Department in Washington. Papadopoulos comments in his book that Dibble was in close touch with Gregory Baker and Terrence Dudley, the two presumed CIA agents posing as military attachés to the U.S. embassy in London. We will soon see that Baker and Dudley were monitoring Papadopoulos in London, possibly from the first moment he arrived there in March 2016.

The suspicion is that once the information from Downer reached the State Department in Washington, it was conveyed to the FBI by Jonathan Winer, the former deputy assistant of state who was in communication with Christopher Steele during the summer of 2016. Reporter Kimberley A. Strassel at the *Wall Street Journal* correctly noted that the information from Downer about Mifsud's conversation with Papadopoulos reached the FBI outside normal channels.[145]

The United States is part of what is known as "Five Eyes," an intelligence network that includes the U.K., Canada, Australia, and New Zealand. As Strassel correctly reports, the Five Eyes agreement provides that any intelligence goes through the intelligence system of the country

---

144   Margot Cleveland, "Papadopoulos Hints Conversation That Launched Trump-Russia Probe Was FBI Setup," op. cit.

145   Kimberley A. Strassel, "The Curious Case of Mr. Downer," *Wall Street Journal*, May 31, 2018, https://www.wsj.com/articles/ the-curious-case-of-mr-downer-1527809075.

that gathered it. This is done to help guarantee intelligence information is securely handled, subjected to quality control, and not made prey to political manipulation. "Mr. Downer's job was to report his meeting back to Canberra and leave it to Australian intelligence," Strassel wrote. "We also know that it wasn't Australian intelligence that alerted the FBI. The document that launched the FBI probe contains no foreign intelligence whatsoever. So, if Australian intelligence did receive the Downer info, it didn't feel compelled to act on it." But when the information reached Winer through State Department channels, he passed it on to the FBI. If the FBI received the Downer information through unauthorized channels, it was arguably illegal to use that information to initiate a national security investigation or to advance a FISA Court application.

This is an issue raised by former CIA analyst Larry Johnson. Emails Papadopoulos is believed to have sent in 2015 to Corey Lewandowski after Lewandowski was appointed Trump's first campaign director may have been intercepted by both GCHQ and the NSA. Possibly, the CIA was receiving intelligence on Trump campaign officials in 2015 from British intelligence monitoring Trump. Under British law, the GCHQ is not restricted under British law from placing U.S. citizens under electronic surveillance. Again, the question of how the CIA, FBI, and DOJ got information used to implicate Trump in "Russian collusion" is important. If the CIA, FBI, or DOJ, in their hate-Trump zeal, circumvented U.S. law in order to receive intelligence from unauthorized sources, the entire Russia-collusion investigation—including all applications to the FISA Court—may have been illegal.

As noted earlier, on July 31, 2016, the FBI formally opened the Operation Crossfire Hurricane investigation, looking into possible coordination between the Russian government and the Trump campaign. I noted that on the day before, July 30, 2016, DOJ officer Bruce Ohr and his wife Nellie met with Christopher Steele at the Mayflower Hotel. As we saw in the previous chapter, subsequent to this meeting, Ohr communicated to the FBI information from the Steele dossier. It also appears that the opening of the Operation Crossfire Hurricane investigation was triggered in part by information about the Downer cable that the Australian government had communicated to the United States through diplomatic channels.

In July 2016, CIA Director John Brennan wrote a two-page EC, or "electronic communication," to FBI Director James Comey. In the EC, Brennan communicated to Comey details of the meeting between Papadopoulos and Mifsud, as reported by Downer. According to GOP Representative Devin Nunes, the former chairman of the House Intelligence Committee, Brennan's EC was not an official product of the U.S. intelligence communities, nor was Brennan using information gained through official partnerships with Five Eyes partner intelligence agencies. Rather, John Brennan appears to have enlisted the assistance of foreign intelligence assets to run operations against the Trump campaign, perhaps starting as early as late 2015. It also appears that two of the foreign intelligence assets Brennan recruited were Stefan Halper and Joseph Mifsud, both with extensive ties to the CIA. Brennan's EC to Comey and the information Mifsud shared with Papadopoulos at their famous breakfast meeting at the Andaz hotel in London on April 26, 2016, were the final pieces of evidence needed to trigger the FBI into opening Operation Crossfire Hurricane as a counterintelligence investigation.[146]

Almost immediately upon the opening of Operation Crossfire Hurricane, text messages exchanged between Peter Strzok and Lisa Page further indicate that Strzok was in London on August 3, 2016. In London, Strzok met with Claire Smith, a member of the U.K. Joint Intelligence Committee, realizing she had worked with Mifsud at three different institutions—the London Academy of Diplomacy, the University of Stirling in Scotland, and Link University Campus in Rome. Smith was also a member of the U.K. security vetting panel and was in a position to brief Strzok on Mifsud, given that she had followed him from the London Academy of Diplomacy to Stirling University and then to Link University Campus in Rome. Smith and Mifsud were photographed together in October 2012 in Rome at Link University Campus, where they were involved in training

---

146 Much of the analysis in this paragraph and in subsequent paragraphs owes a debt of gratitude to an author known as "sundance" writing on The Conservative Treehouse blog, particularly the post titled "Devin Nunes: The Spying Began in 2015…" April 11, 2019, https://theconservativetreehouse.com/2019/04/11/devin-nunes-the-spying-began-in-2015/.

Italian law enforcement on intelligence operations.[147] At the time of his trip to London, Strzok was running the Mifsud case for the FBI. Strzok's meeting with Smith appears to tie British intelligence into the sting operation carried out by Mifsud on Papadopoulos, as sanitized through a leak engineered by Erika Thompson and/or Alexander Downer.

In London, just days after the FBI opened Operation Crossfire Hurricane, Strzok met with Downer. McCarthy noted the extraordinary nature of the Strzok meeting with Downer. "Breaking with diplomatic protocol after tense negotiations, the American and Australian governments had agreed that Strzok and another agent would be permitted to interview High Commissioner Alexander Downer Canberra's top emissary to London," McCarthy wrote. "Downer had informed the American embassy that he believed Trump-campaign advisor George Papadopoulos had tipped him off to a Russian scheme to swing the presidency to Trump—mainly by hacking and releasing information that could damage Clinton, such as the tens of thousands of Democratic party emails now in circulation."[148] So now, the FBI was involved in international diplomatic affairs, mixing responsibilities with the State Department and the CIA, interviewing Downer in London with the obvious consent of British intelligence GCHQ and Australian intelligence.

When Mifsud's role with Papadopoulos became known, Link Campus University officially terminated Mifsud's contract, according to reports published in Italy. Then, in November 2018, Mifsud went missing; U.S. authorities presumed he was deceased. Seven months later, however, Mifsud resurfaced; it turns out he never left Rome. Italian newspapers reported that the entire time Mifsud was missing and presumed dead, he

147   Elizabeth Vos, "A Conversation With Chris Blackburn on the Contradictions Surrounding Mifsud," *Disobedient Media*, April 23, 2018, https://disobedientmedia.com/2018/04/a-conversation-with-chris-blackburn-on-the-contradictions-surrounding-mifsud/.

148   McCarthy, *Ball of Collusion*, op. cit, p. 213. See also: Matt Apuzzo, Adam Goldman, and Nicholas Fandos, "Code Name Crossfire Hurricane: The Secret Origins of the Trump Investigation," *New York Times*, May 16, 2018, https://www.nytimes.com/2018/05/16/us/politics/crossfire-hurricane-trump-russia-fbi-mueller-investigation.html.

was living comfortably in an apartment near the U.S. embassy in Rome. The apartment was owned by a Greek diplomat, and the rent was paid by Link Campus University.[149]

Did Mifsud Actually Whisper Anything?

Despite the enthusiasm of Peter Strzok and those involved in the Mueller investigation to take the Mifsud-Downer story at face value, doubts have continued to circulate about whether or not Mifsud actually said anything about Clinton's emails at his breakfast meeting with Papadopoulos. In an interview with the Italian newspaper *La Repubblica*, Mifsud denied telling Papadopoulos anything about the Russians having Clinton's missing thirty thousand emails, or about any other emails (including those WikiLeaks published on July 22, 2016, or Podesta's stolen emails).

"'Dirt on Hillary Clinton? This is nonsense,'" Mifsud told the Italian newspaper *La Repubblica*. "Friendship is friendship, but Papadopoulos does not tell the truth. The only thing I did was to facilitate contacts between official and unofficial sources to resolve a crisis. It is usual business everywhere. I put think tanks in contact, groups of experts with other groups of experts." In the interview, Mifsud claimed he was "a member" of the Clinton Foundation. "Between you and me, my thinking is left-leaning. But I predicted Trump's victory as well as Brexit. Everyone wants peace. If the governments don't talk to each other, we citizens must keep talking."[150]

No recording has surfaced to corroborate Downer's meeting at the London wine bar with Papadopoulos on May 10, 2016. Had Mifsud and

---

149   Paolo G. Brera, "*Il prof dei contatti russi-Trump*" "*É vero, ho fatto da mediatore ma sono clintoniano e di sinistra*," *La Repubblica*, November 1, 2017, https://www.repubblica.it/esteri/2017/11/01/news/il_prof_dei_con-tatti_russi-trump_e_vero_ho_fatto_da_mediatore_ma_sono_clinto-niano_e_di_sinistra_-179918121/. In English: Paolo G. Brera, "Russiagate, Mystery Professor Joseph Mifsud Speaks Out: 'Dirt on Hillary Clinton? Nonsense,'" *La Repubblica*, November 1, 2017, https://www.repubblica.it/esteri/2017/11/01/news/russiagate_mystery_professor_joseph_mifsud_speaks_out_dirt_on_hillary_clinton_nonsense_-179948962/.

150   Paolo G. Brera, "Russiagate, Mystery Professor Joseph Mifsud Speaks Out: 'Dirt on Hillary Clinton? Nonsense,'" op. cit.

Downer simply invented the comments Downer sent in his cable back to the Australian government in Canberra? Investigative reporter Kimberley Strassel, writing in the *Wall Street Journal* on May 31, 2018, was struck by an important discrepancy between Downer's account of the conversation, as published in an Australian newspaper, and the version being leaked by the U.S. government to the media. "In his Australian interview, Mr. Downer said Mr. Papadopoulos didn't give specifics," Strassel wrote. She noted that the Australian newspaper quoted Downer as saying, "He [Papadopoulos] didn't say dirt, he said material that could be damaging to her [Clinton]." Also, Strassel wrote, "nothing he [Papadopoulos] said in that conversation indicated Trump himself had been conspiring with the Russians to collect information on Hillary Clinton."[151]

If our suspicions prove true that Erika Thompson was the source of the information about Mifsud's alleged comments to Papadopoulos during their meeting on April 26, 2016, it is possible that Mifsud never spoke those words to Papadopoulos. This explains why Mifsud has always denied whispering to Papadopoulos anything about the Russians being in possession of emails stolen from Clinton. It is hard to imagine that Mifsud would have forgotten comments that were explosive about Russia and dirt in stolen emails, and the Clinton campaign comment—even if they were made out of context.

The meeting with Mifsud on April 26, 2016, would have been the first time Papadopoulos could have heard anything about Clinton's emails having been stolen by anybody, including the Russians. The Democrats waited until June 2016 to issue a public statement that their computers had been hacked. Prior to that, the only relevant email scandal involved Hillary Clinton's private email server. That scandal was not that Secretary Clinton's private email server had been hacked, but that she chose to use an offline computer server to transmit and receive classified information, in apparent violation of national security laws.

---

151 Kimberley A. Strassel, "The Curious Case of Mr. Downer," *The Wall Street Journal*, May 31, 2018, https://www.wsj.com/articles/the-curious-case-of-mr-downer-1527809075.

From his first meeting with the FBI, in February 2017, Papadopoulos has never wavered in his insistence that Mifsud told him, "The Russians have dirt on Hillary." Mifsud, as noted above, denies the allegations. Papadopoulos has also been consistent in saying he gave little thought to Mifsud's comments about Russia having dirt on Clinton. He has consistently claimed that his only real interest in Mifsud was that Mifsud might be able to help him set up a meeting between Putin and Trump.

From my own experience with the Mueller prosecutors and the FBI, I believe it is entirely possible that the FBI and prosecutors on Mueller's team suggested to Papadopoulos that they had evidence to "prove" that Mifsud made the Clinton comments. Rather than risk disputing "proof" that the FBI and the Mueller prosecutors may have claimed to have in their possession, Papadopoulos might have decided it was best to go along, hence "remembering" Mifsud's words. This may explain why Papadopoulos went from dismissing Mifsud as "a nothing" and "just a guy talking up connections or something" in his first interview with the FBI on January 27, 2017, to acknowledging in his second interview with the FBI on February 16, 2017, that Mifsud was "important" and had serious connections to Russian officials in Moscow.

Erika Thompson, Secret Agent

Let's backtrack and establish more carefully just who Erika Thompson actually is.

A close reading of the Mueller report reveals that on page eighty-six, Mueller notes the following: "On May 6, 2016, 10 days after that meeting with Mifsud, Papadopoulos suggested to a representative of a foreign government that the Trump Campaign had received indications from the Russian government that it could assist the Campaign through the anonymous release of information that would be damaging to Hillary Clinton." A strong argument can be made that "a representative of a foreign government" refers to Erika Thompson, not Alexander Downer. Also lending weight to this conclusion, May 6, 2016, was the day Thompson telephoned Papadopoulos in London to set up the meeting with Downer.

A few days earlier, on May 3, 2016, Papadopoulos got a phone call from Christian Cantor, an acquaintance at the Israeli embassy in London.

Cantor explained that he wanted to introduce Papadopoulos to his girl-friend, Erika Thompson. The three of them met at a pub. Cantor intro-duced Thompson as a staff member of the Australian High Commission (the Commonwealth equivalent of "embassy"), where she claimed to be an assistant to Alexander Downer, the high commissioner (equivalent to "ambassador"). Next, Papadopoulos remembers that "on or about May 6, 2016," he got an email from Thompson, inviting him to meet with her and Downer. In his book, Papadopoulos comments that an unnamed "high-profile reporter based in Washington" told him that Cantor and Erika Thompson were both intelligence officers for their respective coun-tries. The email on May 6, 2016, was the setup for the fateful meeting that Papadopoulos had with Thompson and Downer at the London wine bar.

The Mueller report goes on to mention in footnote 465 on page eighty-nine: "The foreign government conveyed this information to the U.S. govern-ment on July 26, 2016, a few days after WikiLeaks's release of Clinton-related emails. The FBI opened its investigation of potential coordination between Russia and the Trump Campaign a few days later based on the information." The date, July 26, 2016, is likely the date Brennan sent his EC to Comey, de-tailing for Comey the Mifsud-Papadopoulos meeting. Like Mifsud, Downer has consistently said he does not remember the subject of Russia and emails coming up in his meeting with Papadopoulos on May 10, 2016. If Mifsud's supposed comments to Papadopoulos were relayed by Thompson through intelligence channels to the FBI, it is possible that Thompson invented words for Mifsud that he never said at all.

That the Papadopoulos setup was an intelligence operation organized and implemented by Brennan at the CIA with the help of CIA foreign operative Joseph Mifsud makes even more sense with the knowledge that a large portion of the CIA's work overseas is done through U.S. embassies, with CIA foreign agents positioned as State Department officials. In his book, Papadopoulos also comments that in the setup for the meeting with Downer, he was contacted by two military attachés at the U.S. embassy in London, Terrence Dudley and Gregory Baker. Papadopoulos knew that while most embassy staff work for the State Department, he commented in his book that "it is common knowledge in diplomatic communities that many embassy employees designated as 'diplomats' are, in fact, intelligence operatives affiliated with the CIA or military intelligence divisions."

Dudley and Baker took Papadopoulos out to an expensive dinner at "The Rag"—the name given to the Army and Navy Club in London's tony Mayfair district. During the dinner, Dudley and Baker presented themselves as being in favor of reaching out to Russia. Papadopoulos says that in their subsequent meetings, Dudley and Baker seemed to be recruiting him to become an intelligence agent, suggesting he could make contact with the military attaché of the U.S. embassy in Greece the next time he visited the country. Papadopoulos was also curious about how Dudley and Baker tried "to ingratiate themselves" into the Trump campaign, asking if Papadopoulos could get them a job. Papadopoulos noted that they kept messaging him until the inauguration.

In his congressional testimony, all references made by FBI director of counterintelligence Bill Priestap to cities where he had been traveling were redacted. But on May 4, 2016, Strzok sent Page a text message that read: "Going back to that [redacted] memo, just remembered Jones wants something soon (tonight or tomorrow). I don't know that Bill [Priestap] will read it before he gets back from London next week, but last thing I want is him launching it upstairs with 3rd party review in there." Priestap was one of Strzok's bosses. This also puts Priestap as well as Strzok in London around May 10, 2016, the day when Papadopoulos and Downer had their famous wine bar discussion.[152]

The Downer Cable: Just Another DOJ Cover-Up

It appears that Priestap may have been in London to oversee the steps taken to arrange the Papadopoulos meeting with Downer. It does not appear

---

152 Much of the analysis in this paragraph and in subsequent paragraphs owes a debt of gratitude to an author known as "sundance" writing on The Conservative Treehouse blog, particularly the post "'Unofficial Channels'—Reconciling Mueller's Strategically Worded Origin of Operation Crossfire Hurricane," April 20, 2019, https://theconservativetreehouse.com/2019/04/20/unofficial-channels-reconciling-muellers-strategically-worded-origin-of-operation-crossfire-hurricane/.

coincidental that Priestap was in London when Papadopoulos met Downer at the wine bar. Neither does it seem coincidental that Priestap was in town when two likely CIA intelligence agents contacted Papadopoulos, or that Priestap was in town when Christian Cantor called Papadopoulos out of the blue to introduce him to his girlfriend, Erika Thompson.

Papadopoulos was set up to meet Downer precisely because the DOJ and FBI needed a way to get word back to the United States that on April 26, 2016, Mifsud had whispered to Papadopoulos that Russia was in possession of emails stolen from Hillary Clinton. Given that the DOJ had not yet opened a counterintelligence investigation on Trump and Russia, Priestap's involvement in London was possibly illegal and certainly "unofficial." Priestap understood that, for reasons of law and protocol, word of Mifsud's comments to Papadopoulos needed to reach the DOJ and FBI in Washington through official channels. Given that Thompson was an Australian intelligence agent operating from within the Australian embassy in London, she could have composed the Downer cable and arranged to have it sent back to Canberra without consulting with Downer or being told by Downer to do so.

What we know for sure is that this was a complicated sting in that it took until July 26, 2016, for the "foreign government"—that is, the Australian embassy in London—to report Downer's cable to the U.S. government. The information had to have traveled from Australia's equivalent of the State Department in Canberra to the Australian embassy in London. From there, Australian diplomats in London could relay the information to U.S. diplomats in London, confident that U.S. diplomats in London would relay the information to the U.S. State Department in Washington. The State Department could then inform the DOJ and FBI, with the information passing through "official" channels. July 26, 2016, was also the likely date of the Brennan EC to Comey that triggered the opening of Operation Crossfire Hurricane.

Yet there can be no doubt that Assange's decision to start making the stolen Democrat emails public on July 22, 2016, formed an important context for the shifting of the DOJ and FBI investigation of Russian collusion into the full-scale Operation Crossfire Hurricane. McCarthy in his 2019 book *Ball of Collusion* speculates that "…the Trump campaign must have known that Russia possessed emails somehow related to Hillary Clinton before WikiLeaks caused the dissemination of hacked Democratic National Committee emails to the media, beginning on July 22, 2016." Starting from that premise, McCarthy further surmises "…the foreign ministries of the United States and Australia, through mendacity or incompetence, erected a fraudulent story that warped the Trump campaign's purported foreknowledge of Russia's perfidy into a potential espionage conspiracy."[153]

McCarthy goes on to consider that Downer, prompted by WikiLeaks beginning to release DNC emails on July 22, 2016, on the eve of the Democrats' national nominating convention in Philadelphia, and some two months after the famous Papadopoulos-Downer meeting, went into high gear. "From this occurrence [WikiLeaks actions on July 22, 2016], Downer suddenly drew the unfounded inference that *these emails* [the ones Papadopoulos mentioned to Downer in their meeting at the London wine bar on May 10, 2016] *must have been what Papadopoulos was talking* about when he said Russia had damaging information about Clinton." McCarthy next suggests that the High Commissioner, after realizing this, "decided that, rather than just letting whatever he'd fleetingly reported to his government gather dust in the archives, he'd better raise it directly with his American counterparts—his friends at the U.S. embassy, then being run by U.S. Ambassador Matthew Barzun, the mega-fundraiser for President Obama and then-Secretary of State John Kerry, who had labored to retire the campaign debt from Hillary Clinton's first White House run, clearing the way for her to become Obama's Secretary of State."[154]

Interestingly, McCarthy notes the decision by WikiLeaks to begin releasing the DNC stolen emails on July 22, 2016, also affected Christopher Steele. Having begun his famous dossier before that date, Steele and Simpson were required to weave WikiLeaks into the Trump-Russia conspiracy narrative. In what ended up being an evolving document, the narrative of the Steele dossier after July 22 was altered to insist Russia stole the emails and gave them to Assange to publish. But to complete the "collusion" circle back to Trump, Steele (and Mueller) had to find some way Trump connected

---

153 McCarthy, *Ball of Collusion*, op. cit., p. 125.
154 Ibid, p. 135, italics in original.

with Assange so as to instruct Assange how best to drop the emails remaining after the July 2016 dump in a manner aimed at doing Hillary's campaign the maximum harm. The point is that Steele did not attribute the DNC hack to Russia until a few days after July 22, 2016. Before that, Steele had based his Russia-collusion argument largely on the fabrication that Trump had been compromised by perverted sexual behavior when visiting Russia.[155]

Still, the problem remains that the Downer cable yet could be nothing more than a cover story designed to hide the fact that Papadopoulos was set up, very likely by Priestap and Strzok, in an international intelligence sting operation organized by Brennan and the CIA. The point was to tag Papadopoulos with having advance knowledge that Russia possessed the stolen Clinton emails. That the FBI "officially" got word of the Downer cable through diplomatic channels makes the Obama State Department an instrumental player at the heart of the coup d'état. In the previous chapter, I established the pains that Christopher Steele took to communicate details of his anti-Trump dossier to Jonathan Winer, the State Department special coordinator for Libya, and to Victoria Nuland, the assistant secretary of state for European and Eurasian affairs. The DOJ and FBI could not begin Operation Crossfire Hurricane unless the State Department played along. It strains credibility to believe that Australian intelligence in Canberra and in London participated in this scam with someone of Priestap's rank and with two CIA agents assigned as military attachés to the U.S. embassy in London unless British intelligence knew exactly what was going on and gave a nod of approval.

Much of the confusion about Mifsud comes from the fact that he was acting as a Western intelligence agent, working in London and Italy to recruit and train agents for British intelligence while also acting as a CIA asset. However, for the CIA to establish that Mifsud knew as early as April 26, 2016, that Russia had Clinton's emails, the CIA had to present Mifsud as an intelligence agent working as a Russian asset. Papadopoulos would not have any reason to believe Mifsud's out-of-context remarks to him suggesting that Russia was in possession of stolen Clinton emails unless Papadopoulos believed Mifsud was working with Russians. In his

---

155 Ibid., pp. 171-174.

book, Papadopoulos details the many hints Mifsud gave him that he visited Russia frequently and had excellent intelligence sources of information in Moscow. This appears not to have been idle conversation by Mifsud, but rather part of the script written for Mifsud by Brennan to create in Papadopoulos's mind the impression that Mifsud was a Russian asset.

In 2018, Swiss-German lawyer and entrepreneur Stephan C. Roh and his coauthor Thierry Pastor, a French political analyst, published a book in London titled *The Faking of Russia-Gate: The Papadopoulos Case—An Investigative Analysis*. The book was published by ILS Publishing, which is owned by ILS Energy, an energy research and consulting company based in Hong Kong. ILS Publishing and ILS Energy are controlled by the international law firm RoH Attorneys at Law, based in Zurich, Switzerland, with offices in London, Berlin, and Hong Kong, and with affiliated operations in Moscow, Dubai, Beijing, and Monaco. The principal of RoH Attorneys and the principal author of the book, Stephan Roh, is also an investor who holds a 5 percent stake in Link Campus University in Rome. In this context, Roh worked with Professor Joseph Mifsud. In their book, Roh and Pastor describe Mifsud as "a distinguished Maltese academic, a seasoned civil servant, a lecturer on international relations and diplomatic studies in Rome, as well as at several distinguished U.S. and European universities."

The authors readily concede that Mifsud is a "Clintonist" who "was embedded in the network of Clintonian and Democratic institutions, employed by and befriended with Christian mega-donors, with supporters and followers of the Democratic Party and of the Hillary Clinton 2016 Presidential Campaign." They insist that Mifsud was also "deeply embedded in the network of Western Intelligence Services" and has never worked for Russian intelligence in any capacity. The authors comment on their curiosity when Papadopoulos was styled as the "smoking gun" for the alleged collusion between the Russian government and Donald Trump. They were even more curious when Papadopoulos became the critical element of the scandal, the first "domino" to fall in Russiagate. They compare him to "John Dean of Watergate," the person responsible for the fall of President Nixon. Meanwhile, the authors insist, because Mifsud "disappeared" for a few "scandalous months" while still cooperating with "his Western spy masters," he was unable to defend himself and tell the truth while the press portrayed him wrongfully as a "mysterious and shady Russian spy."

The book argues it is "unproven" that Papadopoulos ever received from Mifsud the message that the Russians had emails with dirt on Hillary Clinton. Roh and Pastor point out how important it was to the "Russian collusion" hoax to establish that Mifsud told Papadopoulos Russia had stolen emails. Roh and Pastor note this constitutes "the main narrative to support the idea of collusion and it is nowadays the official version of why the Obama Administration's anti-Trump spying and intelligence operation found justification and for what reason it was commenced." The authors also claim that Mifsud went into hiding because he was disgraced by the international publicity that tagged him as a Russian spy. Even more frightening, Mifsud feared for his life and his health.

The key point here is that the growing documentary record available to the public proves that in the Papadopoulos sting, U.S. intelligence agents worked in conjunction with the CIA to establish that Mifsud gave Papadopoulos information that Russia had stolen Clinton emails. Ultimately, the Mifsud story about Russia's having dirt on Clinton had to be sanitized through State Department diplomatic channels—an effort that took from May 6, 2016, until July 26, 2016—to give the DOJ and the FBI confidence the story about the Mifsud-Papadopoulos meeting was true. The State Department diplomatic channel came into play because the DOJ and the FBI needed the Downer cable not only to establish the credibility of the Mifsud-Papadopoulos story, but as a pretext to open Operation Crossfire Hurricane. Once the FBI had Ohr's report on the Steele dossier implicating Carter Page and Downer's report implicating Papadopoulos, the FBI had all the justification needed to spy on the Trump campaign and possibly even Trump himself. Comey's receipt of the Brennan EC placed the CIA blessing for the DOJ and FBI to begin counterintelligence investigations on Trump absent evidence Trump or anyone in his campaign had committed crimes. On July 31, 2016, with the opening of the Operation Crossfire Hurricane investigation, the DOJ and FBI set their path to the FISA Court to get permission to conduct electronic surveillance of the Trump campaign.

But what remains inexplicable in the Papadopoulos story that Brennan and DOJ/FBI coconspirators manufactured is why Mifsud, a known

Hillary Clinton supporter, would act as a shill for Russia in an attempt to help Trump defeat Clinton. And why would Mifsud, a professor with vast experience in foreign policy and a history of training diplomats on how to work for MI6, pick Papadopoulos, an inexperienced research fellow at the Hudson Institute, to relay the one critical piece of information—advance knowledge that Russia had stolen "Clinton emails"—a "fact" on which the entire Russia-collusion narrative rested?

It appears that on May 16, 2019, the Italian government stopped covering up for the U.S. Justice Department and the CIA. That was the day Prime Minister Giuseppe Conte fired six deputy directors of Italy's intelligence agencies. While government sources in Italy have described this unusual move as "business as usual," Giulio Occhionero—an Italian hacker arrested in Rome on January 9, 2017—begs to differ. Occhionero was charged with having hacked some eighteen thousand email accounts, including those belonging to former Italian prime minister Matteo Renzi. But Mario Monti, an Italian economist who served as Italy's prime minister from 2011 to 2013, tweeted on May 16, 2018, "But in Rome, everybody knows it's all about SpyGate and Trump sabotage."[156]

Why Bother Setting Up George Papadopoulos?

On June 14, 2019, the Australian Information Commission announced its agreement with "foreign officials" not to release to the public the diplomatic cable that Downer sent back to the Australian government within days of his meeting with Papadopoulos on May 10, 2016. The commission explained that publishing the diplomatic cable that sparked the Trump-Russia investigation would damage Australia's ability to build a good relationship with

---

156 Jon Dougherty, "Unprecedented: Italian PM Reportedly Fires Several Top Intelligence Agency Chiefs over Their Cooperation with Obama Deep State in 'Spygate,'" *The National Sentinel*, May 17, 2019, https://thenationalsentinel.com/2019/05/17/unprecedented-italian-pm-fires-several-top-intelligence-agency-chiefs-over-their-cooperation-with-obama-deep-state-in-spygate/.

the United States.[157] Clearly, the Australians had joined in taking the vow of silence intended to continue the Clinton/Obama coup d'état cover-up.

That vow of silence also extends to the Mueller report, which does not mention Downer's name—not even once. Yet the Mueller report mentions Mifsud by name eighty-seven times. This again raises the question of whether the Downer cable exists, or whether it was manufactured after the fact to substantiate the also questionable claim Mifsud told Papadopoulos that Russia had Clinton emails. The Downer cable and the Brennan EC were necessary to set up Papadopoulos, tying him to Julian Assange and the WikiLeaks publication of emails stolen from the Democrats. That really became relevant only after July 22, 2016, when Assange made public the first round of DNC emails designed to expose Hillary's rigging the primaries with the help of Debbie Wasserman Schultz to make sure that Bernie Sanders did not get the nomination.

Note that prior to July 22, 2016, the information planted with Carter Page and George Papadopoulos was vague, stressing only that Russia had stolen "Clinton emails." Page and Papadopoulos could easily have assumed the reference was to emails destroyed by Clinton from the private email server she had used while she served as secretary of state. After July 22, 2016, when Assange publicized the first round of stolen DNC emails, the DOJ, the FBI, the State Department, the CIA, and other intelligence agencies including James Clapper's Office of the Director of National Intelligence went into overdrive. They worked in conjunction with British, Italian, and Australian intelligence. The coconspirators now had to establish not only that Russia stole the DNC emails, but that Trump induced Russia to steal the emails (through the offering of a quid pro quo benefit after Trump was elected), that Russia gave the emails to Assange for WikiLeaks to publish, and that Trump established contact with Assange

---

157   Mark Di Stefano, "Australia's Account of the London Meeting that Led to the Trump-Russia Investigation Will Remain Secret," BuzzFeed News, June 14, 2019, https://www.buzzfeed.com/markdistefano/australia-account-trump-russia-papadopoulos-downer.

so as to instruct Assange to make the remaining stolen DNC emails public to do maximum harm to Hillary's campaign.[158]

If Papadopoulos knew as early as April 2016 that Russia had these stolen DNC emails, it's highly possible that he was the link between the Russian intelligence agents who had stolen the emails and Assange, who ultimately published the stolen emails with WikiLeaks. This type of reasoning is identical to the way the FBI formulated the central hypothesis pursued by the Mueller prosecutors during my forty-hour inquisition, as described in Chapter 1 and in all its excruciating detail in my book *Silent No More*. Mueller's team of hate-Trump prosecutors became abusive with me when I insisted I never contacted Assange or Wikileaks. As we shall see in the next chapter, the hate-Trump FBI and Mueller prosecutors became equally abusive to Papadopoulos when he insisted that he had told no one in the Trump campaign about Mifsud's saying the Russians had stolen DNC emails.

Downer Raised Millions in Australia for the Clinton Foundation

Downer, it turns out, has a history of raising a substantial amount of money for the Clinton Foundation in Australia. In 2006, then Australian foreign minister Downer and Bill Clinton signed a Memorandum of Understanding (MOU) in which Australia pledged to raise $25 million to help the Clinton Foundation fight AIDS in Papua New Guinea and Asia. The terms of the MOU allowed Australia to raise the money over a period of four years. The money initially was allocated to the Clinton Foundation, but later was channeled through a Clinton Foundation structure known as the Clinton Health Access Initiative (CHAI).[159]

---

158 Andrew C. McCarthy, "Disingenuous Denials on FISA Surveillance of Trump," *Real Clear Politics*, March 5, 2017, https://www.realclearpolitics.com/2017/03/05/disingenuous_denials_on_fisa_surveillance_of_trump_404249.html.

159 John Solomon and Alison Spann, "Australian Diplomat Whose Tip Prompted FBI's Russia-Probe Has Tie to Clintons," *The Hill*, March 5, 2018, https://thehill.com/376858-australian-diplomat-whose-tip-prompted-fbis-russia-probe-has-tie-to-clintons.

In my 2016 book *Partners in Crime: The Clintons' Scheme to Monetize the White House for Personal Profit,* I document how the Clintons raised money to fight HIV/AIDS by arguing that the buying power of the Clinton Foundation would allow them to enter the generic drugs market to buy a larger quantity of medications for the amount spent. In that book, I document that from 2002 through 2013, the Clinton Foundation had a history of purchasing from Ranbaxy, an Indian company in the generic-drugs business, which later pled guilty to manufacturing defective HIV/AIDS medications incapable of treating the disease. I also document that the Clinton Health Access Initiative, known by its acronym CHAI, never received from the IRS a determination letter allowing the "charity" to raise tax-free funds to combat the disease. The Clinton scam extended to Unitaid, an international initiative raising funds largely through levies on airplane tickets in Europe, with Unitaid contributing some $500 million to the Clintons' HIV/AIDS campaign.

Finally, *Partners in Crime* explains the work done by Charles Ortel, a well-known and respected Wall Street analyst, to prove from CHAI financial statements and regulatory filings that the accounting was fraudulent. Ortel's analysis gives reason to question whether the Clintons' CHAI project was "just another Clinton family get-rich-quick investment scheme designed to rip off legitimate charity donors worldwide as well as HIV/AIDS-infected people in the Third World."[160] Australian journalists, alerted in 2018 to allegations of Clinton Foundation fraud involving the $25 million Australian contribution arranged by Downer, have sought to have a formal investigation opened by Australian law enforcement authorities and the FBI.[161]

George Papadopoulos and Carter Page: Easy Marks

It does not take much imagination to understand that for experienced intelligence agents like Downer and Halper, both Carter Page and George

---

160 Jerome R. Corsi, *Partners in Crime: The Clintons' Scheme to Monetize the White House for Personal Profit* (Washington, D.C.: WND Books, 2016), Chapter 5, "The HIV/AIDS Scam." The quotation is taken from page 97.

161 Mark Tapscot, "Aussie Complaints on Clinton Foundation Headed to FBI," Real Clear Investigations, January 16, 2018, https://www.realclearinvestigations.com/links/2018/01/16/aussie_complaints_on_clinton_foundation_headed_to_fbi_108705.html.

Papadopoulos looked like obvious marks for a professional political hit job. Both were relatively young and inexperienced in the cutthroat world of U.S. presidential campaign politics. But both had managed to be named as foreign policy advisors to Trump's presidential campaign—positions that sounded more influential than they turned out to be. In reality, all the efforts Sam Clovis expended to create a policy advisory team of experts for Trump went for naught. In the final analysis, Trump relied on his own political instincts, probably not even taking the time to read any of the policy papers the Clovis-selected experts wrote.

Neither Page nor Papadopoulos understood until too late that each was being set up to look like the crucial link between Trump and Russia. Looked at objectively, it was preposterous for these supposedly world-class intelligence agencies to assume anyone would believe that if Trump had wanted to collude with Putin, someone of Trump's celebrity status would have recruited as a go-between with Putin either Carter Page or George Papadopoulos, two relatively unknown unpaid advisors to the Trump campaign that Trump barely knew. Clearly, Trump could have found a trusted and highly experienced international operative to engineer his planned collusion with Putin. Yet Downer and Halper, as well as their international intelligence agency bosses, correctly calculated that Page and Papadopoulos could be entrapped relatively easily, given their complete lack of experience with presidential politics and the desire both had to prove their importance to the Trump campaign.

The irony of all this is that it is likely that the CIA and the Justice Department concocted the Carter Page and George Papadopoulos entrapment schemes precisely because Hillary Clinton and Barack Obama knew from the start that Trump had committed no crimes in his business dealings in Russia. This ruled out the DOJ and FBI opening criminal investigations against Trump. The only alternative left was for the DOJ and FBI to open a counterintelligence investigation premised on the assumption Trump was a Russian asset. After extensive research, I have concluded the Russians had nothing to do with stealing the DNC emails. That Assange did not get the stolen emails from Russia is a key point that I shall prove in the Chapter 7 discussion of Julian Assange and WikiLeaks.

Chapter Six

MUELLER BAGS
PAPADOPOULOS

The relationship between Mueller's special counsel team and Papadopoulos is complex in that Mueller prosecutors clearly wanted Papadopoulos for testimony. The record shows that the DOJ, the FBI, and Mueller's prosecutors did everything possible to extract from Papadopoulos a confession that Mifsud told him in the April 26, 2016 meeting that Russia had thousands of stolen emails containing dirt on Clinton, and that Papadopoulos then relayed this information to the Trump campaign. Initially, Mueller's prosecutors did not want to indict Papadopoulos. But the prosecutors became aggressive and turned antagonistic because they were frustrated when Papadopoulos failed to deliver the testimony Mueller's team had determined in advance was needed to make a case to impeach Trump.

In this chapter, I will show the abundant evidence that the DOJ, the FBI, and Mueller's prosecutors conspired to put maximum pressure on Papadopoulos by threatening to send him to prison for years over what amounted to little more than a mistaken date that they would easily have forgiven. The prosecutors were willing to allow Papadopoulos to amend his testimony, provided that he told them what they wanted to hear. There is even evidence in the record that Mueller's prosecutors and the FBI made attempts to flip Papadopoulos—to turn him into an FBI asset willing to wear a wire to tape Mifsud.

This chapter and my case with Mueller leave no doubt that Mueller's prosecutors and the FBI employees working with them were desperate to frame Trump as a Russian asset and traitor. Mueller was conducting an investigation to validate a political conclusion the Deep State had already predetermined would destroy Trump's political ambitions. The Papadopoulos case proves the point.

Stefan Halper Shows Up with a Blonde Bombshell Spy

On September 2, 2016, Stefan Halper, representing himself as a professor at Cambridge University, reached out to Papadopoulos in an email, inviting him to London to work on a project on Turkey's relationship with the European Union. In particular, Halper suggested Papadopoulos was invited to show how the Leviathan natural gas fields off the coast of Israel and the gas fields off the coast of Cyprus impact Turkey. Papadopoulos was an expert in these subjects, and he was interested in collaborating, especially after Halper offered to compensate him.

Papadopoulos explained in his testimony to Congress, "And he [Halper] said [in the email], 'I'll pay you three thousand dollars and I'll fly you to London, and let's talk about it for a few days and let's see what you can do, and just write a paper for me.'"

"I said, 'That's great, you know, five-star hotel in London, a free flight, and three thousand dollars for a couple of days to write a 1,500-word paper. That's fine to me.'"[162]

Papadopoulos indicated that he did not know much about Halper at the time, but after a Google search, he found out that Halper had served in the Ford and Reagan administrations. The Google search failed to show the extensive ties Halper had to British and U.S. intelligence over many decades.

On September 15, 2016, Papadopoulos flew to London and checked into the five-star Connaught Hotel. The next thing Papadopoulos knew, Azra Turk, a woman identifying herself as Halper's research assistant,

---

162 "Interview of George Papadopoulos," Executive Session, Committee on the Judiciary, Joint with the Committee on Government Reform and Oversight, U.S. House of Representatives, Washington, D.C., October 25, 2018.

messaged him and suggested, "Let's meet for a drink. I'm looking forward to meeting you." Papadopoulos was in for a surprise. "Azra Turk is a vision right out of central casting for a spy flick," Papadopoulos explains in his book. "She's a sexy bottle blond in her thirties, and she isn't shy about showing her curves—as if anyone could miss them. She's a fantasy's fantasy. 'If this is what academic research looks like, I've been going to the wrong school,' I laugh to myself." Turk told Papadopoulos that she was from a wealthy Turkish family that had relocated to Los Angeles. Then, about five minutes into the conversation, she began asking if the Trump campaign was working with Russia.

Papadopoulos was immediately suspicious. "But she keeps pushing," he explains in his book. "She puts her hand on my arm. She says I'm more attractive in person than in my pictures. She says I've been doing important work. It's all a come-on. Still I want to believe she's a research assistant, because if she isn't this woman is an operative of some kind." Papadopoulos told Congress he was especially suspicious when he realized that "*azra*" in Turkish means "pure," giving Azra Turk the name Pure Turk.

Papadopoulos correctly assumed the name was another fake alias. "Another beautiful young lady—you know, I had many young beautiful ladies coming into my life with Joseph Mifsud and now another professor," he explained to Congress. "The professors liked to introduce me to young beautiful women." Papadopoulos added that while Turk never explicitly said, "I will sleep with you for this," her "mannerisms and her behavior suggested that she was flirtatious, and she was very open to something like that if I ended up providing what she wanted, whatever that was."

On May 2, 2019, the *New York Times* reported that Azra Turk was a government investigator posing as a research assistant and had been sent to London to oversee Stefan Halper's operation.[163] Although the *New York Times* suggested that Turk was with the FBI, we cannot rule out that she was a CIA employee, or at least an FBI employee coordinating with the CIA, given Halper's credentials with the CIA. The newspaper noted that the discovery that Turk was a government employee working in conjunc-

---

163 Adam Goldman, Michael S. Schmidt, and Mark Mazzetti, "FBI Sent Investigator Posing as Assistant to Meet with Trump Aide in 2016," op. cit.

tion with the developing Russia-collusion investigation gives credence to what became known as "Spygate" after President Trump's insistence that the Obama administration was spying on his presidential campaign. The *New York Times*, assuming that Turk was an FBI investigator assigned to Operation Crossfire Hurricane, commented that the FBI "wanted in place a trained investigator for a layer of oversight, as well as someone who could gather information for or serve as a credible witness in any potential prosecution that emerged from the case."

To resume the narrative, on the next day, September 16, 2016, when Papadopoulos met for the first time with Halper at the Travellers Club in London's tony Pall Mall area, he understood why the intelligence community worldwide had tagged Halper as "The Walrus." In his book, Papadopoulos comments, "Stefan Halper is a morbidly obese seventy-three-year-old American. His girth earned him an unflattering nickname in the intelligence community." The location Halper picked for the meeting also made Papadopoulos suspicious. Papadopoulos describes the club's building as an 1832 edifice inspired by Raphael's *Palazzo Pandolfini* in Florence. "I walk in, dwarfed by the high ceilings, and can see why ambassadors and high commissioners and other senior diplomats frequent the club," he observed. "It's genteel—the last place you'd go expecting a hostile interrogation." He went upstairs in the club to find Halper seated with Azra Turk.

"I go upstairs and find the Walrus sitting in a private room," he writes in his book, describing the meeting at the Travellers Club. "He is cartoonishly massive, and the cartoonishly voluptuous Azra Turk is with him. Once again, her provocative outfit defies expectations. But with Halper in the room, her behavior is much more demure than the previous evening. She gets us coffee. I wonder what their relationship is since she really doesn't come across as an academic."

Papadopoulos sensed the meeting was an intelligence operation. "Halper is sweating from the moment I walk in," Papadopoulos continues writing. It is obvious he is connecting the dots. "Like Downer, he immediately launches into a foul-mouthed rant. He's talking to me about Cyprus, Turkey, and energy—just like Alexander Downer had—except, he homes in even more about Turkey, making it clear he's very hostile to my stance on the future of Mediterranean energy alliances."

Not only is Papadopoulos connecting the dots, he is realizing that Mifsud, Downer, and now Halper were all playing roles in the same intelligence agency plot that was aiming to entrap him and force him to confess to statements that, if true, could have been used to build a treason case against Trump.

Papadopoulos Walks Out on Halper

Before he left London, Halper called again and asked Papadopoulos to meet with him at the Sofitel hotel for a goodbye drink. "The next day, I show up at the hotel," Papadopoulos writes, continuing the narrative in his book. "The Walrus is there. Without Azra this time." They ordered gin and tonics and Halper once again pulled out his phone and put it on the table. Papadopoulos observed that Halper pushed the phone toward him, commenting, "Just like Downer." Immediately, Papadopoulos suspected he was being taped.

Almost immediately, Halper launched into a series of leading questions: "It's great that Russia is helping you and the campaign, right George? George, you and your campaign are involved in hacking and working with Russia, right? It seems like you are a middleman for Trump and Russia, right? I know you know about the emails."

This struck Papadopoulos as more than odd. "He's basically making outrageous statements and asking me to confirm them," Papadopoulos writes. He thought that by September 2016, the whole world had been told by the Clinton campaign that Russia had hacked the DNC emails. When Halper pushed that he wanted to know about Papadopoulos and Trump, Papadopoulos became angry. "Well, I have no idea what you are talking about," he told Halper. "What you are talking about is treason. And I have nothing to do with Russia, so stop bothering me about it." He correctly sensed the setup.

Concluding that Halper's $3,000 offer had been a come-on, Papadopoulos felt used. For the CIA fronting Halper, that amount was a pittance. Halper's offer had been calculated to entice Papadopoulos to visit London. There, the CIA would have Papadopoulos where the Justice Department wanted him. In conjunction with British intelligence and the CIA, the Justice Department schemed to get Papadopoulos on tape making statements that would incriminate him in colluding with Russia on behalf of the Trump campaign. Fortunately, Papadopoulos saw through the scheme and would have none of it.

Papadopoulos writes that Halper is basically making "outrageous, bogus statements and asking me to confirm them." Papadopoulos notes that since June 2016 the whole world knew Russia's intelligence operatives had hacked the DNC. Stolen DNC emails had already been published, starting on July 22, 2016. "So these suggestions—about my being involved in some kind of conspiracy—are not just absolutely outrageous and false, they are dangerous," he writes. Again, Papadopoulos ended the meeting, disgusted. "This is the second time in three days that someone has mentioned conspiring with Russia—Halper's honeypot assistant tried to do the same thing," he observes.

He ended the meeting by standing up and telling Halper he planned to turn in the report due in the coming week. "I send him my report," Papadopoulos says. "But I never hear from him again." It is doubtful Halper or anyone else ever read the report Papadopoulos submitted. Papadopoulos never again heard from Halper.

So, the intelligence agency had planned to entrap Papadopoulos, with Erika Thompson and Alexander Downer setting the hook, but Halper failed to reel in the catch.

Halper Meets with Sam Clovis

Before Papadopoulos flew to London on September 15, 2016, and checked into the five-star Connaught Hotel, Halper met with Sam Clovis in Washington. Recall that Clovis was the Trump campaign's former national cochairman who was best known for his attempt to put together for the Trump campaign an advisory board of public policy experts in various fields, to which both Page and Papadopoulos were recruited. On August 29, 2016, Clovis received an email from Halper, a person he did not know. In the email, Halper said he had met with Page in London, commenting that Page had attended "our conference in Cambridge on U.S. elections." Halper also commented in the email that Page had suggested he should meet Clovis.[164] In response to the email, Clovis agreed to meet a couple of days later with Halper for coffee in the lobby of the DoubleTree Inn in Crystal City, Virginia. Clovis later reported that the meeting with Halper was academic, innocuous in that Halper spent much of the time discussing his research on China.

Clovis came away with the theory that Halper had used the meeting to get from Clovis the bona fides that Halper felt he needed to talk to Papadopoulos. One of Clovis's other theories was that Halper was trying to pin down Papadopoulos as the Trump campaign official colluding with Russia to get access to the Clinton emails that Russia supposedly had. Clovis concluded that Halper's goal was motivated by "a deliberate and intentional effort on the part of the leadership of the FBI to create something that did not exist," namely an "audit trail from the campaign or someone associated with the campaign back to those Clinton emails—whether or not they existed, we don't know."[165]

By meeting Clovis, Halper had an opportunity to verify that Papadopoulos was on the advisory team for Trump. But if Halper's purpose in meeting with Clovis was to establish for the FBI that Papadopoulos played a role in Russia gaining possession of stolen emails from Clinton and the DNC, that mission apparently failed.

The Mysterious Sergei Millian

In his testimony to Congress, Papadopoulos mentioned that in late July 2016, a mysterious stranger named Sergei Millian reached out to him on LinkedIn, a professional networking site. Millian introduced himself as an American of Belarus descent who told Papadopoulos he could help the

---

164 Byron York, "Trump Campaign Vet: Informant Used Me to Get to Papadopoulos," *Washington Examiner*, May 28, 2018, https://www.washington-examiner.com/news/trump-campaign-vet-sam-clovis-says-informant-used-him-to-get-to-papadopoulos.

165 Melissa Quinn, "Sam Clovis: FBI, Suspected Informant Wanted to Create 'Audit Trail' to Justify FISA Warrants," *Washington Examiner*, May 22, 2018, https://www.washingtonexaminer.com/news/sam-clovis-fbi-suspected-informant-wanted-to-create-audit-trail-to-justify-fisa-warrants.

Trump campaign understand the U.S.-Russia relationship. He agreed to meet with Millian at the Trump Tower in Chicago.

"I will say I don't remember too much except he [Millian] was very much interested—he was very—he was acting like he was very pro-Trump, that he wanted me to meet with certain Russian-American leaders, especially in the church, and to help get the Russian vote, the Russian-American vote," Papadopoulos said in his closed-door testimony to the House Judiciary Committee in a joint session with the House Committee on Oversight and Government Reform on October 25, 2018.[166] "And that he was a businessman of some sort and, you know, that he was very excited for Trump, something like that." Millian also told Papadopoulos that he knew Trump's lawyer, Michael Cohen, a suggestion apparently meant to trigger in Papadopoulos the thought that Millian could connect him into Trump's business empire.

Papadopoulos further testified that Millian suggested that he could pay Papadopoulos $30,000 a month, plus provide office space in New York, on an outside contract not related to the Trump campaign that was geared toward providing "some sort of PR [public relations] or consultancy for a friend of his or somebody he knew in Russia."

But almost from the beginning of his discussions with Millian, Papadopoulos felt wary. "I felt that he [Millian] wasn't who he seemed to be and that he was working on behalf of somebody else when he was proposing this to me," he testified. "I just felt that when he proposed this deal to me face-to-face that he might have been wearing some kind of a wire," Papadopoulos continued. "And he was acting very bizarre. And I don't know what there was. Maybe I'm a paranoid person. But there were certain other events regarding Sergei Millian that made—that made me believe that he might have actually been working with the FBI."

---

166 Testimony of George Papadopoulos, Executive Session, Committee on the Judiciary, Joint with the Committee on Government Reform and Oversight, U.S. House of Representatives, Washington, D.C., October 25, 2018.

Millian Named as a Source for the Steele Dossier

Papadopoulos also told Congress he felt it was bizarre that just before he was interviewed by the FBI for the first time, the *Wall Street Journal* published a front-page article listing Millian as a key source for the Steele dossier.

The article, published on January 24, 2017, identified Millian as the source of various information contained in the Steele dossier, in particular the suggestion there was a compromising video of the infamous "golden shower" incident involving Trump in Russia. No such video has ever surfaced. But the concern was that the video, if it existed, could have been used to blackmail Trump into a "conspiracy of cooperation." The logic of the Steele dossier was that the Trump campaign had colluded with Russian leadership over the cyberattack on Hillary Clinton and the Democrats in order to keep the video under wraps. Basically, the theory amounted to suggesting that Russia used the video (assuming the video existed) to compromise Trump.[167]

The *Wall Street Journal* also reported that Millian, then thirty-eight years old, used the alias Siarhei Kukuts in legal documents and speaks six languages. The article said that after moving to the United States some fifteen years earlier, he had lived in Atlanta before moving to New York. In Atlanta, Millian reportedly worked for a local law firm and had a translation business on the side. At the same time, he became a licensed real estate broker. According to the *Wall Street Journal*, Millian claimed he had "formal agreements" with the Trump organization to service the real estate needs of Russian clients, but Michael Cohen has denied that any such agreement existed.

On March 29, 2017, the *Washington Post* identified Millian as "Source D" in the Steele dossier, the person responsible for the allegations that Trump had hired prostitutes at the Moscow Ritz-Carlton and that the

---

167   Mark Maremont, "Key Claims in Trump Dossier Said to Come from Head of Russian-American Business Group," *Wall Street Journal*, January 24, 2017, https://www.wsj.com/articles/key-claims-in-trump-dossier-came-from-head-of-russian-american-business-group-source-1485253804.

Kremlin kept evidence of the encounter.[168] The newspaper tied Millian to Papadopoulos, noting that Millian was included among the nearly 240 friends listed on Papadopoulos's Facebook account.

The FBI Drills Papadopoulos about Millian

Papadopoulos told Congress that in his first interview with the FBI, the focus was Millian. The FBI was interested in connecting Millian with Russian interference in the election and with connections Papadopoulos had in Israel.

"It is my belief that the FBI, at the time they came to my home, believed that I was working as some sort of agent of Israel, or that I might have been compromised by the Israeli government or their intelligence agencies, just based on the questions they were asking me," Papadopoulos said.

In his testimony to Congress, Papadopoulos commented that Israel was a recurring theme in many of his campaign-related dealings. Stefan Halper had offered to pay him for information on his ties to Israel; Alexander Downer was also interested in his ties to Israel. "You could see there was a pattern," Papadopoulos continued. "And there's a second encounter I have with the FBI, and they basically tell me—this is where it's very—if Mifsud really was working with the FBI, this is incredibly problematic, because during my second meeting with the FBI agent, Curtis Heide, he tells me basically, 'We want you to go after Joseph Mifsud or to get some sort of information about him.'"

In his congressional testimony, Papadopoulos expanded on why he thought Millian was wearing a wire during their meeting at Trump Tower in Chicago, when Millian offered him the job paying $30,000 a month. During the meeting, Millian made it clear that while he was offering Papadopoulos a contract independent of the Trump organization, he still expected Papadopoulos to keep working for the Trump campaign.

---

168   Rosalind S. Helderman and Tom Hamburger, "Who is 'Source D'? The Man Said to Be Behind the Trump-Russia Dossier's Most Salacious Claim," *Washington Post*, March 29, 2017, https://www.washingtonpost.com/politics/who-is-source-d-the-man-said-to-be-behind-the-trump-russia-dossiers-most-salacious-claim/2017/03/29/379846a8-0f53-11e7-9d5a-a83e-627dc120_story.html?utm_term=.32e18cdceddc.

"And he [Millian] was looking at me with his eyes really bugged out, very nervous," Papadopoulos described. "And I just looked at him, like this guy is on an operation against me right now trying to set me up for something. And I flatly told him, as far as I can remember, 'No, I'm not taking this offer, because it's illegal what you're talking about,' or at least I thought it was illegal." Papadopoulos suspected that Millian wanted him to work with Millian's contacts in Russia, and Papadopoulos was afraid he would be breaking federal law if he accepted an assignment working for the Russians while Russia was under U.S. government sanctions.

Papadopoulos also recalled in his testimony that during the Trump inauguration celebrations in Washington, he met Aziz Choukri, a Moroccan American music producer who invited him for drinks at the Russia House, a restaurant in Washington known for its vodka and caviar. At the Russia House, Papadopoulos found himself seated at a table that included Millian and Choukri.

According to Papadopoulos's description of the incident, Choukri reached over and, in front of Millian, told Papadopoulos, "Sergei, you know, is working for the FBI." Questioned about this by GOP Representative Mark Meadows, Papadopoulos explained, "He [Choukri] certainly said something along those lines, yes, where it left the impression on me that Sergei was not who he seemed to be." He said Millian looked shocked at Choukri's disclosure. "He [Millian] did one of these things where he puts his eyes up, like that," Papadopoulos said, demonstrating the eye roll. "And then I was very cautious about my interactions with them [Millian and Choukri]."

For an article published on February 7, 2019, the *Washington Post* interviewed Choukri on his meeting with Papadopoulos at the Russia House. Choukri denied telling Papadopoulos that Millian worked for the FBI. "I never mentioned that," Choukri insisted. "It's a lie."[169]

---

169 Rosalind S. Helderman and Tom Hamburger, "Sergei Millian, Identified As an Unwitting Source for the Steele Dossier, Sought Proximity to Trump's World in 2016," *Washington Post*, February 7, 2019, https://www.washingtonpost.com/politics/sergei-millian-identified-as-an-unwitting-source-for-the-steele-dossier-sought-proximity-to-trumps-world-in-2016/2019/02/06/c7465a52-ec19-11e8-8679-934a2b33be52_story.html?utm_term=.d6d0bda1a172.

The FBI Asks Papadopoulos to Wear a Wire

Before the Mueller prosecutors charged Papadopoulos with the criminal count of intentionally giving the FBI information that he knew to be false, the FBI offered him the chance to be an informant.

In his book, Papadopoulos recounts that on January 31, 2017, he was at the gym when he got a friendly call—a conversation Papadopoulos remembers as being "peppered" with a lot of "bros"—from Agent Curtis Heide of the FBI.

"Hey, George, I'm not here to trip you up or anything," Heide said, in a manner that Papadopoulos describes as Heide's "best good cop act." On the phone, Heide asked Papadopoulos if the two of them could meet.

"Okay," Papadopoulos agreed. "Let's meet with my lawyer." He said he had just hired an attorney the day before.

"No, no, no. Let's not get lawyers involved," Heide implored. "This is just going to be a quick conversation between you and me, and then I'm not going to bother you again."

Papadopoulos notes that he foolishly agreed to meet Heide at George's cafe in Andersonville, a neighborhood Papadopoulos describes as "vibrant," on Chicago's North Side, not far from his family home in Lincoln Square.

"Did you tell anyone that you were coming here?" Heide asked to begin the meeting. "Did you tell anyone where you are? Are you being followed?"

"No," Papadopoulos answered. "I just came from the gym."

"George, I'm letting you know that we want you to wear a wire," Heide said, getting to the point of the interview. "We want you to work for us. We want you to go to London and meet this guy Mifsud for us. We can pay you, and you can be a key part of an FBI operation. We will let you peek behind an FBI operation."

Papadopoulos was surprised that the FBI wanted to use him as an undercover informant wearing a wire. His first interviews with the FBI had focused on Millian, but now the FBI was shifting its focus to his April 26, 2016 conversation with Mifsud. Papadopoulos was out of his league thinking about wearing a wire for the FBI. He wondered if Mifsud was really a Russian agent. He worried that if he wore a wire, he was going to get caught up working with spies.

"Look, I don't know what to tell you," Papadopoulos told Heide. "This guy [Mifsud] told me that they have Hillary's emails. I told you that. I don't know what more I can do. I haven't seen him or spoken to him in months. I wish you guys came to me sooner. Aren't you the professionals? What do you need me to wear a wire for?"

"To help us," Heide answered.

"I will think about it," Papadopoulos said, wanting to put an end to the conversation. "But I don't think my lawyers are going to want me to do this."

He reported that upon hearing about lawyers, Heide switched from being friendly to being a tormentor, switching into his "bad cop" mode as soon as the "good cop" routine appeared to be failing.

"I know everything about you," Heide said. Papadopoulos took that as a threat, as if he had done something wrong and the FBI was going to make him pay for it. He racked his brain, but couldn't think of anything he had done wrong. He wondered if the FBI had an incriminating video of him jaywalking because he couldn't think of any illegal transactions he might have made.

"Look, Curtis, I'm trying to help you guys," he explained. "But at this point I don't even want to be involved in politics anymore. I just want to go to law school."

"I know everything about you," Heide repeated, letting Papadopoulos know that the FBI knew the identity of his past girlfriend and his current girlfriend. "I know you're at the center of this, and if you don't help us, we're going to bust you for what you're doing in Israel. You're lucky we're not doing it now because they're allies. But Washington wants answers, and Washington wants answers now."

Papadopoulos couldn't figure out what FBI agent Heide meant in bringing up Israel. Was the FBI thinking of charging him with espionage? Yes, Papadopoulos had Israeli friends and business associates. He recalled that Cantor in London had introduced him to Australian high commissioner Alexander Downer, whom Papadopoulos remembered as being hostile to him. But he started to panic, not sure what Heide meant by threatening him about Israel.

Given my personal experience with how the FBI worked with the Mueller prosecutors, I am confident that if Papadopoulos had agreed to flip and become an FBI informer, the FBI would have required him to return to London or Rome to meet with Mifsud again. In that meeting, the FBI would have instructed Papadopoulos that his mission was to wear a wire so he could record Mifsud repeating the comments about the Russians being in possession of stolen emails that supposedly contained derogatory information about Hillary Clinton. The Deep State DOJ and FBI were so outrageously over the cliff in their determination to frame Trump as a traitor that the FBI was willing to have an undercover informant, Papadopoulos, go back to Europe to record Mifsud, a Western intelligence asset most likely working with the CIA, repeating on tape what he had allegedly told Papadopoulos on April 26, 2016.

Obviously, the FBI could not prove that Mifsud had said anything of the kind, especially since Mifsud denied ever making the comments. FBI agents knew that Priestap and Strzok had been in London engineering the transfer of the Downer confirmation of the Mifsud comments from the realm of intelligence gathering to the realm of official diplomatic communications between embassies. But to make their largely manufactured case believable in court, they needed Papadopoulos to cooperate.

The FBI Meetings Suddenly Become Tense

In Papadopoulos's next meeting with the FBI, on February 16, 2017, a particularly aggressive lawyer, Kevin Clinesmith, grilled Papadopoulos about his various meetings with Mifsud and Downer. Unsatisfied with the answers they were getting, the army of FBI inquisitors abruptly stood up, left the room, and returned to Washington—without saying a word to Papadopoulos or his attorneys.

Papadopoulos thought that this behavior was strange, but again, from my experience with Mueller's prosecutors and the FBI, this was typical behavior for them when they did not get what they wanted. The whole army, including three of Mueller's top prosecutors and the eight or ten FBI agents, would suddenly pick up all their materials from the conference table and stomp out together without saying a word. When they deigned to call my attorney out to meet with them separately, I was left alone. I found myself abandoned in an internal conference room without windows, without a clock, and without a cell phone or computer in an unmarked FBI building somewhere in southeast Washington, D.C. I am confident the tactic was strategized and used on many witnesses continually, to make the witness feel afraid, and to throw the witness off balance when Mueller's team was not getting the information they wanted to hear.

After this meeting with the FBI, Papadopoulos consulted his attorneys, and on their advice, deactivated his Facebook account, knowing that in the process he would wipe out some emails and text messages. Mifsud had used Facebook in reaching out to Papadopoulos, and Papadopoulos wanted to "exist in a vacuum" after his most recent experiences with the FBI. Later, this would come back to haunt him, when the FBI threatened to charge him for obstructing justice, arguing that Papadopoulos had intended to destroy evidence by deactivating his Facebook account. Mueller's team also played the same ruse on me, suggesting I had obstructed justice by deleting emails. I had external hard drives that backed up my computers such that emails could be recovered even if they were erased on the laptop computers I was using every day. The truth was that I had to erase emails periodically just to keep the email programs working.

Papadopoulos, however, found some vindication when Clinesmith was later booted off the Mueller special counsel team for making "profoundly anti-Trump" remarks that later surfaced.[170]

The FBI Sets Up Papadopoulos with Ten Thousand Dollars in Cash in Israel

While attending a March 2017 conference in Washington of the American Israel Public Affairs Committee (AIPAC), an Israeli lobbying group, Papadopoulos learned there was an Israeli-American businessman named Charles Tawil who wanted to meet him.

---

170   Paul Sperry, "'Scorched Earth': After Mueller Comes Up Empty, His Targets Speak Out," *Real Clear Politics*, June 8, 2019, https://www.realclear-politics.com/articles/2019/06/08/after_mueller_comes_up_empty_his_tar-gets_speak_out_140524.html.

In March 2017, Papadopoulos was broke, with mounting legal bills. He had already had two interviews with the FBI—the first when the FBI knocked on his mother's door in Chicago on January 27, 2017, and the second on February 16, 2017. After the second interview, as noted above, Papadopoulos deleted his Facebook account and scrubbed other social media. He was beginning to realize he was in serious legal trouble.

Tawil flew to Chicago for a lunch with Papadopoulos at Shallots, a restaurant Papadopoulos describes as "a popular kosher steakhouse in Skokie, a Chicago suburb with a large Jewish population."

"It sounds like Tawil might lead to work," Papadopoulos writes in his book. "I'll take any consulting gig I can get."

At the lunch, Tawil suggested he had ties to Israeli intelligence, putting Papadopoulos on guard. Then, ten minutes into the meeting, he swung the conversation to Russia.

"Obviously a Greek Orthodox guy like you has close ties to Russia," Tawil commented to Papadopoulos. "You were probably viewed as a middleman with Trump and Russia just simply based on those characteristics." At that point, Papadopoulos would have been smart to end the lunch meeting and leave, planning never to see Tawil again. Instead, he allowed Tawil to talk him into going to Israel based on the prospect of doing business together.

In a Tel Aviv hotel room after he arrived in Israel, Papadopoulos found that Tawil had laid out on the bed ten thousand dollars in hundred-dollar bills. This cash, Tawil said, was for Papadopoulos. "Why? What am I doing for this money?" Papadopoulos asked. "I still don't understand our project." Tawil explained that Papadopoulos would work for him as a consultant and this was his retainer.

"At that time, I was incredibly confused," Papadopoulos told the lawmakers in Congress. "I was intimidated. I didn't know what really was going on, except that I started to feel that I was being set up. And just months before that, I saw that the FBI was really going after me for being some sort of agent of Israel. So, it all started to make sense to me, that this potentially was a frame or entrapment of some nature."

Still, Papadopoulos took the cash. But before he returned to the United States, he had the good sense to hand it over to his lawyer in Greece for safekeeping.

The FBI Arrests Papadopoulos at Dulles Airport

On July 27, 2017, when Papadopoulos returned to the United States, landing at Dulles airport in Washington, he was detained by a team of FBI agents looking for the ten thousand dollars in cash. But he knew that bringing that much in cash into the United States from a foreign destination was a felony.

"When I disembarked, a team of FBI hustled me off to a secluded area of the airport and immediately tore through my briefcase and bags, feverishly searching for something," Papadopoulos writes in his book. "I watched the agents rifle through my bags twice. Then I watched them confer with each other, agitated looks on their faces. It was clear to me that they'd expected to find something important. It was equally clear from their pissed-off expressions that they hadn't found it."

Disappointed and angry at not finding what they were looking for, the FBI agents handcuffed Papadopoulos and put his ankles in shackles. When he asked what was going on, one of the agents shot back at him, "This is what happens when you work for Trump." Next, they put Papadopoulos, handcuffed and shackled, into a black SUV with tinted windows and drove him to a detention center in Alexandria, Virginia. There, his mug shot was taken, and he spent the night in a prison cell with other prisoners, finding it impossible to rest on the dirty mattresses lying on the floor.

Clearly, the FBI was attempting to entrap Papadopoulos with the money. But since Papadopoulos did not bring ten thousand dollars in cash into the United States from a foreign destination without declaring it to customs officials, Papadopoulos had committed no crime. Frustrated at not finding the cash, the FBI arrested Papadopoulos as if he were a major international criminal. "Until that moment in Dulles Airport—an army of men in black basically accusing me of working with Russians—I don't think I knew what real terror was," Papadopoulos writes. "I was about to get a crash course."

Mueller Prosecutors Show Up at the Papadopoulos Arraignment

The next morning, Papadopoulos was taken before a magistrate to be arraigned. In court, he was greeted by one of Mueller's top prosecutors, Jeannie Rhee. Rhee was a deputy assistant attorney for the Obama administration from 2009 to 2011 and had served as one of Hillary Clinton's personal attorneys for the Clinton Foundation. Rhee was also the supervising prosecutor on the three-prosecutor team Mueller assigned to grill me in my forty-hour "voluntary interview" ordeal.

Before the magistrate, Papadopoulos learned he was facing federal charges for lying to an FBI agent and obstructing justice, crimes for which he could spend twenty-five years in prison if he was found guilty. These were the same charges Mueller's prosecutors threatened to bring against me, with the same prison sentence: twenty-five years. At my age then, seventy-two, it could easily have become a lifetime sentence.

The prosecutors told the magistrate that Papadopoulos was "willing to cooperate" with the government in its ongoing investigation into Russian efforts to interfere in the 2016 presidential election. Papadopoulos writes in his book that the prosecutors told the magistrate they hoped he would be a "proactive cooperator," a term Papadopoulos interprets as "valuable informant." He was returned to the jail cell, and the next day he was released.

Nothing was mentioned before the magistrate about the ten thousand dollars or Tawil.

The FBI's Ten-Thousand-Dollar Scheme Crashes and Burns

My guess is that if the FBI had found the ten thousand dollars in cash, the government would have leveled against Papadopoulos felony charges for bringing that much cash into the United States undeclared. Mueller's prosecutors would have held off, hoping to use the leverage of those charges to pressure Papadopoulos into a false confession, admitting he told Trump campaign officials what Mifsud supposedly said about Russia having stolen Clinton emails.

But the FBI made a mistake in arresting Papadopoulos. They could re-lease him and create an international incident once Papadopoulos told his story to the press. Or the DOJ would have to charge Papadopoulos with a crime. That is the moment the die was cast. The game of the FBI entrap-ping Papadopoulos into lying about Mifsud, or wearing a wire to record Mifsud, was over. Mueller's prosecutors had no choice but to release Pap-adopoulos and suffer the consequences, or to charge Papadopoulos with a crime to keep their "investigation" going in their increasingly desperate attempt to prove Trump was a Russian asset. Given that Papadopoulos had left the cash with his attorney in Greece, and the FBI had arrested Papadopoulos, the government had no choice but to bring Jeannie Rhee to Chicago to level criminal charges related to the Mueller investigation against him.

What is clear from Rhee's statements to the magistrate in Arlington is that Mueller's prosecutors now expected that Papadopoulos would coop-erate in their investigation in return for the FBI reducing or possibly even dropping criminal charges against him. Clearly, in their two interviews with him, the FBI had failed to get what the Mueller prosecutors needed to make their Russia-collusion case. It would have been no crime for Pap-adopoulos to hear from Mifsud that Russia had the purloined emails with dirt on Clinton. If anyone was facing legal difficulties for advance knowl-edge about the emails Julian Assange had in his possession, it should have been Mifsud, not Papadopoulos. We can add this to the list of the reasons why it is unlikely that Mifsud ever made the comments attributed to him.

The key was to get Papadopoulos to confess that he relayed Mifsud's comments to Clovis (or someone else on the Trump campaign) and that Clovis relayed the comments to Trump. If these links could be established, Mueller's prosecutors would argue that Trump was in a position to co-ordinate—that is, "to collude"—with Russia concerning how and when WikiLeaks would release the emails to do the maximum damage to Clin-ton. Papadopoulos never did relay those comments and he refused to lie by saying he had.

In other words, despite all the effort expended on Papadopoulos by the U.S. government, Mueller's team failed. Papadopoulos never broke down to the point where he was willing to wear an FBI wire, nor did he become so scared that he finally admitted what Mueller's team expected they could force him to admit. Papadopoulos insisted he had not relayed Mifsud's whispered tip to Clovis or to anyone else on the Trump campaign. As a result, Mueller's prosecutors hit a dead end.

But Mueller's team was not finished roughing up Papadopoulos.

The Mueller Prosecutors Abuse Papadopoulos

Papadopoulos faced the same top-tier prosecutorial team that I did: Rhee, Zelinsky, and Goldstein. Not only were the prosecutors the same, the tactics were the same. In Papadopoulos's first interview after his arrest at Dulles airport, the trio of Rhee, Zelinsky, and Goldstein threatened him with charges of lying to the FBI and conspiracy to obstruct justice, insisting they had enough evidence to put him in prison for twenty-five years unless he told them "the truth."

Goldstein presented Papadopoulos the deal the government was willing to make. "This is an agreement for a proffer," he explained—an agreement the prosecutors had prepared for Papadopoulos to sign, admitting his guilt. The Mueller prosecutors planned that after Papadopoulos agreed to the "statement of offense" they had drafted, they would bring him before a federal judge to plead guilty. "This is your last chance to cooperate, or we go to trial," they told him. In his book, Papadopoulos makes it clear that Goldstein used intimidation tactics, making a threat immediately after presenting Papadopoulos with the proffer. Papadopoulos also relates that Zelinsky reinforced Goldstein's threat by telling Papadopoulos, "I'm going to go home, and we will get ready for trial," when Papadopoulos did not answer a question the way Zelinsky wanted.

In debating the plea deal, Papadopoulos felt the pressure from Mueller's prosecutors was relentless. "We go back and forth about whether or not I shared Mifsud's claim with campaign members," Papadopoulos writes. "For seven hours, in every possible manner, I am asked, 'Did you tell him on this day?' or 'Did you tell her?'" The prosecutors went through every person Papadopoulos had contacted on the campaign: Sam Clovis, Trump campaign manager Corey Lewandowski, General Michael Flynn, Carter Page, Trump campaign manager Paul Manafort—person after person.

"There are moments when I feel dizzy, moments when I think about lying to get them off my back," Papadopoulos continues. "But I don't do that. I tell them, 'I don't understand. It's as if you're trying to implant a memory in my mind of something that never happened.'"

Thinking back to my forty-hour ordeal with Mueller's prosecutors, I experienced the same harassment from the tag team of Rhee, Zelinsky, and Goldstein. All the Mueller prosecutors wanted was to know the name of the person who had introduced me to Assange, and then for me to admit that I introduced Roger Stone to Assange after I made contact. My trouble, identical to the difficulty Papadopoulos faced, was simple: what the prosecutors wanted me to confess was pivotal to their hypothesis of the crime they planned to pin on Trump. There is no doubt in my mind that the mission Rhee, Zelinsky, and Goldstein had from the beginning was to charge Donald Trump with treason. Their problem was that Rhee, Zelinsky, and Goldstein could not make this case unless they got Papadopoulos and me, or at least one of us, to confess to their allegations even though the Mueller hypothesis was not true. What Rhee, Zelinsky, and Goldstein wanted us to admit in the plea deal we were offered never happened and neither Papadopoulos nor I was willing to lie to say it had happened.

Papadopoulos admits to being so scared that he would have told the prosecutors anything they wanted to know about him, including "my sex life, my finances, my most embarrassing teenage moment." But the fact remained that he had never told anyone on the Trump campaign that Mifsud said Russia had Hillary Clinton's emails. "Unfortunately, the truth was not what they wanted to hear," Papadopoulos writes. "No matter how much Robert Mueller and his team of FBI agents and prosecutors wished I had told campaign members about Mifsud's claim, I hadn't. It. Did. Not. Happen."

There came a moment when Papadopoulos realized that the FBI had set him up. "Joseph Mifsud is no Russian agent!" Papadopoulos writes, explaining how the light bulb in his head switched on. "I've been duped into pleading guilty," he continues. "What would have happened if I had worn a wire [to record Mifsud] and met once again with the FBI? Maybe I could have asked him [Mifsud] about the Russian email operation," he speculates. "But given the way the FBI has treated me, it's more likely

Mifsud could have been instructed to spew more lies about me. Lies that would be used against me. Maybe he would have gone on wild tangents, talking about how Trump knew everything, and I knew everything."

Mueller Fraudulently Indicts Papadopoulos on Minor Criminal Charges

The problem Mueller's prosecutors had in bringing charges against Papadopoulos was that he had been truthful about admitting that he had met with Mifsud in London and about admitting that Mifsud had told him the Russians had "dirt" on Hillary Clinton in the form of "thousands of emails."

The only fault Mueller's prosecutors could find was that Papadopoulos claimed his meeting with Mifsud came before he joined the Trump campaign. The truth was that Papadopoulos learned in early March that Sam Clovis had accepted him to be a foreign policy advisor to the Trump campaign, and he met with Mifsud after that, on March 14, 2016. In the indictment, Mueller's prosecutors stressed that Mifsud took an interest in Papadopoulos only after his appointment to Trump's campaign, and that the critical meeting with Mifsud was on April 26, 2019, when Papadopoulos had been a Trump foreign policy advisor for over a month.[171]

The indictment also noted that Papadopoulos told the investigating agents that Mifsud was "a nothing" and "just a guy talk[ing] up connections or something." It asserted that the truth was that Papadopoulos "understood that the professor [Mifsud] had substantial connections to Russian government officials and had met with some of those officials in Moscow immediately after telling Papadopoulos about the Clinton emails supposedly in Russian possession." The indictment stressed that after hearing from Mifsud that he could arrange a meeting between Trump and Putin, Papadopoulos "repeatedly sought to use the professor's Russian

---

171 "Statement of the Offense," in the case *United States of America v. George Papadopoulos*, Defendant, filed in U.S. District Court for the District of Columbia, Criminal Case 17 GR. 182 (RDM) SEALED, One Count, Violation of 18 U.S.C. Section 1001 (False Statements), filed October 5, 2017.

connections in an effort to arrange a meeting between the Trump campaign and Russian officials."

Papadopoulos realized that if he did not plead guilty to this one charge, Mueller's prosecutors were likely to pursue charges that he was an Israeli agent and he had committed a crime by failing to register as an agent of a foreign government, as required under the Foreign Agent Registration Act (FARA). "This is as chilling as it is false," Papadopoulos writes. "I never was an Israeli agent. Never. But FARA charges are a whole other life-ruining ballgame." Papadopoulos bent to the pressure and accepted the plea deal.

Struggling to comprehend how all this had happened to him, Papadopoulos asked himself what he had done wrong: "Failed to remember the sequence of events during two of the busiest moments of my life?" It seemed so insignificant, a date easy to confuse when, two years after the fact, Papadopoulos was being questioned by three skilled prosecutors and an army of FBI agents with unlimited resources and no fixed budget to investigate the matter.

Truthfully, Mueller's prosecutors knew the answer to every question they asked. Papadopoulos's interrogation, like mine, was not an effort by them to learn new facts in order to determine the truth. The point was to see if Papadopoulos would make a statement, any statement, that the prosecutors could demonstrably prove to be false according to one of the hundreds of emails or phone calls Zelinsky had documented in a thick binder with Papadopoulos's name on it. With me, Zelinsky paged through the binder as he asked questions. The odds were in Zelinsky's favor that sooner rather than later, Papadopoulos would make a memory error that would allow Zelinsky to create fear in Papadopoulos by threatening to put him in federal prison for intentionally lying in order to obstruct justice.

The Flaw in the Papadopoulos Criminal Charges

As he approached the sentencing hearing, Papadopoulos realized his mistake had been to minimize his interaction with Mifsud. "I never intended to harm the [Mueller] investigation, and I seriously doubt anything I said mattered at all," he writes. "I initially played down Mifsud's importance not to protect the Trump campaign, or 'harm' the investigation, but to protect my own ego." The episode with Mifsud had been an embarrassment to Papadopoulos. "Everything he [Mifsud] said turned out to be smoke and mirrors," Papadopoulos explains. "The man fabricated Putin's niece for me, and I fell for it! Can you imagine how stupid I felt about the whole thing?"

It took an experienced federal prosecutor like Andrew McCarthy to catch the fatal flaw in Papadopoulos's indictment. As McCarthy convincingly argued, Papadopoulos was never charged with meeting any Russian agents, an omission McCarthy interpreted as an admission by Mueller that the various players in the Papadopoulos drama were agents of the FBI or of one or more foreign or domestic intelligence agencies. And all of these actors were working with the CIA and the FBI, playing roles that were scripted by the CIA in advance. Their insidious goal was to entrap the unsuspecting Papadopoulos, a minor figure in the Trump campaign who was naïve and inexperienced in the real politics of foreign affairs at the presidential level. McCarthy wrote:

> When one looks carefully at Mueller's statement of the offense, and at the one-count criminal-information to which Papadopoulos pled guilty, one realizes Mueller is not claiming that Mifsud and his associates truly were Kremlin operatives—*only that Papadopoulos was under the impression that they were.* The information legalistically accuses Papadopoulos of lying about his "interactions with certain foreign nationals *whom he understood to have* close connections with senior Russian government officials" [emphasis added]. That is, Papadopoulos is accused of misrepresenting his subjective state of mind, not objective reality.[172]

If Mueller's prosecutors could have proved that any of the actors in the Papadopoulos setup drama had been Russian agents—Mifsud, Downer, Halper, or Millian—they would have said so in indicting him. This

---

172 Andrew C. McCarthy, "The Papadopoulos Case Needs a Closer Look," *National Review*, June 2, 2018, https://www.nationalreview.com/2018/06/george-papadopoulos-case-needs-closer-look/.

fact goes to the heart of proving that Mueller's role was political. Mifsud, Downer, Halper, and Millian were all playing roles scripted by the CIA and FBI. Entrapping Carter Page and George Papadopoulos was designed not only to incriminate Trump in treason, but to cover up what the FBI and the Justice Department, in cahoots with U.S. and foreign intelligence agencies, were doing illegally. What became a coup d'état to remove Donald Trump from the presidency was initially designed to divert attention from the reality that Hillary Clinton, Barack Obama, John Brennan, and James Comey, to mention just a few, were involved in a covert plan to blame Trump and Russia for the theft of the Democrats' emails. Remember, their initial plan was to defeat Trump, confident that once Hillary was in the White House, their crimes would never be investigated.

The FBI Silences Papadopoulos

The DOJ indicted Papadopoulos on October 5, 2017, but he was not sentenced until nearly a year later, on September 7, 2018. His plea deal was similar to the one the Mueller prosecutors wanted me to sign. I refused and was never indicted. I am convinced that if Papadopoulos had rejected Mueller's plea deal, the DOJ might never have indicted him. Rejecting the government's plea deal, however, would have been a calculated risk.

Papadopoulos was indicted on what in law is known as a "process crime." In other words, Papadopoulos had committed no crime, at least not until he talked with the FBI and Mueller's team. Defense attorneys typically instruct their clients to accept the government's plea deal, knowing that accepting the plea deal is the only way to avoid prosecution and a much more severe punishment if found guilty. Many criminal defendants are guilty, and even the innocent typically run out of money given the expense of hiring defense attorneys for trial. David Gray advised me correctly that accepting Mueller's plea deal was the only sure route I had to avoid prison time. Yet the turning point for me came over Thanksgiving weekend in 2018 when my wife and I were debating what we should do. Monica woke up one morning that weekend and said to me, "I would rather visit you in prison for the rest of my life than have you not be the man I married."

That was all I needed to hear. As I discussed at length in *Silent No More*, my firsthand account of my dealings with the Mueller Office of Special Counsel, how I would handle the plea deal was a family decision. I knew that I could exhaust our resources and possibly have to sell the family house if I chose to let Mueller indict me. But hearing Monica say this, I resolved on the Monday following Thanksgiving to go on national television on *One America News* in New York to announce my decision to tell Mueller to take a hike. I want to stress that Mueller had no case against me, as proved by the fact Mueller did not prosecute me. But we did not know this would be the outcome until March 2019, when Attorney General Barr announced the Mueller Office of Special Counsel investigation was done and there would be no more indictments. From Thanksgiving 2018 until March 2019, Monica and I typically woke up at 4:00 am, wondering if the FBI was assembling in the front yard to storm our home and arrest me. For weeks on end, CNN had a car parked outside our home, hoping to capture my arrest on film. Thank God it never happened. Even after the Mueller investigation was closed down, the DOJ refused to announce that their case against me had been dropped, even though that was the reality.

But because Papadopoulos did not remember a date correctly, and because he tried to minimize Mifsud as "a nothing," and because he downplayed his conversations with Mifsud (which were a Deep State setup in the first place), Papadopoulos admits to having had a guilty conscience. This blocked him from resisting the DOJ charge that he had "lied" to federal agents. The decision Papadopoulos made to plead guilty marked an important milestone for the Mueller team. Yes, Mueller would have gained more had Papadopoulos worn a wire to record Mifsud, or simply by "composing" the narrative the Mueller prosecutors wanted to hear. But by digging in his heels, insisting he did not discuss the Mifsud conversation with the Trump campaign, Mueller's team took their next best option pressuring Papadopoulos to plead guilty to a process crime.

Make no mistake: the plea deal Mueller offered Papadopoulos was calculated and carefully worded by the prosecutors to help Mueller make his case against Trump. The charging document the DOJ prepared for Papadopoulos stressed that on or about March 31, 2016, Papadopoulos attended a "national security meeting" in Washington, D.C., with then candidate Donald Trump and Papadopoulos's fellow foreign policy advisors for the campaign. Although this was the only in-person meeting Papadopoulos ever had with Trump, the charging document stressed that when Papadopoulos introduced himself to the group, he stated he had connections that could arrange a meeting between Trump and Putin. The charging document also stressed Papadopoulos's interaction with Timofeev, noting that the Russian Ministry of Foreign Affairs is the executive entity in Russia responsible for Russian foreign relations. The charging document notes that after being introduced to Timofeev by email on April 18, 2016, Papadopoulos and Timofeev had multiple conversations over Skype about setting the groundwork for a potential meeting between the Trump campaign and Russian officials. The charging document also notes that Papadopoulos emailed Clovis saying, "The Russian government has an open invitation by Putin for Mr. Trump to meet him when he is ready. The advantage of being in London is that these governments tend to speak a bit more openly in 'neutral' cities." In the Mueller charging document, Papadopoulos is transformed from a relatively junior foreign policy advisor to a major go-between in the alleged Russia-collusion hoax.

The moment Papadopoulos pled guilty before a federal judge, he was a convicted felon, even if his crime was relatively minor. From that moment on, he had to get DOJ approval to travel, to give interviews, to write a book, or to speak out in any other manner. By not sentencing Papadopoulos immediately, the Mueller prosecutors knew they could silence him. If Papadopoulos did not do precisely what the government wanted after swearing guilty to the plea deal before a federal judge, the prosecutors could renege on their promise to ask the judge at sentencing for no prison time or a light prison sentence at worst. But if Papadopoulos spoke out or did anything the prosecutors did not approve in advance, then at sentencing, the prosecutors could ask the judge for a maximum sentence.

The ordeal cost Papadopoulos in more ways than he could contemplate at the moment he decided to take the easy way out by pleading guilty. In the year between Papadopoulos's plea and the sentencing hearing, Mueller owned him. In that one-year period, Mueller predictably placed a gag order on Papadopoulos that kept him silent, unable to tell his side of the story.

In his book, Papadopoulos admits that the most frustrating aspect of his plea deal was that he could not say anything. "I can't defend myself or explain the nuances of what happened," he writes. He says that listening to the mainstream media report on his case was tough. "I am itching to get out there," he writes, suffering as he watched his reputation being destroyed on a national stage. "But I have to wait until I am sentenced before I utter a word in public or risk the wrath of the special prosecutor and the judge presiding over my case." Meanwhile, Mueller's team allowed the sentencing hearing to drag on for nearly a year. "The prosecution keeps asking for extensions, so they don't expose other aspects of their investigation," Papadopoulos continued. "Even though I want to put this behind me and eliminate the lawyer fees that every delay costs me, I agree to the postponements. It's the right thing to do."

Obviously, it never occurred to Papadopoulos what was evident to me from the first moments of my "voluntary interview" with Mueller's team. The Mueller special prosecutor had gone rogue, and only a criminal would have offered me the fraudulent plea deal that ended my forty-hour ordeal with these politically motivated, hate-Trump "law enforcement" officials.

A Criminal Sentence of Fourteen Days

At Papadopoulos's sentencing hearing, on September 7, 2018, nearly a full year after he pleaded guilty, Mueller's prosecutors wanted the judge to impose a six-month federal prison sentence. U.S. District Judge Randolph Moss, in a direct rebuke to Mueller's prosecutors, instead imposed a minimal sentence of fourteen days. "I don't have any reason to believe and I don't think there's any reason in the record to conclude that Mr. Papadopoulos had any desire to aid Russia in any way, to do anything that was contrary to the national interest," Judge Moss explained.

Mueller's prosecutors knew the "lie" of getting the dates wrong was trivial. Clearly, if Mueller's prosecutors had succeeded in getting Papadopoulos to give them the testimony they wanted, Papadopoulos would never have been charged with a criminal offense. If Papadopoulos had lied to testify that he had repeated Mifsud's comments to various members of Trump's campaign team, Mueller's prosecutors would have excused the "lie" over dates by allowing Papadopoulos to amend his testimony. If Mueller's prosecutors had gotten the testimony they wanted, their goal would have shifted instantly. To preserve Papadopoulos's credibility as a key government witness, they would have been forced to allow Papadopoulos to correct his testimony to retract all alleged "lies."

Mueller's prosecutors knew they could not both charge Papadopoulos as a liar under Title 18, United States Code, Section 1001 and put him on the stand as a key government witness. It had to be one or the other. The fact that Mueller's prosecutors proceeded to indict Papadopoulos shows their vindictiveness. What Rhee, Zelinsky, and Goldstein wanted was for Papadopoulos to agree to their script, giving Mueller the dirt (even if fabricated) needed to implicate Trump and his campaign in Russian collusion.

With prosecutors like Weissmann on Mueller's team, committing prosecutorial misconduct to get a witness like Papadopoulos to "compose testimony" to incriminate Trump was a means to an end. As journalist Gregg Jarrett points out in his most recent book, *Witch Hunt*, when Trump's lawyers got hold of the proposed indictment and the allocution the Mueller prosecutors had prepared for me to read before a federal judge during the plea hearing, Rudy Giuliani immediately reported to the FBI and the Department of Justice that the Mueller team was attempting to suborn perjury, which is a felony. "They [the Mueller prosecutors] were dangling an offer that he'd [i.e., me] get probation and never have to go to jail if only he agreed to say things that were false," Giuliani told Jarrett. "They were threatening him to get him to lie."[173]

Convinced from the start that Trump was a traitor, or at least that Trump had to be portrayed credibly as a traitor, Mueller's prosecutors appeared willing to employ a Weissmann technique, pressuring witnesses like Papadopoulos and me to suborn perjury or do whatever else it took to accomplish their end goal of destroying Donald Trump. The only reason Carter Page avoided the government's entrapment schemes and "perjury traps" was because, at trial, the government would have had to admit

---

173   Gregg Jarrett, *Witch Hunt: The Story of the Greatest Mass Delusion in American Political History* (New York: Broadside Books, 2019), p. 386.

Carter Page had been working with the CIA and the FBI as an unpaid undercover informant for decades. That disclosure would have opened up the FBI and the DOJ to more embarrassing questions regarding why those facts were not disclosed to the FISA Court in four separate applications—applications that included placing Donald Trump under electronic surveillance during the first year of his presidency.

If Papadopoulos had decided to launch a defense, going public with his plea deal and claiming he was the victim of a government-concocted international entrapment scheme, it is highly doubtful that DOJ prosecutors would have indicted him. The U.S. government and foreign intelligence agencies involved in the Russia-collusion hoax never would have allowed a Papadopoulos defense team to proceed with pretrial discovery. Nor could the Obama administration ever allow a Papadopoulos defense team to prove in court before the world the treasonous nature of their entrapment schemes. At trial, lawyers for Papadopoulos would argue that the U.S. government had set out to entrap Papadopoulos in an international conspiracy that involved informants and spies working for one or more of the following: the FBI, the DOJ, the CIA, the NSA, the Office of the Director of National Intelligence, British intelligence, Italian intelligence, and Australian intelligence, with active assistance from the Clinton campaign, the DNC, and the Obama White House.

A Presidential Pardon for Papadopoulos?

Papadopoulos should be placed at or near the top of President Trump's pardon list.

Papadopoulos, if he had been willing to take the risk of being found guilty at trial, with the consequence of facing a long and painful prison term, had in his hands the key to turn the tables on Mueller. Had he pursued a strategy of resisting Mueller's plea deal, he might have been able to unravel the Clinton-Obama coup d'état right then and there. But in 2016, Papadopoulos was twenty-nine years old with a fiancée he planned to marry in what he hoped would be a partnership for life. Clearly, he did not want to risk everything by defying Mueller to prosecute him in anger.

Summing up his experience, Papadopoulos felt that as an advisor to the Trump campaign, he found himself in a house of mirrors. He sought to work with the Trump campaign as a young man with a strong interest in international politics. But almost immediately, he found himself in a world filled with influence peddlers who had stepped out of the pages of *The Maltese Falcon* and the Jason Bourne novels. "Almost everyone I met—and I found this out much later—had ties to intelligence outfits," he writes in his book. In the end, he came to realize the extent to which the government he once trusted had abused him.

"Diplomats and academics recorded conversations with me," he continues. "Businessmen offered me tens of thousands of dollars to work with them—without ever specifying what the work was. In the middle of this, I met a stunning Italian woman—a brainy blonde who spoke five languages—and I became smitten." But what came next quickly changed him from being the young, earnest, hardworking man from Chicago he had been before he sought to work on the Trump campaign. "What happened next...well, you know a bit about the FBI," Papadopoulos says. "But I've left out the CIA, MI6, Australian intelligence, Turkish operatives, private intelligence companies, and a university that specializes in training spooks."

In the final analysis, the cases of George Papadopoulos and Carter Page provide crucial evidence documenting that the Clinton-Obama coup d'état was international in scope and rogue, if not outright criminal, in nature. By exposing the Clinton-Obama coconspirators, Papadopoulos and Page deserve to be seen as the American heroes they truly are.

Chapter Seven

WHY IS JULIAN ASSANGE IN JAIL?

The case of Julian Assange disrupts the narrative of the Deep State coup d'état in several very important ways. This chapter will argue that Assange's repeated assertion that he did not get the stolen Democratic Party emails from Russia is correct. Consistently, Assange has pointed the finger at Seth Rich, a DNC staffer who was shot and killed mysteriously during the 2016 election. Rich's murder case has never been solved.[174]

Still, the United States government has chosen to indict Assange under the Espionage Act, a piece of old legislation that was originally passed in 1917 over concerns of the Woodrow Wilson administration about anarchists who violently opposed U.S. involvement in World War I. The DOJ's two criminal indictments against Assange surprisingly are not for anything related to Russia or the 2016 theft of Democratic Party emails.

Instead, these indictments involve the 2010 case of documents stolen by Bradley Edward Manning (now known as Chelsea Elizabeth Manning), then a U.S. Army intelligence agent. Apparently, even with Attorney General William Barr in place, Deep State agents continue to call the shots within the DOJ. Assange, I will argue in this chapter, is being

---

174 "Julian Assange on Seth Rich," YouTube video, 2:02, "Nieuwsuur," a
Dutch public broadcasting service, August 9, 2016, https://www.youtube.
com/watch?v=Kp7FkLBRpKg.

persecuted for publishing government secrets—an act that should be his right under the First Amendment. Assange's prosecution strongly suggests that the Deep State, loathe to see its secrets exposed to the light of day, remains in control of the intelligence apparatus of the nation.

Assange's case is pivotal to the argument of this book: namely that the Russia-collusion hoax was launched by the Clinton campaign and the Obama administration to make sure Donald Trump was denied the presidency. As long as Assange remains in jail, a captive of the Deep State, free press rights under the First Amendment are in jeopardy.

As long as Assange remains in prison, the American public will never know the truth about who stole the Democrats' emails in 2016. Freeing him is essential to killing the Deep State and bringing the Clinton-Obama coup d'état traitors to justice.

A Useful Informant

My insight into Assange began in February 2016, when an initially anonymous source whom I will call "Madam LH" began emailing me the first of what ultimately became dozens of emails explaining in detail how the Democrats put together their computer systems in 2016.[175]

Madam LH instructed me that the brain behind the Democrats' 2016 computer system architecture was little-known leftist operator Zack Exley. In 2000, George W. Bush dubbed Exley "the garbage man" after Exley hacked Bush's 2000 presidential campaign website to post doctored

---

175 Ultimately, I identified Madam LH, confirming her identity in a telephone call to her former husband, a retired National Security Agency employee who cautioned me that his former wife had psychological problems. Despite that warning, I quickly found I could independently corroborate everything Madam LH had told me. In my forty-hour interrogation by the FBI and Mueller's prosecutors, I confirmed that the FBI knew all about Madam LH, with the FBI going so far as to send agents to visit her too in her home. But despite my efforts to argue that I could prove the Russians did not steal the Democrats' emails, Mueller's henchmen were not interested. This reaffirmed my belief that Mueller's prosecutors were politically motivated, interested only in information that had the potential to threaten Donald Trump's presidency.

images of Bush from the political-satire campaign website Exley had created in 1999. What most upset Bush was that Exley had posted on his website a photograph of Bush lifted from Bush's official website, altered to show Bush with a straw up his nose and inhaling white lines in an obvious parody designed to suggest a history of cocaine use. In 2004, Exley served as the director of online communications and online organizing for the unsuccessful 2004 presidential campaign of senators John Kerry and John Edwards.

Exley rapidly became a leader in the vanguard of hard-left operators arising during the presidential campaigns of 2000 and 2004 who argued the importance of developing sophisticated computer technology aimed at mining all available sources of information, including social media, to gather a proactive database of potential Democratic Party small-dollar donors and likely voters. In Barack Obama's presidential campaigns of 2008 and 2012, Exley applied his Saul Alinsky-like experiences in labor union organizing to working with Obama's army of computer experts. The goal was to develop advanced techniques of transforming thousands of campaign volunteers into effective field organizers capable of increasing voter turnout, to propel Obama to victory with a "get out the vote" strategy.[176]

In 2015, Bernie Sanders's presidential campaign hired Exley to run his nationwide ground game. Previously, Exley had cofounded the New Organizing Institute (NOI) as a think tank to produce computer-savvy field operatives for left-oriented Democratic electoral campaigns. Serving with Exley on the advisory board of NOI was Nathaniel G. Pearlman, another leftist political operative. Pearlman produced a key component of the DNC's 2016 computer system. In 1997, Pearlman founded NGP Software, a computer-oriented company organized to provide political software identifying Democratic voters. Hillary Clinton first used the NGP system in her unsuccessful 2008 presidential bid, after hiring Pearlman to be her chief technology officer. Pearlman had a history with Clinton, having worked for her in 1999 during her first campaign for the U.S. Senate.

---

176 Zack Exley, "Obama Field Organizers Plot a Miracle," *Huffington Post*, August 27, 2007, https://www.huffpost.com/entry/obama-field-organizers-pl_b_61918.

Pearlman's job back then was to clean up campaign data on donors who had contributed some $30 million.

In 2010, NGP merged with the Voice Activation Network to form NGP VAN.

How the DNC Used NGP VAN

In 2016, the DNC used the NGP VAN system as its core computer data-processing machine. It was created by combining Pearlman's NGP system, or the National Geographical Political system—a name Pearlman insists was not created based on his initials—with the VAN system, or Voice Activated Network system, created in 2001 by Mark Sullivan. In 2016, the NGP VAN system ran the voter-builder database that was originally developed for Obama's presidential campaign. All Democratic Party candidates in 2016 used the same NGP VAN system to build their own voter and donor databases. That year, the NGP system operated out of Washington, D.C., and was used exclusively to manage donor contributions. The VAN system operated out of Somerville, Massachusetts, and was used primarily to manage voter data.

So, even though the Clinton campaign and the Sanders campaign in 2016 each had its own databases for donors and for prospective voters, both campaigns had to access the DNC to use the NGP VAN system to manage those databases. In December 2015, software technology expert Will Conway explained the DNC's relationship to the NGP VAN technology as follows:

> NGP VAN has a contract with the Democratic National Committee in which their customers' data is owned and retained by the DNC. In exchange, the DNC provides data to NGP VAN customers—those using NGP VAN get the data of every previous NGP VAN user and the DNC, which basically covers every Democrat to run for office in modern history.

Conway also noted the following problem:

…campaigns don't actually own the relationships they build in the software. The Democratic National Committee does. The deal struck with the DNC ensures an incredible competitive advantage for NGP VAN: use our software or be cut off from all Democrats' data. Moreover, if you break our rules, we'll kick you off the platform and cut you off from *your own data*.[177] [Emphasis in original.]

Please note, the private email server Hillary Clinton used at the State Department involved email technology that was separate and distinct from the NGP VAN technology used by both the Clinton and Sanders campaigns to manage their donor and voter databases. Clinton's private email system was created by Bryan Pagliano, one of the many computer experts Exley recruited from his "Colorado computer mafia" to work on the computer systems Clinton used both at the State Department and in her 2016 presidential campaign. Also note that the DNC maintained an email server separate from the NGP VAN system. Thus, hacking into the NGP VAN would not allow the hacker also to steal DNC emails or Clinton's emails from the State Department. As seen in the next paragraph, the private email server the Clintons set up when Hillary became Obama's secretary of state involved yet another computer server, one initially installed to operate out of the Clintons' home.

In March 2009, Pagliano installed Hillary's private email server in the basement of the Clintons' Chappaqua, New York, home.[178] Bill and Hillary Clinton personally paid Pagliano $5,000 for "computer services" prior to his becoming a State Department employee, according to a financial disclosure form Pagliano filed in April 2009. This payment evidently was for establishing a private server for the Clintons in their Chappaqua home. In May 2009, the State Department hired Pagliano as a special

---

177 Will Conway, "Why the NGP VAN Model Hurts Democracy," Medium.com, December 21, 2015, https://medium.com/@heywillconway/why-the-ngp-van-model-is-hurting-democracy-d9893d3d28f7.

178 Matthew Dean, "Timeline of Clinton Email Server Setup," Fox News, September 2, 2016, https://www.foxnews.com/politics/timeline-of-clinton-email-server-setup.

advisor. The record shows that Pagliano lied to the State Department to hide payments the Clintons continued to make to him privately to maintain the Chappaqua email server. He neglected to list the outside income in the required financial disclosures he filed with the State Department each year until concluding his full-time employment in February 2013, coincident with Hillary Clinton's departure as secretary of state. Pagliano played no role in the creation of the DNC computer system in 2016.

The point is that Hillary Clinton's private email system operated completely separately from the DNC's computer system in 2016. Thus, hacking into her emails would not permit the hacker also to access DNC emails or DNC donor and voter data. That data could be stolen only by hacking into the DNC email server or the NGP VAN system.

Over the course of the 2016 campaign, Hillary Clinton's personal email server was hacked, the NGP VAN system was hacked, and the DNC email server was hacked—with the possibility that each hack job was done by a different person or cybertheft group.

The Sanders Campaign Breaks into Clinton Voter Data

On Wednesday, December 16, 2015, NGP VAN released a software modification. Unfortunately, it contained a bug that dropped a firewall, opening a window of approximately forty minutes during which IT specialists on Bernie Sanders's campaign were allowed to view and copy voter data proprietary to Clinton's campaign.[179]

A DNC email released by WikiLeaks made clear that Amy Dacey, communications director for the Clinton campaign, had concluded that the data breach was serious. "As a result of this analysis, NGP VAN found that campaign staff on the Sanders campaign, including the campaign's national data director, had accessed proprietary information about which voters were being targeted by the Clinton campaign—and in so doing

---

179 Maggie Haberman and Nick Corasaniti, "Democrats and Bernie Sanders Clash over Data Breach," *New York Times*, December 18, 2015, https://www.nytimes.com/politics/first-draft/2015/12/18/sanders-campaign-disciplined-for-breaching-clinton-data/.

violated their agreements with the DNC," Dacey said. "These staffers [in the Sanders campaign] then saved this information in their personal folders on the system, and over the course of the next day, we learned that at least one staffer appeared to have generated reports and exported them from the system."[180] The *New York Times*, in reporting on the data breach, quoted an unnamed Clinton staffer who compared the data breach to "the opposing general getting your battle plans."[181] This confirmed that through the VAN system, the DNC provided all Democratic presidential campaigns with the same access to Democratic voters' names, phone numbers, and addresses, protected only by a VAN firewall designed to protect the proprietary data each Democratic campaign created from being viewed by competing Democratic campaigns.

On December 18, 2015, a Twitter user called "Iowa Starting Line" posted the logbook data from NGP VAN documenting by name four Sanders campaign staffers, including Sanders's national data director, Josh Uretsky.[182] The clear implication was that those named were the Sanders campaign staffers who accessed various Clinton campaign data files and saved them into their own computers, appearing to steal the data from the Clinton campaign. The logbook entries show that the proprietary VAN voter data the Sanders campaign took was potentially useful tactical information. Among the files identified as stolen were, for instance, data regarding turnout of voters age sixty years or older, "Turnout 60+," from the folder "Ranged Targets"; in the same folder were the files "Turnout 40–60" and "Not Sanders."

---

180 Amy Dacey, "Here's What Happened with the NGP VAN, the Sanders Campaign, and the Clinton Campaign," contained in an email released by WikiLeaks, addressed to John Podesta on December 19, 2015, https://WikiLeaks.org/podesta-emails/emailid/15792.

181 Emma Roller, "The Democrats' Database Fight," *New York Times*, December 22, 2015, https://www.nytimes.com/2015/12/22/opinion/campaign-stops/the-democrats-database-fight.html.

182 Iowa Starting Line (@IAStaringLine), "Here are the actions in the VAN the 4 Sanders users took with the Hillary data," Tweet, December 18, 2015, https://twitter.com/IAStaringLine/status/678011156791877632.

The logbook entries show that four Sanders IT specialists spent two hours in the database without notifying NGP VAN that the firewall was down.[183] In those two hours, the Sanders team called up Clinton information from about a dozen states, downloading data that included a voter-turnout variable that showed on a scale from one to one hundred how likely a person is to vote. That scoring was valuable because it aimed to give a high-priority score to someone the campaign should make an effort to contact and persuade. David Atkins, a campaign consultant and county official in the California Democratic Party, told PolitiFact that the information would give the Sanders campaign a view of how the Clinton campaign was targeting voters, as well as a view of polling data indicating how well Clinton was doing in various states.[184]

When the breach became known, a huge controversy developed, in which the DNC cut off Sanders from DNC proprietary data in the NGP VAN system, forcing Sanders to sue the DNC.[185] The matter was resolved acrimoniously but quickly, in a midnight settlement on Friday, December 18, 2015, that allowed Sanders to regain access to VAN. As the settlement was being reached, Sanders fired Uretsky.[186] Reacting to being fired, Uretsky insisted that, in breaking into the Clinton campaign's proprietary database, he was only doing his job by diligently documenting the seriousness of the breach. He insisted his motivation was to make sure NGP VAN could install a patch to make sure the firewall

---

183   Jon Greenberg, "Sanders Spins the Facts when He Says Campaign Did Not 'Go out and Take' Clinton Data," PolitiFact.com, December 22, 2015, https://www.politifact.com/truth-o-meter/statements/2015/dec/22/bernie-s/Sanders-take-Clinton-voter-data/.

184   Ibid.

185   John Wagner, Abby Phillip, and Rosalind S. Helderman, "Accord Reached after Sanders Sues the DNC over Suspended Access to Critical Voter List," *Washington Post*, December 19, 2015, https://www.washingtonpost.com/politics/sanders-threatens-to-sue-dnc-if-access-to-voter-list-isnt-restored/2015/12/18/fa8d6df8-a5a2-11e5-ad3f-991ce3374e23_story.html?utm_term=.1ba10c4e1637.

186   Dan Merica, "Fired Sanders Aide: I Wasn't Peeking at Clinton Data Files," CNN, December 18, 2015, https://www.cnn.com/2015/12/18/politics/sanders-dnc-data-breach-josh-uretsky/.

was never again breached. There was some speculation that Seth Rich, an IT employee of the DNC who was later murdered, felt that Amy Dacey, his boss on the voter mobilization campaign, used the incident to embarrass the Sanders campaign. On the DNC organizational chart, Rich was identified as the campaign's voter expansion data director, reporting to Technology Director Andrew Brown. Sanders said Brown, along with Bryan Whitaker, the former chief operating officer of NGP VAN, recommended he hire Uretsky as the national data director for the campaign.[187]

In the aftermath of the incident, Sanders went so far as to allege that the breach of the Clinton voter data may have been a "false flag" attack staged by the DNC and carried off by a "plant"—namely, Uretsky.[188] "I mean here we are being attacked for the behavior of an individual [Uretsky], which we ultimately fired," Sanders said. "We agree he acted improperly, but it's just amazing to me that this…individual that actually caused this trouble in our campaign was recommended by these guys [Brown and Whitaker]. It's not as if we conjured this guy Josh from thin air." Sanders insisted his campaign had not hacked the DNC's NGP VAN system but had taken advantage of a computer glitch.

Guccifer Hacks Hillary's Private Email Server

In March 2013, Romanian hacker Marcel Lazar, who went by the username Guccifer, a combination of "Gucci" and "Lucifer," shocked the world with the revelation that Hillary Clinton had used a private email server while secretary of state.

On March 15, 2013, the Smoking Gun website broke the story, disclosing that Guccifer had spent the past several months "breaking into

---

187   Democratic National Committee 2016, Organizational Chart, no date, http://www.p2016.org/parties/dnc16.html.

188   Allum Bokhari, "Democrat Turmoil: Bernie Sanders Adviser Claims DNC Planted a Rogue Staffer to Steal Clinton Data," Breitbart, December 27, 2015, https://www.breitbart.com/politics/2015/12/27/democrat-turmoil-bernie-sanders-adviser-claims-dnc-planted-a-rogue-staffer-to-steal-clinton-data/.

the e-mail accounts of family, friends, and political allies of the Bush family."[189] While hacking into the Bush family's accounts, Guccifer "crossed party lines" and illegally accessed the AOL account of a former senior White House advisor to president Bill Clinton, Sidney Blumenthal, a longtime confidant of Hillary Clinton. Guccifer entertained himself by reading the cache of Blumenthal emails that went back to 2005 and had been sent to "an array of Washington insiders, including political operatives, journalists, and government officials." This is the same Sidney Blumenthal referenced earlier who was willing to conduct for Hillary Clinton the opposition research on Donald Trump that was ultimately conducted by Fusion GPS.

Guccifer noticed that emails between Blumenthal and Hillary involved an email address she used, hdr22@clintonemail.com—which was clearly affiliated with the Clintons. Guccifer experienced a "wow" moment when he realized that the initials matched Clinton's maiden name, Hillary Diane Rodham—and that clintonemail.com was a private, unsecured email server.[190] During an interview given in Romania in 2015, Guccifer commented from prison to a reporter that he accessed emailed memos that Hillary had gotten as secretary of state, with CIA briefings attached. "I used to read her memos for six or seven hours then I'd get up and do the gardening in the yard," Guccifer said.

Guccifer was arrested in Romania on January 22, 2014, and sentenced to four years in prison, where he remained until he was extradited to the United States in March 2016 to face U.S. federal criminal charges. On September 1, 2016, a U.S. district judge in Alexandria, Virginia, sentenced Guccifer to four years in federal prison, after he pleaded guilty to one count each of aggravated identity theft and unauthorized access

---

189 "Hacker Targets Clinton Confidant in New Attack," TheSmokingGun. com, March 15, 2013, http://www.thesmokinggun.com/documents/ sidney-blumenthal-email-hack-687341.

190 "Hacker Begins Distributing Confidential Memos Sent to Hillary Clinton on Libya, Benghazi Attack," TheSmokingGun.com, March 18, 2013, http://www.thesmokinggun.com/buster/sidney-blumenthal/ hacker-distributes-memos-784091.

to a protected computer.[191] While Guccifer is responsible for alerting the world to the fact that Hillary Clinton was using a private email server while she was secretary of state, he was not responsible for the theft of data from the DNC's NGP VAN system or the DNC email server. Clinton appears to have destroyed the approximately thirty thousand emails that went missing from her private email system. These "lost" emails were most likely never hacked simply because they were never made public.

Guccifer 2.0 Hacks into the NGP VAN System

On June 15, 2016, an identified hacker using the moniker Guccifer 2.0 published on WordPress an opposition research report the DNC had prepared on Donald Trump, marked "Confidential" and dated December 19, 2015. It contained several pages of donor lists but no emails, suggesting that Guccifer 2.0 might have breached the NGP database. Guccifer 2.0 claimed to have sent the main part of the hacked documents, "thousands of files and mails," to WikiLeaks, bragging that WikiLeaks "will publish them soon."

From June 15, 2016, through October 18, 2016, Guccifer 2.0 published a series of documents, demonstrating extensive access to DNC internal memorandums and donor lists. But what was missing in the Guccifer 2.0 publication of DNC hacked documents were emails, suggesting that Guccifer 2.0 had penetrated the NGP VAN system, not the DNC email server, Hillary Clinton's private email server, the private Gmail accounts of John Podesta, or the private email accounts of any other Clinton campaign officials.

The Guccifer 2.0 controversy flared again when the *Wall Street Journal* published a May 25, 2017 article claiming that Guccifer 2.0 had sent Aaron Nevins, a GOP consultant in Florida, 2.5 gigabytes of documents

---

191   Rachel Weiner and Spencer S. Hsu, "Hacker Known as Guccifer Sentenced to 52 Months in Prison," *Washington Post*, September 1, 2016, https://www.washingtonpost.com/local/public-safety/guccifer-hacker-who-revealed-clintons-use-of-a-private-email-address-sentenced-to-52-months/2016/09/01/4f42dc62-6f91-11e6-8365-b19e428a975e_story.html?utm_term=.f5305e405fcf.

from the Democratic Congressional Campaign Committee (DCCC), a group housed in the same building as the DNC.[192] Nevins published some of these documents on a blog called HelloFLA! using a pseudonym. He told the *Wall Street Journal* he had set up a Dropbox account "so whoever was using the Guccifer 2.0 name could send large amounts of material."

In a WordPress site post on January 12, 2017, Guccifer 2.0 confirmed having hacked only the DNC computers, the donor data in the VAN computer servers in Massachusetts, and the voter data in the NGP computer servers in Washington: "I already explained at The Future of Cyber Security Europe conference that took place in London in last September, I had used a different way to breach into the DNC network. I found a vulnerability in the NGP VAN software installed in the DNC system."[193]

Guccifer 2.0, identified by the U.S. intelligence agencies and by the Mueller report as a Russian entity, is a different entity from the first Guccifer, Lazar, whose hacking capabilities have been severely limited during his continuing imprisonment since January 2014. Comparing all of Guccifer 2.0's publications of material hacked from the Democrats in 2016, and the stolen Democrats' emails that WikiLeaks published in 2016, it is clear that although Guccifer 2.0 may have offered the stolen material to WikiLeaks, Guccifer 2.0 does not appear to have stolen DNC emails and there is no proof Assange ever published any DNC material Guccifer 2.0 claimed to have stolen.[194]

Guccifer 2.0 has never confirmed various assertions that Guccifer 2.0 is a Russian entity. Unlike the first Guccifer, Guccifer 2.0 has never been arrested. As I shall show in the next chapter, the Obama administration's

---

192   Alexandra Berzon and Rob Barry, "How Alleged Russian Hacker Teamed Up with Florida GOP Operative," *Wall Street Journal*, May 25, 2017, https://www.wsj.com/articles/how-alleged-russian-hacker-teamed-up-with-florida-gop-operative-1495724787.

193   Guccifer 2.0, "Here I Am Again, My Friends!" Guccifer2.wordpress. com, January 12, 2017, https://guccifer2.wordpress.com/2017/01/12/fake-evidence/.

194   Daniel Lazare, "The 'Guccifer 2.0' Gaps in Mueller's Full Report," ConsortiumNews.com, April 18, 2019, https://consortiumnews. com/2019/04/18/the-guccifer-2-0-gaps-in-muellers-full-report/.

claim that Guccifer 2.0 is Russian is by no means certain. Former CIA analyst Larry C. Johnson claims that Guccifer 2.0 "appears to be a creation of the CIA and was one character in a broader scheme assembled to paint Donald Trump as a lackey of Vladimir Putin."[195]

July 22, 2016: WikiLeaks Starts Publishing DNC Emails

On Friday, July 22, 2016, WikiLeaks began releasing, in two batches, 44,053 emails and 17,761 attachments from seven key figures in the DNC, none of whom included then DNC chair Debbie Wasserman Schultz.[196]

By far, the largest number of emails were from DNC Communications Director Luis Miranda (10,520 emails), who had three times more emails released than the next-highest person on the list, National Finance Director Jordan Kaplan (3,799 emails). Finance Chief of Staff Scott Comer came in third (3,095 emails). The emails covered the period from January 2015 to May 25, 2016. In all of the emails, one or more of the "From," "To," and or "Cc" fields indicate that the message was sent by or to an addressee using the DNC email server, identified as dnc.org.

While the DNC email server could have been hacked, it's equally plausible that someone on the inside (perhaps an employee with a dnc.org email address) could have discerned the username (possibly identical to the name used in the email address) and the password for each of the seven DNC officials included in the WikiLeaks release. Or that someone within the DNC who had access to the DNC server—perhaps as an administrator—could simply have accessed the emails on the computer without knowing the individual passwords. If obtaining the DNC emails was an inside job, downloading the emails would have been as simple as accessing

---

195   Larry C. Johnson, "Nope, Guccifer 2.0 Was Not a Russian Creation," turcopolier.typad.com, May 22, 2019, https://turcopolier.typepad.com/ sic_semper_tyrannis/2019/05/nope-guccifer-20-was-not-a-russian-creation-by-larry-c-johnson.html.

196   WikiLeaks, "Search the DNC Email Database," WikiLeaks.org, no date, https://WikiLeaks.org/dnc-emails/?q=%222016-05-27%22&m-from=&mto=&title=&notitle=&date_from=&date_to=&nofrom=&noto=&count=50&sort=0#searchresult.

each official's email account and downloading all the emails listed there. Unless each DNC official made sure that emails on the DNC email server were truly erased (not simply erased as viewed by the email user), the leaker could have downloaded conceivably every email that users had written or received from the first email archived in the DNC email server.

The *New York Times*, reporting on Friday, July 22, 2016, commented that the DNC emails released by WikiLeaks showed that top officials at the DNC "criticized and mocked Senator Bernie Sanders of Vermont during the primary campaign, even though the organization publicly insisted it was neutral in the race."[197] Released starting that Friday through Saturday, the days immediately before the first day of the Democratic National Convention in Philadelphia on Monday, July 25, 2016, the emails had the immediate impact of forcing DNC Chair Debbie Wasserman Schultz to resign under fire on that Sunday, July 24, 2016. The publication of the DNC emails threw the national nominating convention into disarray by giving Sanders supporters abundant email evidence that Hillary Clinton and Debbie Wasserman Schultz had conspired to make sure Sanders did not win the primary battle to secure the nomination.[198]

October 7, 2016: Assange Deploys the Podesta File as an "October Surprise"

WikiLeaks began publishing the Podesta emails on October 7, 2016, approximately one hour after the *Washington Post* published an *Access* video

---

197   Michael D. Shear and Matthew Rosenberg, "Released Emails Suggest the D.N.C. Derided the Sanders Campaign," *New York Times*, July 22, 2016, https://www.nytimes.com/2016/07/23/us/politics/dnc-emails-sanders-clinton.html.

198   Anne Gearan, Philip Rucker, and Abby Phillip, "DNC Chairwoman Will Resign in Aftermath of Committee Email Controversy," *Washington Post*, July 24, 2016, https://www.washingtonpost.com/politics/hacked-emails-cast-doubt-on-hopes-for-party-unity-at-democratic-convention/2016/07/24/a446c260-51a9-11e6-b7de-dfe509430c39_story.html?utm_term=.2265f58256e0.

with Trump making lewd comments to *Access*'s Billy Bush.[199] WikiLeaks published a total of 57,153 Podesta emails in a series of drops, with the final drop, part thirty-four, being published on November 7, 2016, the day before Election Day.[200]

The last date of a Podesta email published by WikiLeaks is March 21, 2016, approximately two months earlier than the last date of the DNC emails (those published by WikiLeaks starting July 22, 2016). This allows us to conclude that the Podesta emails were stolen first, though published by WikiLeaks last. The emails attacking Sanders were stolen last, though published by WikiLeaks first. This confirms the brilliance Assange has demonstrated in manipulating the media to serve his purposes in the dozen or so years he has been publishing stolen classified documents.

Assange obviously had both the Podesta and Schultz emails in his possession before he began publishing on Friday, July 22, 2016. He knew that the DNC's national nominating convention was beginning that Monday, July 25, 2016, and decided to use the Schultz emails first. Having studied the entire lot of stolen DNC emails in his possession, Assange obviously concluded (correctly) that the information contained in the first batch of emails that WikiLeaks released had the potential of harming Clinton's campaign by antagonizing the Sanders delegates and denying her the benefit of a unified, supportive convention. Even though Assange got the Podesta emails first, he held off publishing them until October 2016 because he realized Podesta emails had the greatest chance of destroying Clinton's presidential chances beyond any hope of recovery. Realizing this, he decided to save the Podesta emails for his "October surprise."

To eliminate Schultz, Assange dropped the 44,053 emails over a two-day period, Friday and Saturday, July 22 and 23, 2016, when he knew that key Democrats were in transit to Philadelphia. He knew that dropping the

199 Aaron Sharockman, "It's True: WikiLeaks Dumped Podesta Emails Hour after Trump Video Surfaced," PolitiFact.com, December 18, 2016, https://www.politifact.com/truth-o-meter/statements/2016/dec/18/john-podesta/its-true-wikileaks-dumped-podesta-emails-hour-afte/.

200 WikiLeaks, "The Podesta Emails," WikiLeaks.org, no date, https://wikileaks.org/podesta-emails/?q=%222016-03-22%22&m-from=&mto=&title=&notitle=&date_from=&date_to=&nof-rom=&noto=&count=50&sort=6#searchresult.

emails precisely in this manner would make it impossible for the Clinton campaign and the heads of the DNC to manage the adverse news cycle. As noted above, Assange was right. Schultz resigned on Sunday, July 24, 2016, before the gavel went down to open the convention on the next day.

Assange also calculated correctly how and when to drop the Podesta emails. He waited until October 2016, the last full month before Election Day, scheduled for Tuesday, November 8, 2016. He knew that October is the month in a presidential election year when candidates are trying to deliver their closing arguments and the public is finally paying attention. By dropping the Podesta emails serially, drip by drip, a few every day, Assange again dominated the news cycle from the first day he released the Podesta emails, October 7, 2016, to the day before Election Day, when he released the last one. This strategy forced the media to search each day for new and potentially explosive disclosures.

Assange designed his strategy of releasing the Podesta emails to force the media and the public to stay interested, anticipating each day what new information that could be damaging to Clinton would be released in that day's drop. Again, Assange's strategy worked. Clinton lost the election, and the WikiLeaks release of the Podesta emails was a major factor contributing to her defeat.

Of the 57,153 Podesta emails, 48,862 contain "Podesta@"—making it clear that whoever stole Podesta's emails breached his private Gmail account. The released Schultz emails were stolen from the DNC email server, dnc.org, while Clinton's emails had been stolen from her private email server and the @clintonemail.com email account. While it is possible that the same person hacked both Podesta's Gmail account and the DNC email account @dnc.org, the only conclusions we can draw for certain are that Guccifer hacked into @clintonemail.com and Guccifer 2.0 hacked into the NGP VAN system. There is no evidence that the original Guccifer or Guccifer 2.0 hacked into any Democratic email server or into Podesta's private Gmail account in 2016, or at any other time.

That Podesta was lax about cybersecurity is obvious from emails in the WikiLeaks drop that discuss how Podesta lost his cell phone in a taxicab[201]

---

201   WikiLeaks, "The Podesta Emails," email titled "Lost Phone," sent to John Podesta on July 19, 2015, https://www.wikileaks.org/podesta-emails/emailid/6040#searchresult.

and, in a different incident, fell victim to a phishing attack.[202] He apparently shared the username and password to his Gmail account with his assistant.[203] Given that Podesta used john.podesta@gmail.com as his username and "Runner4567" as his password, it is likely (given his apparent disregard for internet security) that he used this username and password for all, or most, of the internet websites to which he subscribed, as well as for other transactions, maybe even including credit card and ATM transactions. Again, an insider familiar with Podesta's use of his Gmail account for virtually all of his campaign email correspondence would need to know or guess only his password to gain access to all undeleted emails that remained on the @gmail.com server, possibly back to the very first one he had sent or received.

Assange Denies Russian Involvement in Theft of Democrats' Emails

The strongest indication that Seth Rich leaked the DNC and Podesta emails to WikiLeaks comes from Julian Assange himself. In interview after interview, he has insisted that Russia had nothing to do with the stolen Democrats' emails that WikiLeaks published in 2016.

It is not central to the thesis of this book whether or not Rich stole Podesta's emails from his private Gmail account or from the DNC email server. I make no claim here to be able to prove that he was involved.

About all that the Washington, D.C. police department (Metropolitan Police of Washington, D.C.) has released with certainty is that Rich was shot to death in the Bloomingdale area of Washington, D.C., in the early hours of Sunday, July 10, 2016. To date, the Washington police have refused to release any investigative report or autopsy that precisely describes his wound. It appears that there are some two and a half hours unaccounted for between 1:15 a.m., when Rich left a local bar, and 4:25 a.m., when he was shot near his home, even considering the time Rich

---

202 WikiLeaks, "The Podesta Emails," email titled "Someone has your password," sent to John Podesta on March 19, 2015, https://www.wikileaks.org/podesta-emails/emailid/34899#searchresult.

203 WikiLeaks, "The Podesta Emails, email titled "Apple ID," sent to Podesta on May 16, 2015, https://wikileaks.org/podesta-emails/emailid/6589.

would have required in order to walk home. Sorting through the thin evidence is unlikely to produce a conclusive breakthrough in the case, as long as the Metropolitan Police withhold all investigative reports and the family of Rich actively discourages further inquiries. The Democratic National Party continues to dismiss Rich's involvement in the theft of the DNC emails as a "conspiracy theory," to deflect any threat to its Russia-collusion story, which itself lacks evidence.

What is central to the thesis of this book is that Assange insists that the Russians had nothing to do with the stolen emails that WikiLeaks published in 2016.

In an interview broadcast on Dutch television on August 9, 2016,[204] host Eelco Bosch van Rosenthal asked Assange, "The stuff that you're sitting on, is an October surprise in there?" Assange insisted, "WikiLeaks never sits on material," even though he had previously said that WikiLeaks had more material related to the Hillary Clinton campaign that had yet to be published. Then, on his own initiative, without being specifically asked, Assange began talking about Seth Rich.

"Whistleblowers go to significant efforts to get us material, and often very significant risks," Assange volunteered. "There's a twenty-seven-year-old that works for the DNC who was shot in the back, murdered, just a few weeks ago, for unknown reasons, as he was walking down the streets in Washington." Van Rosenthal argued that the basis of Rich's murder was robbery. "No, there's no findings," Assange answered. "What are you suggesting?" Van Rosenthal countered. "I'm suggesting that our sources take risks—and they become concerned to see things occurring like that," Assange responded obliquely.

There was no reason for Assange to have spontaneously brought up Seth Rich in the context of the risks his sources take if Rich were not responsible for stealing the DNC and Podesta emails published by WikiLeaks.

On August 9, 2016, WikiLeaks offered a $20,000 reward "for information leading to the conviction for the murder of DNC staffer Seth

---

204   "Julian Assange on Seth Rich," YouTube video, 2:02, "Nieuwsuur," a
       Dutch public broadcasting service, op. cit.

Rich." Again, why would WikiLeaks do this if Rich were not the leak in question? Repeatedly, Assange has denied that the Russians "or any state party" supplied WikiLeaks with the DNC and/or Podesta emails.[205]

March 2018: The U.S. Government Files a Secret Indictment Against Assange

A sealed indictment against Assange was filed by the DOJ in U.S. District Court in Alexandra, Virginia, on March 6, 2018, when the Mueller Office of Special Counsel was reporting to Deputy Attorney General Rod Rosenstein.[206] Recall that on May 17, 2017, Rosenstein appointed Mueller to take over the supervision of the Russia-collusion investigation through the Office of Special Counsel following the decision of Attorney General Jeff Sessions to recuse himself from the Russia-collusion investigation. The DOJ kept Assange's indictment secret for nearly a year. Attorney General Barr made it public on April 11, 2019, on the very day British law enforcement officers barged into the Ecuadorian embassy in London to arrest Assange, removing him forcibly from the asylum he had sought in the embassy since June 2012.[207]

While Rosenstein and Mueller were running the Russia-collusion investigation, clearly the political left was raging against Assange for publishing the DNC emails. Yet the March 2018 indictment against Assange is

---

205 Michelle Ye Hee Lee, "Julian Assange's Claim That There Was No Russian Involvement in WikiLeaks Emails," *Washington Post*, January 5, 2017, https://www.washingtonpost.com/news/fact-checker/wp/2017/01/05/julian-assanges-claim-that-there-was-no-russian-involvement-in-wikileaks-emails/?utm_term=.f84c2c59de46.

206 Indictment, *U.S. v. Julian Paul Assange, Defendant*, filed on March 6, 2018, in the U.S. District Court for the Eastern District of Virginia, Alexandria Division, Under Seal, Criminal Case No. 1:18cr, One Count, Conspiracy to Commit Computer Intrusion (18 U.S.C. Sections 371, 1030(a)(1), 1030(a)(2), 1030(c)(2)(B)(ii), https://www.justice.gov/opa/press-release/file/1153486/download.

207 U.S. Department of Justice, Office of Public Affairs "WikiLeaks Founder Charged in Computer Hacking Conspiracy," April 11, 2019, https://www.justice.gov/opa/pr/wikileaks-founder-charged-computer-hacking-conspiracy.

surprising in that the DOJ did not charge him with any offense related to the 2016 publication of the emails.

The final Mueller report continued to insist that the theft of the DNC emails was accomplished by agents of the Russian Federation's Main Intelligence Directorate of the General Staff (GRU) operating under the umbra of the shadowy Guccifer 2.0. persona. The faulty assumption behind the Russia-collusion hoax is that the Trump campaign coordinated with Assange, directing him to release the DNC emails stolen by Russia in a fashion designed to do the most harm to Hillary Clinton's presidential campaign.

That Russia stole the DNC emails was a Mueller conclusion buttressed (as I shall show in the next chapter) by politically motivated intelligence agency assessments. Those assessments were directed by John Brennan as head of the CIA and by Director of National Intelligence James Clapper to advance the Clinton/Obama coup d'état efforts these intelligence agencies were orchestrating with the FBI and DOJ. But here, I must emphasize again that the March 2018 indictment of Assange had nothing to do with the emails stolen from the Democrats in 2016 or with Russian involvement in the 2016 election.

Instead, the March 2018 indictment alleges that in March 2010, Assange entered into a conspiracy with Chelsea Manning, a former U.S. Army intelligence analyst, to crack a password stored on a U.S. government network used to communicate classified documents.

Obviously, the DOJ realized the indictment would have been on shaky ground if the charges had been related to Assange's role publishing classified documents, due to the Supreme Court case *New York Times v. United States*, 403 U.S. 713 (1971). In that case, the 1971 Pentagon Papers led to the Supreme Court's six-to-three landmark decision that journalists have a right to publish stolen classified government documents, provided the journalists did not participate in the theft. The Pentagon Papers case involved the theft by Daniel Ellsberg, an employee of the Rand Corporation, of a highly classified secret Pentagon study of the Vietnam War.

That study was explosive because the Pentagon Papers provided evidence from classified documents that established the government of the

United States lied to the American people about the premises for the Vietnam war, as well as the conduct of that war. Following the assassination of President John F. Kennedy in 1963, President Lyndon Johnson and Secretary of Defense Robert McNamara knew that the U.S. was doomed to lose, given the strategy to fight a limited foreign war in what was truly a Vietnam civil war. In 1971, the U.S. government went to the Supreme Court to demand that the *New York Times* and the *Washington Post* be prohibited from publishing Ellsberg's stolen Pentagon Papers study. The Supreme Court ruled in favor of extending to the newspapers First Amendment rights, rejecting the government's argument that the legal theory of prior restraint could be used to prohibit the newspapers from publishing (that is, due to the anticipated harm to the national security of the United States).

In the March 2018 indictment of Assange, the DOJ avoided charging him with a Pentagon Papers offense regarding the publication of the 2016 emails stolen from the Democrats. The March 2018 indictment of Assange goes so far as to avoid charging Assange or WikiLeaks with any crime related to publication. Instead, it charges that Assange allegedly became a coconspirator to the theft when he agreed to assist Manning by cracking a password that would allow Manning to steal more documents from government computers. Interestingly, despite Assange's insistence that Russia had nothing to do with the theft of the DNC emails, the Mueller prosecutors never sought to interview him.

In reverting to the old 2010 case to indict Assange, the DOJ appears to have punted, admitting by default that Mueller could not prove that Assange committed a crime in 2016. But in doing so, the DOJ created a major problem. In 2013, the DOJ had passed on prosecuting Assange, arguing appropriately that if he were prosecuted for publishing Manning's documents, the DOJ would also have to prosecute publications like the *New York Times*, the *Washington Post*, and the *Guardian* in London, all of which had also published the Manning documents.[208]

---

208   Sari Horwitz, "Julian Assange Unlikely to Face U.S. Charges over Publishing Classified Documents," *Washington Post*, November 25, 2013, https://www.washingtonpost.com/world/national-security/julian-assange-unlikely-to-face-us-charges-over-publishing-classified-documents/2013/11/25/dd27decc-55f1-11e3-8304-caf30787c0a9_story.html?utm_term=.bbc7b7ea1551.

In returning to the 2010 case to charge that Assange was a coconspirator in Manning's document theft, the DOJ put itself on shaky ground. In the final analysis, it is not credible to believe the DOJ had acquired new evidence since 2010 proving that Assange assisted Manning in cracking a password—evidence that somehow was not available to the U.S. intelligence agencies, the FBI, and the DOJ in 2013, when the DOJ declined to prosecute Assange for publishing the documents stolen by Manning in 2010.

Seriously detrimental to the government's case is the fact the indictment makes clear that Assange had "no luck" cracking the password, despite his repeatedly telling Manning that he would try to do so—in conversations the two conducted over the Jabber chat server that were evidently intercepted by government investigators. Evidently, as a hacker, Assange was a failure. The critical flaw in the government's case is revealed in the last two sentences of the March 2018 indictment: "On or about March 10, 2010, Assange requested more information from Manning related to the password. Assange indicated that he had been trying to crack the password by stating that he had 'no luck so far.'" With this statement, the DOJ undermines the premise of the indictment, making it clear that Assange played no material role in Manning's document theft, except perhaps to promise assistance in cracking a password that Assange was then unable to deliver.

This makes it clear that all the stolen classified documents from Manning published on WikiLeaks were obtained without Assange's actually participating in the theft. Or did the DOJ charge Assange with a crime under the espionage acts simply because he offered to help Manning crack a password? What if Assange had just been boasting in his effort to help Manning crack the password? What if Assange made no serious efforts to crack the password? Then the DOJ's indictment would come down to charging him with a criminal offense simply because he encouraged Manning to keep stealing documents. The problem is that in the 1971 Pentagon Papers case, both the *New York Times* and the *Washington Post* took many affirmative steps to find Daniel Ellsberg precisely in order to encourage him to give them the documents for publication. If Ellsberg was available to steal classified documents in addition to the Pentagon Papers, the *New York Times* and the *Washington Post* would have been happy to publish them as well.

May 23, 2019: The DOJ Hits Assange with a Second, Superseding Indictment

On May 23, 2019, the DOJ hit Assange with a much more serious superseding eighteen-count indictment, charging him with various offenses related to obtaining and disclosing national defense classified information, as well as for the original offense involving a conspiracy to commit computer intrusion.[209] In announcing the second indictment on May 23, 2019, the DOJ made it clear that central to the government's case in the second indictment was the allegation that Assange engaged in a conspiracy with Manning not only to encourage Manning to steal classified information, but that Assange had published on WikiLeaks a narrow subset of documents that identified the names of human sources—including local Afghans and Iraqis who were assisting U.S. military forces in theater, and those of journalists, religious leaders, human rights advocates, and political dissidents living in repressive regimes. Assange was thereby alleged "to have created grave and imminent risk to their lives and liberties" by making this classified information identifying human sources available to "every terrorist group, hostile foreign intelligence service and opposition military." The indictment went on to assert that by doing so, Assange made "our adversaries stronger and more knowledgeable and the United States less secure." Finally, the indictment noted that documents related to these disclosures were even found in the Osama bin Laden compound.[210] The seventeen counts of the superseding indictment under Title 18, United States Code, Section 793 were clearly espionage charges making it clear the United States government now considered Assange a spy, not a journalist.

---

209 Indictment, *U.S. v. Julian Paul Assange*, Defendant, filed on May 23, 2019, in the U.S. District Court for the Eastern District of Virginia, Alexandria Division, Under Seal, Criminal Case No. 1:18-cr-111 (CMH), Seventeen Counts involving a Conspiracy to Obtain and Disclose National Security Information under various subsections of 18 U.S.C. Section 793, plus One Count, Conspiracy to Commit Computer Intrusion (18 U.S.C. Sections 371 and 1030).

210 U.S. Department of Justice, "Remarks from the Briefing Announcing the Superseding Indictment of Julian Assange; Remarks as Prepared for Delivery by Assistant Attorney General for National Security John C. Demers," May 23, 2019, https://www.justice.gov/opa/press-release/file/1165636/download.

A serious complication facing the superseding indictment is that President Obama, in his last week in office, used his clemency powers to commute the prison sentence of Chelsea Manning to the seven years already served of a thirty-five-year prison sentence, the longest prison sentence ever imposed in the United States for a leak conviction. Obama's decision was in part motivated by sympathy for Manning, who had twice attempted suicide in prison and was in the throes of a sex-identity crisis. But if the information published by Manning and Assange caused such serious damage to U.S. national security interests, then why did Obama let Manning out of prison?

Clearly, when Obama weighed what he considered to be the severity of Manning's national security crimes against Manning's personal problems, he came down on the side of clemency. In 2016, the *New York Times* noted when reporting Obama's clemency order that none of the documents Manning disclosed were classified above the "secret" level. How serious, then, could the damage have been?

When we examine the history of the Pentagon Papers case, we can see that the success of the government in prosecuting as spies and obtaining convictions against politically motivated thieves of classified documents like Daniel Ellsberg is not particularly good.

On January 3, 1973, the DOJ charged Ellsberg—under the Espionage Act of 1917—with various counts related to a conspiracy to steal national security documents. However, due to government misconduct in the collection of evidence against Ellsberg, his case was dismissed. On April 27, 1973, Judge Matthew Byrne, the presiding judge in Ellsberg's criminal trial in the U.S. District Court for the Central District of California, made public a memo from Watergate prosecutor Earl Silbert documenting that White House-related Watergate burglar Gordon Liddy—in conjunction with CIA-related operative Howard Hunt—had burglarized the offices of Daniel Ellsberg's psychiatrist to obtain files relating to Ellsberg.[211] As a result of this disclosure, on May 11, 1973, Judge Byrne dismissed all charges against Ellsberg, citing government misconduct as his reason.

---

211 Douglas O. Linder, "The Pentagon Papers (Daniel Ellsberg) Trial: An Account," 2011, University of Missouri-Kansas City, School of Law, http://law2.umkc.edu/faculty/projects/ftrials/ellsberg/ellsbergaccount.html.

In the Pentagon Papers case, *New York Times v. U.S.*, Supreme Court Justice Hugo Black, in a concurring opinion with Justice William Douglas, gave a definitive statement of the priority the First Amendment enjoys, even in a case involving the theft of national security documents relevant to an ongoing foreign war. Justice Black wrote:

> In the First Amendment, the Founding Fathers gave the free press the protection it must have to fulfill its essential role in our democracy. The press was to serve the governed, not the governors. The Government's power to censor the press was abolished so that the press would remain forever free to censure the Government. The press was protected so that it could bare the secrets of government and inform the people. Only a free and unrestrained press can effectively expose deception in government. And paramount among the responsibilities of a free press is the duty to prevent any part of the government from deceiving the people and sending them off to distant lands to die of foreign fevers and foreign shot and shell.

Arguably, this language applies to the WikiLeaks decision to publish the classified government documents containing information regarding the Afghanistan and Iraq wars that Manning stole. Under the standard of *New York Times v. U.S.*, the government will have a high threshold of proof to demonstrate that the WikiLeaks publication of the Chelsea Manning documents in 2010 caused the type of damage to national security that would have justified prior restraint of the publication—especially given the clemency that President Obama extended in commuting Manning's sentence to time served.

The decision to prosecute Assange for espionage appears to be an act of revenge taken by Deep State operatives to imprison him for the rest of his life for being a whistleblower who dared to publish the stolen DNC emails in a move that helped end Hillary Clinton's presidential ambitions in 2016. Attorney General Barr has to realize that the DOJ did not initially indict Assange for publishing either the Manning documents in 2010 or the DNC stolen emails in 2016. The superseding indictment charging Assange with espionage in the 2010 case, when the Obama DOJ had already declined to prosecute Assange, has all the earmarks not only of a vengeance prosecution, but also of retroactive punishment of an earlier offense.

The photographs of Assange being carried out of the Ecuadorian embassy are deeply disturbing to those of us who treasure First Amendment free speech rights as part of the bedrock of our freedoms. In Assange's case, the Deep State in the U.S. and the U.K. were more than willing to send British law enforcement authorities to forcefully remove Assange from asylum in order to haul him before a U.K. magistrate as the first step in extraditing him to the U.S. to face trial.

William Barr's primary responsibility as attorney general is to restore the American public's confidence in the FBI and the Justice Department as a whole. Unlike the U.S. intelligence agencies, the FBI, and the DOJ, Assange has a history over the past dozen years of publishing authentic government documents and telling the truth about his operations. In the entire Russia-collusion investigation, it is impossible to understand why Mueller's special counsel investigation never sought to take Assange's testimony in London. Arguably, even now, Attorney General Barr should grant Assange immunity to allow him to bring forth his claimed proof that Russia did not steal the DNC emails in 2016. Barr is not going to restore the public's confidence in the U.S. justice system by pursuing a revenge prosecution against Assange over an old case with a complex history.

Obviously, the Deep State is seriously frightened that Assange can prove that Russia had nothing to do with stealing the DNC emails in 2016. When this is proved conclusively, as I believe it will be, this will be the second shoe to fall on the Russia-collusion hoax. The first shoe to fall came when Mueller's final report concluded "no collusion" and Attorney General Barr decided there was insufficient evidence to charge President Trump with obstruction. Now, should Assange be allowed to prove that Russia did not steal the DNC emails in 2016, we will know once and for all that Russia had nothing whatsoever to do with Hillary Clinton's resounding electoral defeat in 2016. Trump is right: Clinton, a two-time presidential loser, is simply a lousy candidate on the national stage.

Chapter Eight

CIA DIRECTOR JOHN BRENNAN, RUSSIAGATE FABRICATOR-IN-CHIEF

This chapter will establish that former CIA director John Brennan played a central role in the Clinton-Obama coup d'état. Since leaving office, Brennan has written a series of caustic tweets belittling Donald Trump, ceaselessly suggesting that he should be removed from office.

On June 23, 2018, President Trump tweeted, "@Fox News. Poll numbers plummet on the Democrat inspired and paid for Russia Witch Hunt. With all of the bias, lying and hate by the investigators, people want the investigators investigated. Much more will come out. A total scam and excuse for the Democrats losing the Election!"

Brennan tweeted back: "Your fear of exposure is palpable. Your desperation even more so. When will those of conscience among your Cabinet, inner circle, and Republican leadership realize that your unprincipled and unethical behavior as well as your incompetence are seriously damaging our Nation."[212]

212　John O. Brennan (@JohnBrennan), Tweet, June 23, 2018, https://
twitter.com/JohnBrennan/status/1010500990288695298?ref_
src=twsrc%5Etfw%7Ctwcamp%5Etweetembed%7Ctwter-
m%5E1010500990288695298&ref_url=https%3A%2F%2Fwww.
thegatewaypundit.com%2F2018%2F06%2Fjohn-brennan-in-ominous-
tweet-to-pres-trump-calls-for-insurrection-by-cabinet-gop-leadership%2F.

In this tweet, Brennan openly hinted his wish for the cabinet to invoke the Twenty-fifth Amendment to declare that President Trump is unfit to discharge the powers and duties of the presidency and therefore should be removed from office.

John Brennan: A Hard-Left Partisan

Brennan's history leaves no doubt that he is a leftist who displays a partisan devotion to President Obama. As a young man in 1976, he voted for Gus Hall, the Communist Party USA candidate for president. In college, Brennan spent a year in Cairo learning Arabic, ultimately getting a master's degree in Middle Eastern studies at the University of Texas in Austin in 1980. In 1996, he served as the CIA's station chief in Riyadh, Saudi Arabia.

In March 2008, as Obama was in the process of running for president for the first time, an employee of the Analysis Corporation, a private security firm headquartered in McLean, Virginia, of which Brennan was president and CEO, was accused of breaking into and altering Obama's State Department passport records.[213] At the time of the alleged breach, Brennan was advising Obama, then a first-term U.S. senator from Illinois, on foreign policy and intelligence issues. After Obama was elected president, Brennan served in the White House as homeland security assistant to the president from 2009 to 2013. On January 7, 2013, Obama nominated Brennan to direct the CIA.

This chapter will demonstrate that Brennan has reason to fear being investigated. First, we'll examine Brennan's role as architect of the Intelligence Community Assessment (ICA) produced by the CIA, NSA, and FBI on January 6, 2017. This is the key document used by the Mueller report to "determine" that Russia's collusion in the 2016 election was extensive, including regarding the DNC emails, aimed at promoting Donald Trump's candidacy and defeating Hillary Clinton.

---

213 Kate Bolduan, "Chief of Firm Involved in Breach Is Obama Adviser," CNN, March 22, 2008, http://www.cnn.com/2008/POLITICS/03/22/passport.files/index.html.

In the next chapter, I will explain why the infamous meeting with Donald Trump Jr. at Trump Tower that took place on June 9, 2016, was an intelligence operation designed to plant quid pro quo "evidence" that, in the Deep State endgame, would be brought forth to explain what Trump had promised Russia in order to induce Russia to steal the DNC emails.

The Democrats Blame Cyberthefts on Russia

As indicated in the previous chapter, the last date of a Podesta email published by WikiLeaks was March 21, 2016. This strongly suggests that the theft of Podesta's emails did not occur after that month, March 2016.

Assuming the Democrats were astute enough to realize in March 2016 that Podesta's emails had been hacked, why did they delay the public announcement until June 2016, three months later? The answer may be that the three-month delay gave them enough time to develop a cover story blaming the cybertheft on the Russians. In that intervening time, the Democrats hired a Clinton-supporting cybersecurity firm, CrowdStrike, to investigate the theft. As shown in the next few paragraphs, CrowdStrike gave the Russia-collusion hoax its first spark of credibility.

On March 16, 2016, WikiLeaks launched a searchable archive of 30,322 emails and email attachments from Hillary Clinton's private email server that were sent and received while she was secretary of state. The Clinton emails had been published previously, but what was new was WikiLeaks's publication of a search engine that allowed readers to look for specific topics within the emails. None of these emails had anything to do with the emails stolen from the DNC or from John Podesta.

Then, on Sunday, June 12, 2016, the *Guardian* published an article informing the world, possibly including the Democrats, that WikiLeaks was preparing to publish more Clinton emails.[214] The *Guardian* assumed that the new emails WikiLeaks was about to release were more Clinton emails from her time as secretary of state. The Democrats may have known

---

214 Mark Tran, "WikiLeaks to Publish More Hillary Clinton Emails—Julian Assange," *The Guardian*, June 12, 2016, https://www.theguardian.com/media/2016/jun/12/wikileaks-to-publish-more-hillary-clinton-emails-julian-assange.

better. Julian Assange was planning to release the emails stolen from the DNC email server, which would cause Debbie Wasserman Schultz to resign from her position as chair of the DNC. The *Guardian* story focused on a television interview Assange had done earlier that day on the widely watched ITV *Peston on Sunday* show broadcast on British television. "We have upcoming leaks in relation to Hillary Clinton," Assange said. "We have emails pending publication, that is correct."[215] Assange did not specify what emails precisely he planned to publish, and he gave no details when or how they would be published.

Here's why the DNC may have known precisely what Assange was going to talk about. The first published report that hackers had breached the DNC network was published on June 14, 2016, by the *Washington Post*.[216] The article was an obvious plant by the Democrats in an attempt to get ahead of the rapidly developing story. The article told the world, in advance of Assange's next publication of Hillary Clinton emails, that these new emails may have been stolen not from Clinton's State Department cache but from the Clinton campaign and the DNC. The *Washington Post* reported that Russian government hackers had penetrated the DNC computer network, gaining access to the entire database of opposition research on GOP candidates. The article cited unnamed "U.S. officials" who claimed the intrusion into the DNC was one of several by "Russian spies" targeting "American political organizations," including the computer networks of the Clinton and the Trump campaigns, as well as computers of various GOP political action committees.

The website DCLeaks was launched on June 8, 2016, a week before the *Washington Post* article was published. On June 15, 2016, the day after

---

215 "Assange on Peston on Sunday: 'More Clinton Leaks to Come,'" ITV. com, June 12, 2016, https://www.itv.com/news/update/2016-06-12/ assange-on-peston-on-sunday-more-clinton-leaks-to-come/.

216 Ellen Nakashima, "Russian Government Hackers Penetrated DNC, Stole Opposition Research on Trump," *Washington Post*, June 14, 2016, https://www.washingtonpost.com/world/national-security/ russian-government-hackers-penetrated-dnc-stole-opposition-re-search-on-trump/2016/06/14/cf006cb4-316e-11e6-8ff7-7b6c1998b7a0_story.html?utm_term=.f173b6633b06.

the *Post* article appeared, Guccifer 2.0 began publishing on DCLeaks the files stolen from the DNC's NGP VAN computer system. When posting these emails, Guccifer 2.0 claimed to be the hacker responsible for breaking into the DNC's computers. Judging from how CrowdStrike described the DNC computer breach, it was apparent that the DNC itself was making public the breach by Guccifer 2.0 of the NGP VAN system. Also interesting is that in the article published on June 14, 2016, the *Post* identified the hacker as Russian, but made no mention of Guccifer 2.0.

There is no reference in that article indicating that the Democrats were making public the concern that Podesta's personal Gmail account had been breached. By the time the *Post* article was published on June 14, 2016, and Guccifer 2.0 began publishing stolen DNC material from the NGP VAN system on June 15, 2016, someone had already stolen both Podesta's emails and the DNC emails on Debbie Wasserman Schultz. As we saw in the previous chapter, the last date of the emails in the Podesta dump was March 21, 2016 and the last date of the emails WikiLeaks released to embarrass Debbie Wasserman Schultz was May 25, 2016. Yet, in leaking to the *Post* the information that appeared in the June 14, 2016 article, the Democrats made no mention that emails from Podesta or the DNC had been stolen.

WikiLeaks never published Hillary Clinton emails from the State Department until it published the searchable archive on March 16, 2016. As we also saw in the previous chapter, it was the original Guccifer that let the world know Secretary of State Clinton was using a private email server, not Guccifer 2.0. Hillary Clinton's email scandal did not revolve around Guccifer's hacking, but around the likelihood that by using a private email server, Clinton had violated national security laws regarding the handling of classified material. What is clear from the *Post* article is that the Democrats in June 2016 were blaming all the hacks of their NGP VAN system and their various email accounts on Guccifer 2.0. What the Democrats wanted to spread, by leaking the information to the *Post*, was the conclusion that Guccifer 2.0 was a Russian spy.

The *Post* story on June 14, 2016, also makes no reference whatsoever to Julian Assange or to WikiLeaks. That story appears designed to introduce and establish the narrative that Russians hacked the DNC computers to harm Clinton's campaign. That is why linking Guccifer 2.0 to Russia, to Julian Assange and WikiLeaks, as well as to the Trump campaign, became so vitally important for the Mueller investigation. The Russia-collusion narrative, it appears, can be traced back to this *Post* article, which set up the basis for arguing ultimately that Trump was in collusion with Russia. When WikiLeaks began publishing the stolen emails from DNC officials in July 2016, and from Podesta starting in October 2016, the Democrats succeeded in getting the mainstream media and the Obama administration intelligence agencies to parrot the story that Guccifer 2.0, Trump, Russia, Julian Assange, and WikiLeaks were in cahoots.

Roger Stone fell into the trap when he reached out to Guccifer 2.0 during the 2016 campaign and began exchanging emails with the hacker. Since Stone was in regular communication with Trump during the campaign, the Mueller investigation became locked into Guccifer 2.0 as the sole hacker of the Democrats' NGP VAN system, Podesta's emails, and the DNC emails dropped on Debbie Wasserman Schultz. The Mueller hypothesis was that Guccifer 2.0 stole Podesta's emails and the DNC emails and gave them to Julian Assange for WikiLeaks to publish. Trump was assumed to be in the middle of the "collusion" links because the FBI and prosecutors working with Mueller knew Stone had emailed Guccifer 2.0. The Mueller prosecutors also believed, erroneously, that I put Stone in touch with Assange. This the Mueller prosecutors could never prove, again establishing that I was never indicted despite the insistence of the Mueller prosecutors that I was hiding my alleged contacts with Assange in order to protect Roger Stone and Donald Trump.

I note here that the *Post* article on June 14, 2016, was also the Clinton campaign's setup for the intelligence community assessment (examined closely in the next section of this chapter) issued by the CIA, the NSA, and the FBI, under Director of National Intelligence James Clapper on January 6, 2017.

I will argue in this chapter that the Russian narrative was politically motivated, not supported by forensic evidence. There is no evidence that Guccifer 2.0 ever published any of Podesta's stolen emails or the stolen DNC emails. Guccifer 2.0 appears responsible only for stealing documents out of the DNC's NGP VAN systems. In the previous chapter, I said that a proper understanding of how the Democrats constructed their computer systems in 2016 supports the conclusion that the Podesta emails and the DNC emails were stolen by a party other than Guccifer 2.0. This chapter will argue the likelihood that the thefts of Podesta's emails and the DNC emails, as well of the theft of DNC data attributed to Guccifer 2.0, were all done by an insider. In other words, the theft of the NGP VAN data, Podesta's emails, and the DNC emails were all "inside jobs," with employees or other insiders to Clinton's campaign and/or the DNC being responsible for stealing all the documents and emails from the Democrats in 2016, not hackers operating on the outside. To add to the confusion, there is no reason to believe the person or persons who stole the Podesta emails and the DNC emails is or are the same person or persons hiding behind the Guccifer 2.0 identity.

CrowdStrike Provides "Evidence" That Russia Hacked the DNC's Computers

On June 15, 2016, the day after the *Post* article was published, cyber-security firm CrowdStrike posted an article on its website authored by cofounder Dmitri Alperovitch concluding that two separate Russian intelligence-affiliated adversaries began hacking DNC computers in May 2016.[217] Alperovitch, a U.S. citizen born in Russia, is known to be staunchly anti-Russian. In addition to his position as cofounder and chief technology officer of CrowdStrike, Alperovitch is a nonresident senior fellow at the Atlantic Council, a pro-NATO think tank in part funded by George Soros's Open Society Foundation that shares his pro-European Union and anti-Russian sentiments.[218] The appearance of Alperovitch's posting on the CrowdStrike website one day after the *Post* article seemed too conveniently timed to be coincidental. The point of Alperovitch's post

---

217 Dmitri Alperovitch, "Bears in the Midst: Intrusion into the Democratic National Committee," CrowdStrike. com, June 15, 2016, https://www.crowdstrike.com/blog/ bears-midst-intrusion-democratic-national-committee/.

218 "Dmitri Alperovitch," Atlantic Council, https://www.atlanticcouncil.org/ about/experts/list/dmitri-alperovitch.

was to reveal technical cybersecurity information that was aimed at establishing Guccifer 2.0 as the sole hacker who had stolen Podesta's emails, the DNC emails, and the NGP-VAN data, as well as to identify Guccifer 2.0 as a Russian agent. Clinton campaign operatives and the DNC appear to have taken the time between the last date the DNC emails on Debbie Wasserman Schultz were stolen, May 25, 2016, and the date the *Post* article appeared, June 14, 2016, to get their cover story together, blaming the thefts on Guccifer 2.0 and Russia.

Alperovitch's CrowdStrike article discussed a WordPress blog post that was also dated June 15, 2016, "authored by an individual using the moniker Guccifer 2.0," who claimed credit for breaching the DNC servers. "Whether or not this posting is part of a Russian Intelligence disinformation campaign, we are exploring the documents' authenticity and origin," the CrowdStrike article commented. "Regardless, these claims do nothing to lessen our findings relating to the Russian government's involvement, portions of which we have documented for the public and the greater security community."

Guccifer 2.0 in his WordPress blog suggested that he had advance warning of the conclusions CrowdStrike announced to the world. "Worldwide known cyber security company CrowdStrike announced that the Democratic National Committee (DNC) servers had been hacked by 'sophisticated' hacker groups," Guccifer 2.0 wrote under the heading "DNC's Servers Hacked by Lone Hacker."[219] Guccifer 2.0 ridiculed CrowdStrike's conclusions, assuming sole responsibility and bragging that hacking the DNC's servers was "easy, very easy."

Guccifer 2.0 continued: "Guccifer (Marcel Lazar) may have been the first one who penetrated Hillary Clinton's and other Democrats' mail servers. But he certainly wasn't the last. No wonder any other hacker could easily get access to the DNC's servers." Then Guccifer 2.0 crowed: "Shame on CrowdStrike: Do you think I've been in the DNC's networks for almost a year and saved only 2 documents? Do you really believe it? Here are

---

219 Guccifer 2.0, "Guccifer 2.0 DNC's Servers Hacked by a Lone Hacker," guccifer2.wordpress.com, June 15, 2016, https://guccifer2.wordpress. com/2016/06/15/dnc/.

just a few docs from the many thousands I extracted when hacking into the DNC's networks."

CrowdStrike is clearly a Democratic Party-leaning firm, having received at its founding $100 million in a funding drive conducted in 2016 by Google Capital, known as CapitalG, the investment arm of Alphabet Inc. Eric Schmidt, the chairman of Alphabet Inc., is well-known to be a strong supporter of Hillary Clinton and an active donor to the Democratic Party.[220] In 2016, while chairman of Alphabet, Schmidt was also working inside Clinton's presidential campaign to organize its computer-driven get-out-the-vote effort.

Alperovitch has told reporters that the DNC first asked CrowdStrike to investigate a possible breach of the DNC network on May 5, 2016, some two months after Podesta's emails were stolen from his Gmail account, twenty days before the DNC emails on Debbie Wasserman Schultz were stolen, and approximately one month before the DNC went to the *Post* with the allegation that the Russians were responsible for the cyberattack.[221]

The Democrats told the *Post* for the article published on June 14, 2016, that CrowdStrike computer experts had identified the "sophisticated adversaries" attacking the DNC computers as Cozy Bear and Fancy Bear—both identified by CrowdStrike as "Russian-based."

There are two points here of importance:

1. The DNC delayed announcing that its computers had been hacked until after it had hired CrowdStrike and received the final report blaming the hack on the Russians; and
2. The Democrats were the first to blame Guccifer 2.0 for the hack, not realizing that Guccifer 2.0 had stolen information only from

---

220 Aaron Klein, "DNC 'Russian Hacking' Conclusion Comes from Google-Linked Firm," Breitbart, January 6, 2017, https://www.breitbart.com/politics/2017/01/06/dnc-russian-hacking-conclusion-comes-google-linked-firm/.

221 Vicky Ward, "Expat Leading the Fight to Protect America," *Esquire*, October 24, 2016, https://www.esquire.com/news-politics/a49902/the-russian-emigre-leading-the-fight-to-protect-america/.

the NGP VAN system, not from the emails from Podesta's Gmail account or from the DNC email server.

To investigate the cybertheft, CrowdStrike security experts sent the DNC a proprietary software package called Falcon that within ten seconds identified that Russia "was in the network." CrowdStrike experts found code and techniques coming from Cozy Bear and Fancy Bear, two entities that CrowdStrike believed were linked to the GRU, or Russian military intelligence. They told the DNC that Cozy Bear and Fancy Bear had been stealing DNC emails for more than a year, but that the theft from the DNC network (the NGP VAN system) had been going on only for several weeks.

CrowdStrike's Mission: Set Up Russian Hackers as the Villains

What is shocking is the fact that the DNC rebuffed a request from the FBI to independently examine the DNC computers. This left the FBI no alternative to relying upon third-party information developed by Crowd-Strike.[222] "The DNC had several meetings with representatives of the FBI's cyber division and its Washington field office, the Department of Justice's National Security Division, and the U.S. Attorney's offices, and it responded to a variety of requests for cooperation, but the FBI never requested access to the DNC's computer servers," Eric Walker, the DNC's deputy communications director, told reporters.[223]

Even more shocking, court filings by the government in the pretrial phase of Roger Stone's case reveal that the FBI relied on CrowdStrike to conclude that Russia hacked the DNC server, yet CrowdStrike never completed a final report. CrowdStrike turned over to the FBI only three

---

222   Evan Perez and Daniella Diaz, "FBI: DNC Rebuffed Request to Examine Computer Servers," CNN, January 6, 2017, https://edition.cnn.com/2017/01/05/politics/fbi-russia-hacking-dnc-crowdstrike/.

223   Ali Watkins, "The FBI Never Asked for Access to Hacked Computer Servers," BuzzFeed News, January 4, 2017, https://www.buzzfeednews.com/article/alimwatkins/the-fbi-never-asked-for-access-to-hacked-computer-servers#.ulBYYqk7Nl.

redacted drafts of the never-finished final report.[224] The obvious conclusion is that the FBI, under the guidance of FBI director James Comey, went along with the politically motivated narrative desired by the Clinton campaign and the Obama administration—"Russia did it! Don't worry about the awful things DNC officials and Podesta wrote in their emails. Blame Russia and Trump—they were in collusion." CrowdStrike did the job it had been hired to do. It did not matter that CrowdStrike failed to present ironclad forensic proof that Russia hacked the DNC server. Google funded CrowdStrike, an obvious conflict of interest. Yet, by pointing the finger at Guccifer 2.0 and claiming that Guccifer 2.0 was a Russian spy, CrowdStrike handed Hillary Clinton and the DNC the desired narrative, transforming Clinton from the villain using a private email server while secretary of state into the victim, a role she had been rehearsing since she first appeared on the national scene as Bill Clinton's wife.

As further verification of the CrowdStrike narrative, the FBI and the Department of Homeland Security (DHS) issued, on December 29, 2016, a thirteen-page Joint Analysis Report entitled "Grizzly Steppe—Russian Malicious Cyber Activity." In this report, the FBI and DHS concurred that Russia was responsible for hacking the DNC's computers.[225] This was the specific report that generated a media buzz, with left-oriented media talking points insisting that "seventeen intelligence agencies agreed" that Russian hacking of the DNC computer system had been ordered by Putin with the goal of interfering in the U.S. presidential election to help elect Trump and defeat Clinton.[226] In truth, those who read the report realized

---

224 Ray McGovern, "FBI Never Saw CrowdStrike Unredacted or Final Report on Alleged Russian Hacking Because None Was Produced," Consortium News, June 17, 2019, https://consortiumnews.com/2019/06/17/fbi-never-saw-crowdstrike-unredacted-or-final-report-on-alleged-russian-hacking-because-none-was-produced/.

225 The U.S. Department of Homeland Security and the FBI, "GRIZZLY STEPPE—Russian Malicious Cyber Activity," December 29, 2016, https://www.us-cert.gov/sites/default/files/publications/JAR_16-20296A_GRIZZLY%20STEPPE-2016-1229.pdf.

226 Jeff Carlson, "Did Clapper & Brennan Use the Steele Dossier in the Intelligence Community Assessment," TheMarketsWork.com, February 23, 2018, https://themarketswork.com/2018/02/23/did-clapper-brennan-use-the-steele-dossier-in-the-intelligence-community-assessment/.

that it described in vague terms typical hacking activities with no proof of the claims made against Russia.[227] But with the report appearing after the election, it is clear DHS was now working with the FBI counterintelligence investigation to transform the Russia-collusion narrative into a reason to impeach Trump.

This DHS-FBI report was of critical importance to the development of a joint intelligence committee assessment that Russia stole the Democrats' emails. In December 2016, the month before he left office, President Obama ordered the U.S. intelligence community to write an assessment evaluating the existing intelligence on Russian interference in the U.S. 2016 election.

On January 6, 2017, in response to Obama's request, the CIA (headed by John Brennan), the NSA (headed by Admiral Michael Rogers), and the FBI (headed by James Comey) produced a report in both classified and unclassified versions published under the auspices of the Office of the Director of National Intelligence (James Clapper), titled "Background to 'Assessing Russian Activities and Intentions in Recent US Elections': The Analytic Process and Cyber Incident Attribution."[228] This pivotal document in the Russia-collusion drama became known as the ICA, aka the Joint Intelligence Assessment or Joint Analysis Report.

The ICA clearly placed the blame for the breach of the DNC computers, including the theft of John Podesta's messages on Gmail and the DNC server, on Guccifer 2.0. The ICA contained two major conclusions:

- Russia's intelligence services conducted cyber operations against targets associated with the 2016 U.S. presidential election, including targets associated with both major U.S. political parties.

227 Blogger known as "sundance," "The *ACTUAL* 2016 FBI Report on 'Russian Hacking' Does Not Show What Media Claim It Does…" The Conservative Treehouse, November 11, 2017, https://theconservativetreehouse.com/2017/11/11/the-actual-2016-fbi-report-on-russian-hacking-does-not-show-what-media-claim-it-does/.

228 "Background to 'Assessing Russian Activities and Intentions in Recent US Elections': The Analytic Process and Cyber Incident Attribution," Office of the Director of National Intelligence, January 6, 2017, https://www.dni.gov/files/documents/ICA_2017_01.pdf.

- We assess with high confidence that Russian military intelligence (General Staff Main Intelligence Directorate or GRU) used the Guccifer 2.0 persona and DCLeaks.com to release U.S. victim data.

The ICA left no doubt that Guccifer 2.0 was being identified as the Russian entity that stole the DNC emails. "We assess with high confidence that the GRU relayed material it acquired from the DNC and senior Democratic officials to WikiLeaks," the ICA said. The ICA also concluded that although Guccifer 2.0 claimed to be an independent Romanian hacker, this was not true. "Press reporting suggests more than one person claiming to be Guccifer 2.0 interacted with journalists," the ICA stated definitively.

The truth is that ICA published on January 6, 2017, was a coordinated intelligence assessment that actually involved only three agencies—the CIA, the NSA, and the FBI—with the production of the report directed and managed by Clapper's office as Director of National Intelligence (DNI). President Obama asked Clapper in early December 2016 to have the analysis completed and reported to him before he left office the following month. Yet the fact that the ICA was only supported by the CIA, the NSA, and the FBI, with the help of the DNI, did not stop Hillary Clinton from making the claim that the conclusion Russia stole the DNC emails was a conclusion to which all seventeen U.S. intelligence agencies agreed.[229] After the ICA appeared, this bogus claim was widely parroted by the Clinton-supporting media, including CNN and MSNBC.

Yet James Clapper made his sworn testimony to the Senate Judiciary Committee on May 8, 2017. Clapper acknowledged that the ICA report was the work product of no more than two dozen hand-picked analysts.[230]

---

229   Eliza Collins, "Yes, 17 Intelligence Agencies Really Did Say Russia Was Behind Hacking," *USA Today*, October 21, 2016, https://www.usatoday.com/story/news/politics/onpolitics/2016/10/21/17-intelligence-agencies-russia-behind-hacking/92514592/.

230   Testimony of James R. Clapper, Former Director of National Intelligence, before the Committee on the Judiciary, Subcommittee on Crime and Terrorism, U.S. Senate, concerning Russian interference in the 2016 U.S. Election, May 8, 2017.

The claim was finally debunked when Clapper gave testimony to Congress on July 6, 2017, finally admitting that a *New York Times* report that seventeen intelligence agencies had confirmed that Russia interfered in the 2016 election was false.[231] On June 29, 2017, the *New York Times* was forced to print a correction to its reporting that while "all seventeen organizations of the American intelligence community" had approved the ICA conclusions, only four agencies were involved—the Office of the Director of National Intelligence, the CIA, the NSA, and the FBI.[232]

What should be apparent is that Hillary Clinton and Obama administration agencies—including the Office of the Director of National Intelligence, the CIA, NSA, DHS, and FBI—all rushed to judgment to blame Russia for the cybertheft of documents from the Democrats in 2016. Initially, I was surprised when Mueller's prosecutors and the FBI were close-minded in my forty hours of "voluntary interviews" when I tried to explain my reasons for concluding that the Russians hadn't stolen the emails. But then I realized the conclusion Russia had stolen the Podesta and DNC emails was central to the Deep State's case against Trump.

Evidently, the Clinton-supporting mainstream media and the Mueller team saw no reason to consult the intelligence analysts of the thirteen intelligence agencies not participating in the ICA analysis, or to obtain independent corroboration of the ICA conclusions. Mueller's final report makes clear that the Office of Special Counsel investigation accepted as gospel truth the ICA conclusion that Guccifer 2.0, acting as a Russian agent, stole the Podesta and the DNC emails. The point is worth repeating that the FBI investigation working with Mueller did not examine the DNC server and conducted no independent investigation whatsoever to

---

231 Tim Hains, "Clapper Confirms: '17 Intelligence Agencies' Russia Story Was False," *Real Clear Politics*, July 6, 2017, https://www.realclearpolitics.com/video/2017/07/06/clapper_confirms_17_intelligence_agencies_russia_story_was_false.html.

232 The *New York Times* published the correction at the end of the following article: Haberman, "Trump's Deflections and Denials on Russia Frustrate Even His Allies," *New York Times*, June 25, 2017, https://www.nytimes.com/2017/06/25/us/politics/trumps-deflections-and-denials-on-russia-frustrate-even-his-allies.html?module=inline.

examine if the ICA conclusions were true. Mueller's investigation did not question officials from the U.S. intelligence agencies, nor did it seek to interview Julian Assange.

Cracks Develop that Fracture Intelligence Conclusions Blaming Russia

On June 21, 2016, Vice published a report claiming to have conducted an interview with Guccifer 2.0, who accepted responsibility for hacking the DNC computers. Guccifer 2.0 insisted, however, that "he" was not a Russian spy. Guccifer 2.0 told Vice that "he" hacked into the DNC in the summer of 2015, using an unspecified vulnerability in the NGP VAN system. The hacker told Vice that "he" (for lack of a confirmation of the gender of the hacker) left Russian metadata in the leaked documents as his personal "watermark." Guccifer 2.0 also said "he" got kicked out of the DNC computer system on June 12, 2016, when the Democrats "rebooted their system." While I cannot independently corroborate the claim that Vice spoke with the actual Guccifer 2.0, the statement that Guccifer 2.0 hacked the NGP VAN system corresponds with my analysis here. In the interview with Vice, Guccifer 2.0 made no claim to have hacked Podesta's Gmail account or the DNC email server (separate from those on which the NGP VAN system operated).[233]

From the beginning, Admiral Rogers had concerns about the ICA's conclusions. The ICA report documented that Admiral Rogers and the NSA expressed only "moderate confidence" in its conclusion that Russian president Vladimir Putin and the Russian government "aspired to help President-elect Trump's election chances when possible by discrediting Secretary Clinton and publicly contrasting her favorability to him." In contrast, both the CIA and FBI expressed "high confidence" in this conclusion.

Then, on March 5, 2018, Admiral Rogers addressed a letter to Representative Devin Nunes, then the GOP chair of the House Intelligence Committee, informing the committee that a two-page summary of the

---

233 Lorenzo Franceschi-Bicchierai, "We Spoke to DNC Hacker 'Guccifer 2.0,'" Motherboard, Tech by Vice, Vice.com, June 21, 2016, https://www.vice.com/en_us/article/aek7ea/dnc-hacker-guccifer-20-interview.

Steele dossier, described as the "Christopher Steele information," had been added as an appendix to the ICA draft. Rogers informed Nunes for the first time that consideration of the appendix summarizing the Steele dossier was "part of the overall ICA review/approval process." This was shocking in that Rogers's letter alerted Congress that the ICA evaluation was not independent or unbiased, insofar as the CIA, FBI, and NSA had taken into account the unverifiable allegations of the Steele dossier in coming to their conclusion that the Russians were responsible for hacking the DNC computers.[234]

On January 7, 2016, the day after the ICA was released, Obama had held a secret White House meeting to discuss the Steele dossier with Clapper and Comey. By 2018, investigative reporter Paul Sperry was able to put into print his conclusion that Barack Obama's ICA "matches the main allegations leveled by the Clinton-paid dossier [the Steele dossier] on Trump, which wormed its way into intelligence channels, in addition to the FBI, Justice Department and State Department, during the 2016 campaign."[235] As Sperry noted in his *New York Post* article published on February 22, 2018, it seems not a coincidence that the uncorroborated Steele dossier and the ICA make exactly "the same claim—that Putin personally 'ordered' the cyberattacks on the Clinton campaign and leaked embarrassing emails to 'bolster Trump' as part of 'an aggressive Trump support operation.'" Sperry commented that like Obama's ICA, Hillary Clinton's bought-and-paid-for Steele dossier provides no concrete evidence to back up the claim.[236]

---

234 Paul Sperry, "Two Colleagues Contradict Brennan's Denial of Reliance on Dossier," Real Clear Investigations, May 15, 2018, https://www.realclear-investigations.com/articles/2018/05/14/2_colleagues_contradict_brennan_on_use_of_dossier.html.

235 Paul Sperry, "Yet Another Way Obama's Spies Apparently Exploited the Trump 'Dossier,'" *New York Post*, February 22, 2018, https://nypost.com/2018/02/22/yet-another-way-obamas-spies-apparently-exploited-the-trump-dossier/.

236 Ibid.

Forensic Proof that the Theft of the DNC Emails Was an Inside Job

A group of former U.S. intelligence officers known as the Veteran Intelligence Professionals for Sanity, VIPS, has increasingly warned that there is no reliable forensic evidence to support the conclusion that Russia hacked into the DNC system. According to Ray McGovern, a VIPS member with expertise on Russia who was a CIA analyst for twenty-seven years, "The major premise that Russia hacked into the Democratic National Committee and gave WikiLeaks highly embarrassing emails cannot bear close scrutiny." McGovern was responsible for preparing the president's daily briefing for Presidents Nixon, Ford, and Reagan. McGovern insists that VIPS has developed hard forensic evidence that proves the DNC emails were not hacked—by Russia or anyone else—but were copied and leaked by someone with physical access to the DNC computers.[237]

The VIPS group first presented its findings in a memo written for President Trump on July 24, 2017. The VIPS memo concluded: "After examining metadata from the 'Guccifer 2.0' July 5, 2016 intrusion into the DNC server, independent cyber investigators have concluded that an insider copied DNC data onto an external storage device."[238] Specifically, the VIPS analysts concluded that the DNC data was copied onto a storage device at a speed that far exceeds the internet capability for a remote hack. Equally important, the VIPS analysts insist that the copying was performed on the East Coast of the United States, according to the forensics. The memo commented that why the FBI neglected to obtain access to the DNC server or servers in question to perform any independent forensics on the original Guccifer 2.0 material remains a mystery, as does the lack of any sign that the "hand-picked analysts" from the FBI, CIA, and NSA who wrote the ICA dated January 6, 2017, conducted any independent forensic investigation.

---

237   Ray McGovern, "Orwellian Cloud Hovers over Russia-Gate," Consortium News, May 3, 2019, https://consortiumnews.com/2019/05/03/orwellian-cloud-hovers-over-russia-gate/.

238   "Intel Vets Challenge 'Russia Hack' Evidence," Consortium News, July 24, 2017, https://consortiumnews.com/2017/07/24/intel-vets-challenge-russia-hack-evidence/.

The VIPS memo to President Trump commented that it was no surprise to the VIPS analysts when President Obama, in his last press conference, on January 18, 2017, disputed the ICA's "high confidence" that Russia hacked the DNC system to help elect Clinton. In that press conference, Obama said:

> The conclusions of the intelligence community with respect to the Russian hacking were not conclusive as to whether WikiLeaks was witting or not in being the conduit through which we heard about the DNC emails that were leaked.[239]

"Obama's admission came as no surprise to us," the VIPS memo to President Trump noted. "It has long been clear to us that the reason the U.S. government lacks conclusive evidence of a transfer of a 'Russian hack' to WikiLeaks is because there was no such transfer."

On August 9, 2017, the findings of the VIPS analysts went public in an article in *The Nation*—the left-leaning, well-respected journal—that caused editor and publisher Katrina vanden Heuvel much grief due to blowback from her Clinton-supporting readers.[240] The article, written by veteran columnist and essayist Patrick Lawrence, buttressed the VIPS analysis using information from several different independent computer analysts, including one known only as the "Forensicator."

As reported by *The Nation*, the Forensicator's breakthrough analysis resulted from an evaluation of the metadata embedded in the hack of the DNC computers accomplished by Guccifer 2.0 on the evening of July 5, 2016. The Forensicator determined that 1,976 megabytes of data were downloaded from the DNC's server. The operation took eighty-seven seconds. This yields a transfer rate of 22.7 megabytes per second. "No

---

239 "Obama's Last News Conference: Full Transcript and Video," *New York Times*, January 18, 2017, https://www.nytimes.com/2017/01/18/us/politics/obama-final-press-conference.html.

240 Patrick Lawrence, "A New Report Raises Big Questions About Last Year's DNC Hack," *The Nation*, August 9, 2017, https://www.thenation.com/article/a-new-report-raises-big-questions-about-last-years-dnc-hack/.

Internet service provider, such as a hacker would have had to use in mid-2016, was capable of downloading data at this speed," Lawrence wrote.

This conclusion rules out the possibility that a hacker from the outside stole the DNC computer data. The metadata revealed a time stamp indicating that the download from the DNC computers occurred at approximately 6:45 p.m. Eastern Daylight Time. Finally, the analysis of the metadata also revealed that Guccifer 2.0 had placed Russian markings in a cut-and-paste layer of the metadata using a template that emulated Russian "fingerprints." The conclusion was that the metadata had deliberately been altered and pasted into a "Russified" Word document with Russian-style settings and headings.

Trump-Haters Transform the Russia-Collusion Narrative into Ideology

Yet it has become a dogma of hard-left anti-Trump ideology that Guccifer 2.0, as a Russian agent, stole the DNC documents and emails.

Volume one, page forty-one of the Mueller report clearly states: "The GRU's operations extended beyond stealing materials and included releasing documents stolen from the Clinton Campaign and its supporters. The GRU carried out the anonymous release through two fictitious online personas that it created—DCLeaks and Guccifer 2.0—and later through the organization WikiLeaks." In both of its volumes and in all 448 pages, the Mueller report gives no forensic evidence to support this contention, making it clear that Mueller's prosecutors and the FBI regurgitated the ICA as gospel without bothering to subject the conclusion "Russia stole the DNC emails" to a rigorous, independent investigation.

Brennan was the lead cheerleader promoting the conclusions of the ICA in the intelligence community and Congress. In an important article published in the *Wall Street Journal* on July 19, 2018,[241] investigative reporter Kimberley Strassel characterized Brennan as an extremely political CIA director who had served as a campaign and White House advisor to Barack

---

241 Kimberley A. Strassel, "Brennan and the 2016 Spy Scandal," *Wall Street Journal*, July 19, 2018, https://www.wsj.com/articles/ brennan-and-the-2016-spy-scandal-1532039346.

Obama and was allowed to continue his position at the CIA even after he aligned himself publicly with Hillary Clinton's 2016 presidential campaign.

Strassel stressed that Brennan "took the lead on shaping the narrative that Russia was interfering in the election specifically to help Mr. Trump—which quickly evolved into the Trump-collusion narrative." In July 2016, Brennan faced a problem convincing Clapper and other intelligence agency heads, including Admiral Rogers at the NSA, that Russia was responsible for hacking the DNC computers and that Putin was responsible for giving this order with the goal of promoting Trump and defeating Clinton. Strassel documented that Brennan faced a dilemma in that, as head of the CIA, "he had to be careful not to be seen interfering in U.S. politics," nor could he investigate U.S. citizens.

Strassel wrote that Brennan's solution was to recruit the assistance of then Senate majority leader Harry Reid, another staunch supporter of the Democrats. In a briefing in late August 2016, Brennan told Reid that Russia was trying to help Trump win the election and that Trump advisors might be colluding with Russia—two allegations that Strassel commented had yet to be proved. "But the truth was irrelevant," Strassel wrote. On cue, Reid wrote a letter to FBI Director James Comey, asking him to begin an FBI investigation. "The Reid letter marked the first official blast of the Brennan-Clinton collusion narrative into the open," Strassel concluded. "Clinton opposition-research firm Fusion GPS followed up by briefing its media allies about the dossier it had dropped off at the FBI. On September 23 [2016], Yahoo! News's Michael Isikoff ran the headline: 'U.S. intel officials probe ties between Trump advisor and Kremlin.' Voilà. Not only was the collusion narrative out there, but so was evidence that the FBI was investigating."

March 7, 2017: WikiLeaks Publishes "Vault 7"

On March 7, 2017, WikiLeaks began publishing "Vault 7," a drop of CIA cyberwarfare documents containing the startling revelation that the CIA, under a project identified as Umbrage, maintained a substantial library of Russian cyberattack techniques "stolen" from malware produced in other regions, including the Russian Federation.[242]

---

242 WikiLeaks, "Vault 7: CIA Hacking Tools Revealed," WikiLeaks.org,
    March 7, 2017, https://wikileaks.org/ciav7p1/#FAQ.

This revelation yielded a "through the looking glass" possibility that the Obama administration obtained FISA permission to conduct electronic surveillance on Russians believed to be coordinating with the Trump campaign based on intelligence the CIA planted to deceive the NSA into thinking there was actual contact between Russian agents and the Trump campaign. Possibly, what the CIA was monitoring was not actual contacts between Russian agents and the Trump campaign, but CIA-created counterespionage actions designed to implicate Trump and provide the legal context for the DOJ to have enough "evidence" to obtain a FISA green light. The WikiLeaks Vault 7 drop is also startling in the realization that the Obama administration CIA went rogue, in that it "had created, in effect, its 'own NSA' with even less accountability and without publicly answering the question as to whether such a massive budgetary spend on duplicating the capabilities of a rival agency could be justified."

The VIPS analysts have raised the possibility that Guccifer 2.0 used the CIA's hacking tools revealed in the WikiLeaks release of Vault 7 to plant Russian metadata into the documents Guccifer 2.0 stole from the NGP VAN system: "The list of the CIA's cyber-tools WikiLeaks began to release in March [2017] includes one called Marble that is capable of obfuscating the origin of documents in false-flag operations and leaving markings that point to whatever the CIA wants to point to." Patrick Lawrence, in his article published in *The Nation*, commented that it is not known whether or not Guccifer 2.0 used this tool, "but it is there for such a use."

Former CIA intelligence analyst Ray McGovern has commented that "it should just be a matter of time before [Justice Department investigators] identify Brennan conclusively as fabricator-in-chief of the Russiagate story." McGovern has noted that Brennan and his partners Comey and Clapper "were making stuff up and feeding thin but explosive gruel to the hungry stenographers that pass today for Russiagate obsessed journalists."[243]

---

243 Ray McGovern, "DOJ Bloodhounds on the Scent of John Brennan," Consortium News, June 13, 2019, https://consortiumnews.com/2019/06/13/ray-mcgovern-doj-bloodhounds-on-the-scent-of-john-brennan/.

"By the end of 2016, the CIA's hacking division, which formally falls under the agency's Center for Cyber Intelligence (CCI), had over 5,000 registered users and had produced more than a thousand hacking systems, Trojans, viruses, and other 'weaponized' malware," WikiLeaks disclosed in releasing Vault 7. That a secret CIA cyberwarfare operation of this magnitude had remained hidden from congressional committees assigned to CIA oversight reveals how politically inept Congress has become under an elite Washington-based leadership. Traditional liberal Democrats and moderate Republicans have coalesced into a Washington elite that rules Congress regardless of whether the majority in the House and Senate is Republican or Democratic.

The two parties have even begun trading successive presidencies: eight years of Republican George W. Bush followed by eight years of Democrat Barack Obama. With the core of the Democratic Party becoming rapidly socialist, if not outright communist, it is increasingly likely that Trump will have eight years in office to follow Obama. The point is that those who rule Congress are increasingly susceptible to corruption as they are re-elected, often for multiple terms, and become cozy with the money that lobbyists are anxious to pass around. The swamp in Washington is almost impossible to drain because the real power brokers in Congress have become cozy, allowing the Deep State bureaucracy to run the government by issuing a mountain of regulations. As the Obama presidency progressed through its eight years in power, the Deep State bureaucracy burgeoned in an unprecedented way.

With the publication of Vault 7, Wikileaks once again managed to change the national political dialogue, simply by revealing to the American public the details of a secret CIA cyberwarfare division clearly operating outside the Constitutional requirement of congressional funding.

The implications of Vault 7 include the realization that the CIA at its highest levels is free to commit criminal violations of U.S. law. Meanwhile, the American people remain blissfully unaware of the extent to which our seventeen intelligence agencies, led by the CIA at the top, are responsible for major developments in the United States and worldwide that are designed to move our politics toward ever-increasing Deep State control.

Chapter Nine

DECONSTRUCTING THE TRUMP TOWER MEETING

On June 9, 2016, a meeting occurred in Trump Tower between a Russian lawyer, Natalia Veselnitskaya, and Donald Trump Jr. that was intended by the CIA to be an important evidentiary linchpin the Deep State would need to convict Donald Trump as a traitor to the United States of America.

This chapter will deconstruct the Trump Tower meeting, explaining how the meeting was set up, who the players were, and the importance of the evidence the Clinton-Obama coup d'état coconspirators intended to plant in the very heart of the Trump campaign.

Identifying the Russian Billionaire Players in the Trump Tower Meeting

The meeting was held in the Trump campaign headquarters in Trump Tower on Fifth Avenue between Fifty-Sixth and Fifty-Seventh Streets in New York City.

The Trump campaign attendees included Donald Trump Jr., Paul Manafort—who was in line to become Trump's new campaign manager—and Trump's son-in-law, Jared Kushner. On June 20, 2016, eleven days after the Trump Tower meeting, Trump fired his campaign manager, Corey Lewandowski, replacing him with Manafort. Candidate Donald Trump did not attend the meeting.

The attorneys on the Russian side were Natalia Veselnitskaya and her colleague Rinat Akhmetshin. Since Veselnitskaya spoke only Russian, she brought with her an interpreter named Anatoli Samochornov. The meeting was originally scheduled for 3:00 p.m. but was pushed back to 4:00 p.m. to accommodate an appearance that Veselnitskaya had to make in federal court in downtown Manhattan earlier in the day for a client. More on all this later.

The setup for the meeting had begun a few days earlier, when Robert Goldstone emailed Donald Trump Jr. to ask for a meeting. Goldstone is a British publicist in the music industry. His client, Emin Agalarov, born in Azerbaijan, is a pop music star in Russia and Azerbaijan. Emin also happens to be the son of Aras Agalarov, an influential Azerbaijani-Russian billionaire real estate tycoon and businessman.

In November 2016, Russian president Vladimir Putin awarded Aras Agalarov the Russian Order of Honor. That same month, Aras was Donald Trump's business partner in hosting the Miss Universe pageant in Moscow. Aras spent an estimated $20 million to host the Miss Universe pageant at Crocus City Hall in his glitzy megamall. In return, Trump agreed to film a cameo of Emin's performance during the Miss Universe pageant, an extremely valuable opportunity to produce a music video. While Trump was in Russia, Agalarov's Crocus Group negotiated with Trump to develop plans to build a Trump Tower in Moscow.[244]

Donald Trump Jr. was certain to read any email Robert Goldstone sent him, given Goldstone's closeness to the Agalarovs.

In May 2016, the month before the Trump Tower meeting, Aras's Russian-born accountant set up for him a new U.S. shell company, into which he was planning to move $20 million into the United States. On

---

244   Anthony Cormier and Jason Leopold, "A Series of Suspicious Money Transfers Followed the Trump Tower Meeting," BuzzFeed News, September 12, 2018, https://www.buzzfeednews.com/article/anthony-cormier/trump-tower-meeting-suspicious-transactions-agalarov. See also: Jon Swaine and Scott Stedman, "Revealed: Russian Billionaire Set Up Company before Trump Tower Meeting," *The Guardian*, October 18, 2018, https://www.theguardian.com/us-news/2018/oct/18/russian-billionaire-aras-agalarov-company-trump-tower-meeting.

June 11, 2016, two days after the Trump Tower meeting, an offshore company controlled by Aras wired more than $19.5 million to Aras's U.S. shell company's account at Morgan Stanley in New York. A second infusion of cash occurred shortly after Trump was elected president, when the Agalarov family sent some additional $1.2 million from their bank in Russia to a New Jersey bank account controlled by Emin and two of his friends. Subsequently, the money from the New Jersey account was sent to Corsy International, a company controlled by Irakly "Ike" Kaveladze, a longtime business associate of the Agalarovs' and the person representing the Agalarovs in the Trump Tower meeting. Between July 2015 and January 2017, Goldstein's music business, Oui 2 Entertainment, received more than a half million dollars from Corsy International. According to reports published by BuzzFeed, Corsy International was an import-export business, while Oui 2 was involved with music. BuzzFeed further reported that the New Jersey address of Corsy International was a "small, windowless office in a remarkable building near the Hudson River. When bank examiners began investigating this address, they discovered at least eight other companies located there, all of them controlled by Kaveladze, Emin Agalarov, or their associates.[245]

These financial connections only came to light in 2017, when U.S. law enforcement officers instructed financial institutions to search their records for suspicious financial transactions made by Russians who were "of interest" to the increasingly broad reach of the Mueller investigation. Under Department of the Treasury anti-money laundering rules and regulations, financial institutions, including banks, are required to file suspicious-activity reports on any suspicious transaction. The government's interest is triggered by transactions as low as ten thousand dollars, especially if the transaction is in cash.

The Goldstone Setup to the Trump Tower Meeting

In setting up the Trump Tower meeting, Goldstone emailed Donald Trump Jr. to relay to him an offer from Russia's "crown prosecutor" to "the Trump campaign" of "official documents and information that would incriminate

---

245 Ibid.

Hillary and her dealings with Russia and would be very useful to [Trump Jr.'s] father." According to the Mueller report, the email described this as "very high level and sensitive information" that was "part of Russia and its government's support to Mr. Trump." Responding to this offer, Donald Trump Jr. sent an email to Goldstone stating, "If it's what you say I would love it especially later in the summer." The hook had been sent. Donald Trump Jr. was intrigued at the possibility of obtaining opposition research that potentially could be very damaging to the Clinton campaign.

"The communications setting up the meeting and the attendance by high-level Campaign representatives support an inference that the Campaign anticipated receiving derogatory documents and information from official Russian sources that could assist candidate Trump's electoral prospects," the final Mueller report noted in volume one, page 185. The Mueller prosecutors were determined to find out whether what transpired at the meeting violated the federal election-law ban on donations by foreign nationals. "Specifically, Goldstone passed along an offer purportedly from a Russian government official to provide 'official documents and information' to the Trump Campaign for the purposes of influencing the presidential election," the Mueller report continued. "Trump Jr. appears to have accepted the offer and to have arranged a meeting to receive those materials. Documentary evidence in the form of email chains supports the inference that Kushner and Manafort were aware of that purpose and attended the June 9 meeting anticipating the receipt of helpful information to the Campaign from Russian sources."

For the pro-Clinton Mueller prosecutors, this meeting appeared to be at the heart of establishing Russian collusion, showing that the Trump campaign welcomed the receipt from the Russian government of information believed to be derogatory to Hillary Clinton. But even this was not the Deep State's central purpose in orchestrating the meeting.

Enter Bill Browder, the Ziff Brothers, and Sergei Magnitsky

The meeting at Trump Tower turned out to be a disappointment. According to the Mueller report, Veselnitskaya began the meeting by stating that the Ziff brothers (three sons who inherited the Ziff Davis magazine empire built by their father, William Bernard Ziff) had broken Russian laws in their partnership with Bill Browder, a controversial American-born British investor. Veselnitskaya asserted that the Ziff brothers had engaged in tax evasion and money laundering in both the United States and Russia. But when Trump Jr. asked how the alleged payments could be tied specifically to the Clinton campaign, Veselnitskaya indicated that she could not trace the money once it entered the United States. At this point, Kushner became aggravated and asked, "What are we doing here?"

Next, Veselnitskaya pivoted to talk about Russia's prohibiting U.S. citizens from adopting Russian children in retaliation for the sanctions the U.S. government had placed on Russia under the Magnitsky Act. All of this requires some explanation, but what quickly became apparent to Trump Jr., Manafort, and Kushner was that Veselnitskaya had nothing of value to give them regarding Hillary Clinton. After listening to Veselnitskaya rail against the Magnitsky Act, the three quickly figured out that Goldstone had requested the meeting under false pretenses.

Here, in order to understand what Veselnitskaya's real purpose was in the Trump Tower meeting, we have to deconstruct the unfortunately complicated backstory context to the meeting.

The Magnitsky Act was named after Bill Browder's tax attorney in Russia, Sergei Magnitsky. Browder, as mentioned above, is an American-born British financier; he made his first fortune as a U.S. hedge fund manager. In the 1990s, Browder left the United States to head to Russia, calculating correctly that his next fortune could be made there. Perhaps not coincidentally, Browder's grandfather, Earl Browder, was a former general secretary of the Communist Party USA, appointed by Joseph Stalin in 1932, and ran for U.S. president in 1936 and 1940. Growing up, Bill Browder learned about Communism simply by listening to the stories told about his grandfather within the family. On November 9, 1989, when the Berlin Wall fell, Browder, a shrewd investor, knew there would be opportunities to make a fortune as the former Soviet Union struggled to transform into a capitalist system.[246]

---

246 Jimmy S. Llama, "Part 2: Hermitage Capital," jimmysllama.com, April 8, 2017, https://jimmysllama.com/2017/04/08/9410/.

In 1996, Browder opened Hermitage Management Capital in Russia. His first partner at the company was Edmond Safra, a Jewish banker born in Lebanon to a family with roots tracing back to Aleppo, Syria. In 1966, Safra founded the Republic National Bank of New York, headquartered in Manhattan; Republic National Bank of New York had a counterpart bank in Geneva, Switzerland. In the 1990s, Safra's fortune was estimated to exceed $2.5 billion. In December 1999, Safra died mysteriously in a fire following an apparently bungled robbery in his Monte Carlo home; the initial suspects ranged from the Russian mafia to Colombian drug cartels. At the time of Safra's death, the *Guardian* reported that he was rumored to have had connections to "drug cartels, gold and currency trafficking, money laundering and organized crime."[247]

After Safra died, Browder sold Safra's Hermitage Management Capital shares to the Hongkong and Shanghai Banking Corporation (HSBC), originally established as the Hongkong and Shanghai Bank in 1865 by British banker Thomas Sutherland, created in part to help finance the opium trade in China. In 2012, Loretta Lynch, James Comey, and Robert Mueller all played a role in allowing HSBC to avoid criminal penalties after the discovery of a multibillion-dollar scheme in which HSBC was laundering money from Mexican drug cartels and Middle Eastern terrorist organizations. Lynch, then the U.S. attorney for the Eastern District of New York, was responsible for negotiating the deferred prosecution settlement that allowed HSBC to pay the $1.9 billion fine and admit willful criminal conduct in exchange for the dropping of criminal investigations and prosecutions of HSBC directors, who at that time included James Comey. In 2012, when Comey was a member of the HSBC board of directors, Robert Mueller was FBI director.[248]

---

247 Andrew Anthony, "The Strange Case of Edmond Safra," *The Guardian*, October 28, 2000, https://www.theguardian.com/theobserver/2000/oct/29/features.magazine47.

248 Aruna Viswanatha and Brett Wolf, "HSBC to Pay $1.9 Billion U.S. Fine in Money-Laundering Case," Reuters, December 11, 2012, https://www.reuters.com/article/us-hsbc-probe/hsbc-to-pay-1-9-billion-u-s-fine-in-money-laundering-case-idUSBRE8BA05M20121211.

Through HSBC, Browder set up the Hermitage Fund as a unit trust, with HSBC Management Limited in Guernsey (one of the Channel Islands off the coast of Normandy) as the trustee. Browder's goal was to profit from the privatization movement developing in Russia after the fall of the Berlin Wall. He saw that his Hermitage Fund could buy enough shares to control Russian companies that were being transformed from state-owned businesses into private enterprises. Specifically, he specialized in investing in formerly state-owned corporations where he could bring in professional business managers to turn the companies around privately. Browder calculated, again correctly, that this strategy would cause a dramatic and quick increase in the share prices of the companies in which he invested. In a relatively short time, he was typically able to sell his stake in these Russian privatized companies for a price that was a handsome multiple of his initial investment.[249]

In 2005, however, Russia expelled Browder, with orders never to return. Why? What had Browder done to merit being banned from Russia by Putin?

The Russian government had come to realize that the problem in Browder's scheme was that the quick increase in share prices realized by his strategy was often illusory, reflecting the stock market's enthusiasm for the professional management Browder inserted, but ultimately disappointing when the anticipated profits failed to materialize. Putin's government in Russia charged Browder with taking over $1.5 billion in profits out of Russia without paying any Russian taxes. When Browder was banned from Russia, the Russian government seized his companies, handing them over to new owners. Soon, the new owners complained that Browder's companies had not earned any real profits. They then demanded huge refunds from the Russian government for the taxes they had paid on the nonexistent profits.

---

249 Joshua Yaffa, "How Bill Browder Became Russia's Most Wanted Man," *The New Yorker*, August 13, 2018, https://www.newyorker.com/magazine/2018/08/20/how-bill-browder-became-russias-most-wanted-man.

What Is the Magnitsky Act?

In 2007, after Browder was expelled from Russia, Sergei Magnitsky, Browder's tax attorney in Russia, began investigating the activities of the corrupt Russian government officials who were involved in a scam setting up shell companies under Hermitage Capital. Magnitsky discovered that two interior ministry officials, along with tax officials and judges, were involved in the scam. According to U.S. investigators and independent Russian groups that have studied the affair, in 2007, the Klyuev group, a Russian criminal network, colluded with tax and law enforcement authorities to steal the corporate identities of three Hermitage Capital companies and use them fraudulently to embezzle some $230 million. The scheme essentially involved setting up shell companies using the stolen identity of Hermitage Capital.

Instead of pleading guilty, two of the Russian interior ministry officials that Magnitsky's investigations had implicated in the scheme went after Magnitsky, accusing him of tax fraud.[250] These Russian government officials and their organized criminals had perpetrated their scam by doctoring documents, applying for a tax refund in the name of Hermitage Capital, and in return receiving $230 million from the Russian government on profits that no longer existed on paper. Once the criminals received the money, they allegedly laundered the money out of Russia through a series of transactions that ultimately involved New York banks.[251] In December 2007, Hermitage filed criminal complaints with law enforcement authorities naming the Russian government officials who had been involved. In response, the Russian government assigned the case to the very law enforcement officials involved in the crime. The Russian government arrested Magnitsky, charging him with tax fraud, alleging that he was responsible for the theft.

Magnitsky was left to languish in pretrial detention for a year. Then, on November 16, 2009, after spending a year in jail, he died under

---

250   Anna Arutunyan, "The Magnitsky Affair and Russia's Original Sin," *Foreign Policy*, July 21, 2017, https://foreignpolicy.com/2017/07/21/the-magnitsky-affair-and-russias-original-sin-putin/.

251   Llama, "Part 2: Hermitage Capital," op. cit.

mysterious circumstances in Moscow's Matrosskaya Tishina prison. Magnitsky's death was officially recorded as a heart attack, but rumors persist that he was beaten to death by prison guards. With Browder expelled and his $1.5 billion in "profits" safely out of Russia, Russia's only chance to exact punishment was to make sure that Magnitsky never left prison alive.

In 2012, Browder, who by then had become a British citizen (after renouncing his U.S. citizenship in 1998), was residing in London. Traveling as needed to Washington, he succeeded in convincing the U.S. Congress to enact the Magnitsky Act. The goal of the act was to punish Russia for human rights abuses, in retaliation for allegedly torturing Magnitsky in prison and beating him to death.

In December 2012, Congress passed Magnitsky Rule of Law Accountability, signed into law by President Obama. That law, known commonly as the Magnitsky Act, sought to punish the Russians involved in the tax scam that led to Magnitsky's detention and death; those who financially benefited from the tax scam; and those involved in the criminal conspiracy that Magnitsky had exposed. The law also authorized the U.S. president to determine persons responsible for other extrajudicial murders, torture, and human rights violations committed against individuals seeking to promote human rights or expose illegal activity carried out by Russian government officials. The act authorizes the president to use the International Emergency Economic Powers Act to freeze the property of those under the terms of the law found to be guilty of human rights abuses.[252] Specifically, the Magnitsky Act bars named Russians and other foreign individuals involved in human rights abuses from traveling to the United States, from owning assets in the United States, and from using the financial system of the United States.[253]

---

252 Letter from Senator Charles Grassley, Chairman of the Senate Committee on the Judiciary, to Dana Boente, Acting Deputy Attorney General, U.S. Department of Justice, March 31, 2017.

253 Vladimir Kara-Murza, "What's Really behind Putin's Obsession with the Magnitsky Act," *Washington Post*, July 20, 2018, https://www.washingtonpost.com/news/democracy-post/wp/2018/07/20/whats-really-behind-putins-obsession-with-the-magnitsky-act/?utm_term=.d51341930dbc.

On April 12, 2013, the U.S. Treasury Department released a list of the names of eighteen individuals targeted under the Magnitsky Act, including Russian citizens and citizens of Ukraine, Azerbaijan, and Uzbekistan.[254]

To retaliate against the United States for passing the Magnitsky Act, the Russian government enacted the "anti-Magnitsky law" banning Americans from adopting Russian children.[255]

The Magnitsky affair ended up hardening relations between the Obama administration and the Putin government, effectively putting an end to the "reset" policy implemented by Secretary of State Hillary Clinton.

The Trump Tower Meeting Collapses

To continue with the narrative of the meeting at Trump Tower on July 9, 2016, at some point fairly early in the meeting, Kushner sent an iMessage to Manafort (who was sitting right there with him) stating that the meeting was a "waste of time." Evidently, Manafort did not disagree, because next Kushner sent two separate emails to assistants at his Kushner Companies, asking them to call and give him an excuse to leave. Kushner left before the meeting ended. In wrapping up the twenty-minute meeting, Donald Trump Jr. declined to accept Veselnitskaya's four-page memo regarding the Magnitsky Act and U.S. sanctions against Russia.

In his testimony to the Senate Judiciary Committee, Trump Jr. described his irritation at how Veselnitskaya had begun the meeting. "After perfunctory greetings, the lawyers began telling the group very generally something about individuals connected to Russia supporting or funding Democratic presidential candidate Hillary Clinton or the Democratic National Committee," Trump Jr. testified. "It was quite difficult for me to understand what she was saying or why. Given our busy schedules, we

---

254 Natalya Kovalenko, "Magnitsky List Release: Severe Blow on Moscow-U.S. Ties," *Voice of Russia*, April 12, 2013, https://web.archive.org/web/20130617090515/http://english.ruvr.ru/2013_04_12/Magnitsky-List-release-severe-blow-on-Moscow-US-ties/.

255 Anna Arutunyan, "The Magnitsky Affair and Russia's Original Sin," *Foreign Policy*, op. cit.

politely asked if she could be more specific and provide clarity about her objective for the meeting."

What happened next surprised him. "At that point Ms. Veselnitskaya switched gears and began talking about the adoption of Russian children by U.S. citizens and something called the Magnitsky Act," Trump Jr. continued. "Until that day I'd never heard of the Magnitsky Act and had no familiarity with this issue. It was clear to me that her real purpose in asking for the meeting all along was to discuss Russian adoptions and the Magnitsky Act." He testified that this was when Kushner excused himself from the meeting to take a phone call. "I proceeded to quickly and politely end the meeting by telling Ms. Veselnitskaya that because my father was a private citizen there did not seem to be any point for having this discussion. She thanked us for our time, and everyone left the conference room. As we walked out, I recall Rob [Goldstone] coming over to apologize."

Trump Jr. told the Senate Judiciary Committee he had no recollection of documents being offered or left for the meeting participants. He said the meeting lasted twenty to thirty minutes. "I do not ever recall discussing it with Jared [Kushner], Paul [Manafort] or anyone else," he said. "In short, I gave it no further thought." In answering questions, Trump Jr. made it clear that neither he nor anyone else on the Trump campaign had communicated with Veselnitskaya prior to the meeting. He said the Magnitsky Act was not a campaign issue at the time of the Trump Tower meeting and it was not going to become a campaign issue as a consequence of the meeting. He further testified that he had no further meetings or communications with Veselnitskaya after the meeting had finished.

At the time of the Trump Tower meeting, legislation was pending in the U.S. Congress—legislation that was passed and signed into law by President Obama, on December 23, 2016, as he was preparing to leave office—to make the Magnitsky Act global, expanding the power of the president to impose sanctions on those responsible for human rights abuses around the world. According to Veselnitskaya's memo—a memo that demonized Browder and the Ziff brothers, in obvious sympathy for Putin—Browder was pushing the Global Magnitsky Act in Congress to "prevent the new Administration from revising the interstate relations between the

United States and Russia, so diligently antagonized at the instigation of Browder and those interested in it."[256]

Apparently, Veselnitskaya never had in her possession any official documents or information that would incriminate Hillary Clinton over her dealings with Russia. In other words, Goldstone had set up the Trump Tower meeting under false pretenses, telling Donald Trump Jr. that the purpose of meeting was to allow Veselnitskaya to turn over to the Trump campaign derogatory information regarding Clinton's financial dealings in Russia that were certain to damage her chances of becoming president. That simply never happened. Discussing Browder and the Magnitsky Act, it turns out, was the real reason Veselnitskaya wanted to meet with Trump Jr.

For the purpose of this book's narrative, it is not important to sort out all the complicated charges and countercharges regarding Browder's financial dealings in Russia, nor will I affirm Putin's allegations that Browder is a tax criminal. What is important for this narrative is to understand that the purpose of the meeting with Veselnitskaya was to deliver to Trump Jr. a four-page memo prepared by Veselnitskaya asking Trump to repeal the Magnitsky Act and remove the sanctions imposed by the act against Russia once Trump was elected president. Donald Trump Jr., Manafort, and Kushner all refused to take a copy of Veselnitskaya's memo, concluding that the memo and its discussion of the Magnitsky Act were irrelevant to the Trump campaign.

Putin Sounds Off in Helsinki

On July 16, 2018, as President Donald Trump and Vladimir Putin were concluding their summit at the Presidential Palace in Helsinki, Putin dropped a bomb at the final joint press conference.

"According to our investigative officers, a group of people—Mr. Browder's business partners—who illegally made over $1.5 billion in

---

256 Elias Groll, "Here's the Memo the Kremlin-Linked Law-yer Took to the Meeting with Donald Trump Jr.," *Foreign Policy*, October 16, 2017, https://foreignpolicy.com/2017/10/16/heres-memo-kremlin-lawyer-took-to-meeting-donald-trump-jr/.

Russia, did not pay taxes, either in Russia or the United States," Putin said through a translator. "They contributed $400 million to Ms. Clinton's election campaign. This is official information included in their reports—$400 million." With these statements, Putin was sure to make international news. "We have grounds to suspect that U.S. intelligence officers supported these illegal transactions." Putin continued, "So, we have an interest in questioning them. That would be a first step."

Two days later, a Russian government spokesperson walked back Putin's claims. What Putin intended to say, the spokesperson insisted, was that business associates of the U.S.-born investor William Browder had donated $400,000 to Clinton's campaign. According to federal campaign finance records, it appears that Ziff Brothers Investments gave $315,000 to Clinton's campaign and the Democratic National Committee and about $1.1 million to Democratic campaign committees around the United States.[257] This is a substantial sum, but far short of the $400 million Putin had claimed.

Alexander Kurennoi, a spokesperson for Russia's prosecutor general, had a slightly different story. Kurennoi told reporters that Putin stood by his demand that the United States should make Browder, as well as a number of former American diplomats and intelligence officers described as his accomplices in a criminal plot, available for questioning.[258] "Browder's criminal group funneled $1.5 billion from Russia into tax havens," Kurennoi told Russian news agency TASS.[259] "Of this sum, at least $400 million was transferred to the Democratic party's accounts. Afterward, our president asked us to correct the sum to $400,000 from $400 million."

---

257 Jon Greenberg, "Putin's Pants-on-Fire Claim about $400 Million Donation to Clinton from Bill Browder Partners," Politifact.com, July 16, 2018, https://www.politifact.com/truth-o-meter/statements/2018/jul/16/vladimir-putin/putins-pants-fire-claim-about-400-million-donation/.

258 Robert Mackey, "Putin Says He Misspoke Too, Withdrawing Claim Clinton Got Millions Stolen from Russia," *The Intercept*, July 18, 2018, https://theintercept.com/2018/07/18/putin-says-misspoke-withdrawing-claim-clinton-got-millions-stolen-russia/.

259 "Russia Ready to Send Request to U.S. over Questionings in Browder Case," TASS, July 17, 2018, https://tass.com/world/1013707.

In his request to interview U.S. government authorities about Browder, Kurennoi noted that on July 13, 2013, Moscow's Tverskoy District Court found Browder guilty in absentia of large-scale tax evasion estimated at 522 million rubles and sentenced him to nine years in prison. In July 2014, Russia placed Browder on Interpol's most wanted list.

John Brennan decided to get into the act, expressing outrage that in the Helsinki joint press conference, President Trump refused to condemn Putin for the "solid evidence" that Russia had engaged in sustained efforts to interfere in the 2016 U.S. election that U.S. intelligence agencies (through the ICA) claimed to have known at the time. In the White House-published version of the transcript and the video of the joint press conference in Helsinki, the Trump White House edited out what happened when Reuters's Jeff Mason asked Putin if he had wanted Trump to win the 2016 election and whether he had directed any of his officials to help him do that. The White House edited out the question and Putin's response. "Yes, I did. Yes, I did," Putin had replied at the joint press conference. "Because he talked about bringing the U.S.-Russia relationship back to normal."[260] Predictably, former CIA head John Brennan called Trump's performance "nothing short of treasonous."[261]

Putin's comments in Helsinki occurred three days after Mueller published his first indictment against the Russians, charging twelve members of Russia's military intelligence service, the GRU, with hacking into Democratic Party servers and disseminating emails during the 2016 election.[262]

---

260   Katelyn Caralle, "Here's Why the White House Transcript of Trump-Putin Presser Is Missing a Piece," *Washington Examiner*, July 25, 2018, https://www.washingtonexaminer.com/news/white-house/heres-why-the-white-house-transcript-of-trump-putin-presser-is-missing-a-piece.

261   Dan Mangan, "Outrage at Trump's Summit Comments: Ex-CIA Chief John Brennan Calls President's Performance 'Nothing Short of Treasonous,'" CNBC, July 16, 2018, https://www.cnbc.com/2018/07/16/outrage-at-trump-performance-with-putin.html.

262   Vladimir Kara-Murza, "What's Really behind Putin's Obsession with the Magnitsky Act," *Washington Post*, op. cit.

How Did Veselnitskaya Get a Visa to Enter the U.S. for the Trump Tower Meeting?

The answer to this question is that several Obama administration federal agencies were involved in getting Veselnitskaya a special visa to enter the United States for the Trump Tower meeting on June 9, 2016. Over a year after the meeting, on July 17, 2017, the Department of Homeland Security finally admitted that the State Department had issued Veselnitskaya a B1/B2 nonimmigrant visa in June 2016 after the intervention of the DOJ in Washington, and with the agreement of Preet Bharara's U.S. Attorney's Office of the Southern District of New York, which paroled Veselnitskaya into the United States.[263] She had been denied by Preet Bharara's office an extension of a special type of "parole" visa that allowed her to be in the United States from September 2015 through February 2017 to work on the Prevezon Holdings Ltd. case (more on this starting in the next few paragraphs), which was then being litigated in federal district court in Manhattan. Her "parole" visa expired on January 7, 2016, and she would not have been allowed back into the United States for the Trump Tower meeting on June 9, 2016, unless the Obama administration directly intervened.

Responding to a question in a joint press conference with French president Emmanuel Macron in Paris on July 13, 2017, President Trump claimed that Veselnitskaya's visa to come into the country had been approved by then attorney general Loretta Lynch.[264] Gillian Christensen, acting chief of media relations for U.S. Citizenship and Immigration Services, explained to Fox News the unusual nature of the visa granted to Veselnitskaya. She explained that the type of parole she received is given

---

263   Brooke Singman, "Mystery Solved? Timeline Shows How Russian Lawyer Got into U.S. for Trump Jr. Meeting," Fox News, July 14, 2017, https://www.foxnews.com/politics/mystery-solved-timeline-shows-how-russian-lawyer-got-into-us-for-trump-jr-meeting.

264   Stefan Becket, "Why Did Obama's DOJ Let Natalia Veselnitskaya into U.S.?" CBS, July 14, 2017, https://www.cbsnews.com/news/did-the-obama-doj-let-russian-lawyer-natalia-veselnitskaya-into-the-u-s/.

"sparingly" and in "extraordinary circumstances," including for humanitarian reasons, such as medical or family emergencies.

What Is Veselnitskaya's Involvement in the Legal Case *U.S. v. Prevezon?*

In 2013, the U.S. Justice Department opened a civil asset forfeiture case against Prevezon Holdings, a Cyprus-based real estate holding company that was owned by Russian Denis Katsyv, the son of Pyotr Katsyv, one of Putin's closest advisors, a transportation minister who rose to the position of vice president in Russia's state-owned national railroad monopoly. The DOJ alleged that Prevezon had received millions of the $230 million stolen through tax refunds in Russia and laundered through New York banks in the conspiracy that Magnitsky discovered. Veselnitskaya was one of the attorneys representing Prevezon in the DOJ civil case being litigated by Preet Bharara's office in Manhattan. The case was still proceeding when President Trump fired Bharara on March 11, 2017, after Bharara refused to accept an order to resign from Attorney General Jeff Sessions. Two months later, the Justice Department announced it settled the $230 million case for $5.9 million.[265]

On July 12, 2017, Browder told Fox News that a Kremlin-connected group had given Veselnitskaya "unlimited resources" to get the Magnitsky Act repealed.[266] By June 2016, Prevezon Holdings and the Russian government had begun an aggressive campaign to get the Magnitsky Act repealed

---

265 "Natalia Veselnitskaya," Committee to Investigate Russia, no date, https://investigaterussia.org/players/natalia-veselnitskaya. See also: U.S. Attorney's Office, Southern District of New York, Department of Justice, "Acting Manhattan U.S. Attorney Announces $5.9 Million Statement of Civil Money Laundering and Forfeiture Claims Against Real Estate Corporations Alleged to Have Laundered Proceeds of Russian Tax Fraud," May 12, 2017, https://www.justice.gov/usao-sdny/pr/acting-manhattan-us-attorney-announces-59-million-settlement-civil-money-laundering-and.

266 Christopher Wallace, Alex Diaz, and Jason Kopp, "Shadowy Company Tied to Russia Meeting Linked to Trump Jr. Troubles," Fox News, July 12, 2017, https://www.foxnews.com/politics/shadowy-company-tied-to-russia-meeting-linked-to-trump-jr-troubles.

and to get the name Magnitsky removed from the Global Magnitsky Act, then in Congress, seeking to extend the Magnitsky sanctions framework to human rights abusers across the globe.[267] The Russian government working with Prevezon was seeking to clear Prevezon in the theft of $230 million from Hermitage's companies.

To represent Prevezon in the federal law case, Denis Katsyv hired BakerHostetler, one of the U.S.'s largest law firms with a global reach, established in 1916 by Newton D. Baker, President Woodrow Wilson's secretary of war in World War I. Browder, in his testimony to the Senate Judiciary Committee, revealed that Veselnitskaya, through BakerHostetler, hired Glenn Simpson of Fusion GPS to manage the public relations campaign that Katsyv was launching to get the Magnitsky Act repealed. Browder further testified that as part of Veselnitskaya's lobbying, former *Wall Street Journal* reporter Chris Cooper of the Potomac Square Group was hired to organize the Washington premiere of a documentary produced to discredit Browder and Magnitsky. Browder asserted that Veselnitskaya had hired Howard Schweitzer of Cozen O'Connor Public Strategies and former congressman Ronald Dellums to lobby members of Congress to repeal the Magnitsky Act and to remove Sergei Magnitsky's name from the global bill. Finally, Browder told the Senate Judiciary Committee that on June 13, 2016, Veselnitskaya and Denis Katsyv funded an event at the Newseum in D.C. to show the documentary to invited members of Congress and the State Department. Browder alleged that at no time did any of these groups or individuals register disclosures under the Foreign Agent Registration Act, FARA.[268]

The most explosive of Browder's charges was the disclosure that Veselnitskaya, at the time of the Trump Tower meeting with Trump Jr., had been a client of Glenn Simpson and his company, Fusion GPS, who hired Christopher Steele to write the Steele dossier.

---

267 Letter from Senator Charles Grassley, Chairman of the Senate Committee on the Judiciary, to Dana Boente, Acting Deputy Attorney General, U.S. Department of Justice, op. cit.

268 Rosie Gray, "Bill Browder's Testimony to the Senate Judiciary Committee," *The Atlantic*, July 25, 2017, https://www.theatlantic.com/politics/archive/2017/07/bill-browders-testimony-to-the-senate-judiciary-committee/534864/.

Veselnitskaya Meets with Fusion GPS Glenn Simpson in New York

In his testimony before the Senate Judiciary Committee on August 22, 2017, Glenn Simpson clarified that in the Prevezon case, Veselnitskaya retained BakerHostetler, which in turn retained Fusion GPS. This is identical to the strategy the Clinton campaign and the DNC used to hire Fusion GPS, laundering the Fusion GPS contract though a law firm—in that case, Perkins Coie. Simpson testified that Veselnitskaya arranged for BakerHostetler to be paid, and BakerHostetler in turn paid Fusion GPS. Simpson testified that although he did not know where Veselnitskaya got the money to fund these payments, he understood she was the attorney managing the case for Prevezon.[269]

Simpson also testified that he had dinner with Veselnitskaya in New York City on June 8, 2016, the day before the Trump Tower meeting, and again on June 10, 2016, in Washington, the day after the Trump Tower meeting. Simpson indicated that on June 9, the day of the meeting, he had been with Veselnitskaya in federal court in lower Manhattan for the Prevezon case being heard. It appears that the Trump Tower meeting was moved from the originally scheduled 3:00 p.m. to 4:00 p.m., to allow Veselnitskaya more time for her appearance in court for the Prevezon case.

In his testimony before the Senate Judiciary Committee, Simpson denied any knowledge about the Trump Tower meeting, and he testified under oath that he did not discuss the meeting with Veselnitskaya at dinner the day before or the day after the meeting.

In a letter Senator Chuck Grassley sent to Browder on August 12, 2017, he made it clear that Browder told the Senate Judiciary Committee that Fusion GPS had received money from the Russian government—a logical conclusion given that the Russian government funded Veselnitskaya, who in turn hired BakerHostetler, which in turn hired Fusion GPS. The money Veselnitskaya used to make these payments rather obviously traced back to the Russian government. This would mean Fusion GPS had been paid by the Clinton campaign and the DNC (via Perkins Coie), by

---

269 Interview with Glenn Simpson, Senate Judiciary Committee, U.S. Senate, Washington, D.C., August 22, 2017.

the Obama administration (via the FBI), and by the Russian government (via Veselnitskaya and the contract with BakerHostetler).

Browder also insisted to the Senate Judiciary Committee that the work Fusion GPS did in the Prevezon case was not limited to litigation support research, but also included work on Veselnitskaya's anti-Magnitsky propaganda.[270] In a statement to Politico, Fusion GPS admitted that Simpson and Fusion GPS had found records on Browder's property and finances and tracked down potential witnesses in the Prevezon case. Fusion GPS also admitted to discussing the case record with several reporters.[271]

Why Did Akhmetshin Attend the Trump Tower Meeting?

Although Rinat Akhmetshin did not play a speaking role in the Trump Tower meeting, it was clear he was there for a purpose. Born in Kazan, Russia, Akhmetshin now resides in Washington, D.C., and holds dual U.S. and Russian citizenship. He is a media consultant and a lobbyist by trade with a history of service in the Russian military, having served in the Soviet army, where he worked as a counterintelligence officer. In his testimony before the Senate Judiciary Committee on November 14, 2017, Akhmetshin said he was born in 1967, arrived in the U.S. in 1994 to pursue his graduate studies, and became a U.S. citizen in 2009. He claimed to hold a doctorate in biochemistry, but he did not specify the university from which he received the degree.

Akhmetshin further testified that he met Veselnitskaya in 2014, having been introduced to her by a partner in BakerHostetler. After meeting Veselnitskaya, he was hired by BakerHostetler to work on the Prevezon

---

270 Letter from Senator Charles Grassley, Chairman of the Senate Committee on the Judiciary, to William Browder, CEO, Hermitage Capital Management, dated August 12, 2017, https://www.grassley.senate.gov/sites/default/files/constituents/2017-08-12%20CEG%20to%20Browder%20%28Washington%20Post%20article%20follow-up%29.pdf.

271 Isaac Arnsdorf, "FARA Complaint Alleges Pro-Russian Lobbying," Politico, December 8, 2016, https://www.politico.com/tipsheets/politico-influence/2016/12/fara-complaint-alleges-pro-russian-lobbying-217776.

case. Akhmetshin and Veselnitskaya created the nonprofit Human Rights Accountability Group International (HRAGI) in February 2016, to lobby for the repeal of the Magnitsky Act; it was set up by one of Denis Katsyv's lawyers. Akhmetshin testified that he lobbied for HRAGI, working to help promote the showing of the anti-Magnitsky documentary and urging various members of Congress and reporters to attend the showing at Newseum.

Senator Grassley, then chairman of the Senate Judiciary Committee, in a letter to Dana Boente, acting deputy attorney general, dated March 31, 2017, noted that Rinat Akhmetshin, along with former congressman Ron Dellums, reportedly lobbied the House Foreign Affairs Committee, telling staffers they were lobbying on behalf of a Russian company named Prevezon. Grassley continued that Akhmetshin and Dellums asked these staffers to delay the Global Magnitsky Act, or to at least remove Magnitsky's name from the legislation. Akhmetshin and Dellums commented to the staffers, "[I]t was a shame that this bill has made it so Russian orphans cannot be adopted by Americans."[272]

Grassley's letter to Boente also commented that it was particularly disturbing that Mr. Akhmetshin and Fusion GPS were working together on this pro-Russia lobbying effort in 2016 in light of Mr. Akhmetshin's history and reputation. Grassley cited published reports that Akhmetshin was an English-speaking former Soviet army counter-intelligence officer[273] whom Radio Free Europe had hired as "a gun-for-hire [who] lurks in the shadows of Washington's lobbying world."[274] Grassley said in the letter that it was unclear whether the FBI was aware of Fusion GPS's pro-Russian lobbying in the Prevezon case and the connection to Akhmetshin, or "that these events coincided with the creation of the [Steele] dossier."

---

272 Letter from Senator Charles Grassley, Chairman of the Senate Committee on the Judiciary, to Dana Boente, op. cit.

273 Steve LeVine, *The Oil and the Glory: The Pursuit of Empire and Fortune on the Caspian Sea* (New York: Random House, 2007).

274 Mike Eckel, "Russian 'Gun-For-Hire' Lurks in Shadows of Washington's Lobbying World," Radio Free Europe, July 17, 2016, https://www.rferl.org/a/rinat-akmetshin-russia-gun-for-hire-washington-lobbying-magnitsky-browder/27863265.html.

Grassley was also concerned that none of those recruited by Veselnitskaya to participate in the Prevezon case had met the filing and disclosure requirements required by FARA.

In his testimony, Akhmetshin said he knew and had worked with Glenn Simpson and Fusion GPS, but he insisted that on the Prevezon case, he had worked with Glenn Simpson and Fusion GPS as a co-consultant not under contract with Fusion GPS.

Akhmetshin admitted that in the work he had done for BakerHostetler on the Prevezon case, he worked with reporters, naming in particular the courts editor at Bloomberg. In his testimony to the Senate Judiciary Committee, Simpson admitted to sharing his research on the Prevezon case with Akhmetshin, acknowledging that he believed that Akhmetshin used the information supplied by Fusion GPS when lobbying Congress on the Magnitsky Act.

On August 9, 2018, investigative reporter John Solomon published an article in *The Hill* in which he examined handwritten notes that then associate deputy attorney general Bruce Ohr made in his Washington coffee shop meeting with Simpson. "Much of the information about the Trump campaign ties to Russia comes from a former Russian intelligence officer [illegible] who lives in the U.S.," Ohr scribbled.[275] Given that the pool of former Russian intelligence officers currently living in the United States is relatively small, speculation continues that Akhmetshin may have been the Russian referred to in Ohr's note.[276]

Simpson and Akhmetshin have ties to Hillary Clinton through Ed Lieberman, a Washington-based lawyer who has expertise in U.S. and Russian tax laws. Lieberman was also hired by BakerHostetler to provide

---

275 John Solomon, "The Handwritten Notes Exposing What Fusion GPS Told DOJ about Trump," *The Hill*, August 9, 2018, https://thehill.com/hilltv/rising/401185-the-handwritten-notes-exposing-what-fusion-gps-told-doj-about-trump.

276 Brian Cates, "Is Rinat Akhmetshin the 'Former Russian Intelligence Officer' Who Was a Source for the Steele Dossier?" *The Epoch Times*, August 19, 2018, https://www.theepochtimes.com/is-rinat-akhmetshin-the-former-russian-intelligence-officer-who-was-a-source-for-the-steele-dossier_2627738.html.

analysis of the alleged tax evasion scheme involving Bill Browder and Hermitage Capital. In his testimony to the Senate, Akhmetshin said that he first met Lieberman in 1998. In addition to advising BakerHostetler on the Prevezon case, Lieberman served as legal advisor to the nonprofit organization HRAGI that Veselnitskaya and Akhmetshin set up to lobby for the repeal of the Magnitsky Act. Lieberman's late wife, Evelyn, had served as First Lady Hillary Clinton's chief of staff. Evelyn Lieberman had also served as the Bill Clinton deputy chief of staff who famously transferred Monica Lewinsky out of the White House to the Defense Department.

Akhmetshin told the Senate Judiciary Committee that he "may have" taken the Acela train on Amtrak from Washington to New York on June 9, 2016, the day of the Trump Tower meeting. He did remember having dinner with Ed Lieberman that night, but insisted in his testimony that they did not discuss the Trump Tower meeting. Investigative journalist Aaron Klein found this hard to believe. "In other words, Akhmetshin is claiming that he attended a meeting at the campaign headquarters of Clinton's personal challenger with the challenger's son and other top Trump staffers, and that same night Akhmetshin did not even mention the meeting to his friend Lieberman, a Clinton associate," Klein observed.[277]

Even the translator at the Trump Tower meeting had ties to the Democrats. In his testimony to the Senate Judiciary Committee, the Russian-born translator, Anatoli Samochornov, acknowledged that in his work for the U.S. State Department, he had translated for Secretary Hillary Clinton on one occasion, "two or three times" for Secretary John Kerry, and for President Obama's summits at the United Nations.[278]

On May 12, 2017, Joon H. Kim, the acting U.S. attorney for the Southern District of New York, announced that the DOJ had settled the civil money-laundering and forfeiture claims against Prevezon shortly

---

277 Aaron Klein, "Translator at Trump Tower Meeting Personally Served Hillary Clinton, John Kerry, President Obama," Breitbart, August 23, 2018, https://www.breitbart.com/politics/2018/08/23/translator-at-trump-tower-meeting-personally-served-hillary-clinton-john-kerry-president-obama/.

278 Testimony of Anatoli Samochornov, Senate Judiciary Committee, U.S. Senate, Washington, D.C., November 8, 2017.

before the case would have gone to trial, with Prevezon agreeing to pay $5.9 million in the settlement agreement.[279]

On January 8, 2019, the U.S. Attorney's Office for the Southern District of New York indicted Veselnitskaya with obstruction of justice in her representation of Prevezon.[280] The DOJ charged that she had concealed from the court her role in helping to draft part of the investigative findings submitted to the court by the Russian government. It is unlikely that Veselnitskaya will ever return to the United States to face these criminal charges.

Evidence in Plain Sight or a Fusion GPS Setup?

The obvious conclusion is that hate-Trump Democrats and the Mueller investigation took the Trump Tower meeting at face value, concluding that it provided evidence in plain sight that the Trump campaign was actively soliciting information from the Russian government that would implicate Hillary Clinton over dirt with Russia.

Devin Nunes, the former GOP chairman of the House Intelligence Committee, is skeptical. "When you hear the Democrats talk about that there's 'evidence in plain sight,' the Russians that are involved in the infamous Trump Tower meeting in New York, I call them the Fusion GPS Russians," Nunes told the *Washington Examiner*. "Fusion GPS was the company that was working for the Clinton campaign and the Democrats, and somehow Glenn Simpson meets with them [Veselnitskaya] before and

---

279 Department of Justice, U.S. Attorney's Office, Southern District of New York, "Acting Manhattan U.S. Attorney Announces $5.9 Million Settlement of Civil Money Laundering and Forfeiture Claims Against Real Estate Corporations Alleged to Have Laundered Proceeds of Russian Tax Fraud," May 12, 2017, https://www.justice.gov/usao-sdny/pr/acting-manhattan-us-attorney-announces-59-million-settlement-civil-money-laundering-and.

280 Department of Justice, U.S. Attorney's Office, Southern District of New York, "Russian Attorney Natalya [sic] Veselnitskaya Charged with Obstruction of Justice in Connection with Civil Money Laundering and Forfeiture Action," January 8, 2019, https://www.justice.gov/usao-sdny/pr/russian-attorney-natalya-veselnitskaya-charged-obstruction-justice-connection-civil.

after [for dinner on July 8 and again on July 10, 2016], and he's actually, these are Russians he's working for? I mean come on. If Mueller can't get to the bottom of this and answer this for the American people, I don't know what the report was really worth."[281]

Why would the Russian government send a Russian attorney who spoke no English to meet Donald Trump Jr.? It is also a stretch to imagine that the Russian government would need a British music publicist, Robert Goldstone, to be the contact arranging the meeting. Clearly, Veselnitskaya knew she was setting up the meeting on false pretenses. Veselnitskaya's real purpose was to use the lure of Russian government dirt on Hillary Clinton to arrange the meeting to deliver the four-page memo on Bill Browder and the Magnitsky Act. Veselnitskaya should have been able to predict that Trump Jr. and the other senior members of the Trump campaign attending the meeting would become irritated by, if not angry at, the waste of time. That the meeting ended after only about twenty minutes should not have been a surprise to Veselnitskaya.

The whole meeting looked staged, not by the Russian government but by Fusion GPS, with the willing assistance of Rinat Akhmetshin, a one-person lobbying organization that appears to operate more like a Russian intel operation. The tie that binds Veselnitskaya, Akhmetshin, and Glenn Simpson together in what appears to have been a comically unprofessional sting is that all three were being paid in Russian government money, laundered through the law firm BakerHostetler, to do Putin's business lobbying for the repeal of the Magnitsky Act. Putin's comments at the Helsinki summit leave no doubt that he was still bristling over Browder, Magnitsky, various privatization swindles, and unpaid Russian taxes. If there was any evidence to come out of the Trump Tower meeting, it was Putin's revelation that money from Browder's investment activities in Russia found its way into Hillary Clinton's presidential campaign—even if Putin was widely mistaken on the amount.

---

281 Daniel Chaitin, "Devin Nunes Looking for 'Some Type of Setup' in 3 Areas of Mueller's Report," *Washington Examiner*, April 16, 2019, https://www.washingtonexaminer.com/news/devin-nunes-looking-for-some-type-of-setup-in-3-areas-of-muellers-report.

The Mainstream Media "Exposes" Soviet Intel within the Trump Camp

The whole Magnitsky saga is so horribly complicated to average Americans that there was no possible way Veselnitskaya could have imagined that Trump Jr. would have any idea what she was talking about in her four-page memo. Yes, the meeting might have been a setup to demonstrate that the Trump campaign was open to receiving opposition research on Hillary Clinton from the Russian government. But it is unclear whether or not this is a crime, especially since the Clinton campaign and the DNC hired a former British intelligence officer to gather dirt on Trump from Russian sources.

It is entirely possible that the goal of Fusion GPS and the Clinton campaign was to plant within the Trump campaign Veselnitskaya's four-page memo arguing for the repeal of the Magnitsky Act. From the perspective of arguing the Russia-collusion narrative in court, what motive would Russia have to steal the DNC emails to elect Trump president? The missing part of the narrative is a convincing argument about what Russia was planning to gain if and when Trump won.

In 2017, the mainstream media picked up the narrative planted by Veselnitskaya. On July 14, 2017, NBC News published an article with the headline "Former Soviet Counterintelligence Officer at Meeting with Donald Trump Jr. and Russian Lawyer."[282] The article was written to frame Trump as a Russian spy without making the allegation directly. The lead paragraph of the article reads:

> Washington—The Russian lawyer who met with Donald Trump Jr. and others on the Trump team after a promise of compromising material on Hillary Clinton was accompanied by a Russian-American lobbyist—a former Soviet

---

282 Ken Dilanian, Natasha Lebedeva, and Hallie Jackson, "Former Soviet Counterintelligence Officer at Meeting with Donald Trump Jr. and Russian Lawyer," NBC, July 14, 2017, https://www.nbcnews.com/news/us-news/russian-lawyer-brought-ex-soviet-counter-intelligence-officer-trump-team-n782851.

counterintelligence officer who is suspected by some U.S. officials of having ongoing ties to Russian intelligence, NBC News has learned.

The next paragraph clearly references Natalia Veselnitskaya as the suspicious Russian lawyer and Rinat Akhmetshin as the former Soviet counterintelligence officer. Given my experience with Mueller's prosecutors and the FBI agents working with them, the "unnamed sources" used by the mainstream media regarding this case are almost certain to lead back to Mueller leaks.

Subsequent paragraphs make the reader aware that Mueller is investigating the Trump Tower meeting as evidence that Donald Trump Jr. was willing to accept dirt on Hillary Clinton from the Russian government:

> But, given the email traffic suggesting the meeting was part of a Russian effort to help Trump's candidacy, the presence at the meeting of a Russian-American with suspected intelligence ties is likely to be of interest to special counsel Robert Mueller and the House and Senate panels investigating the Russian election interference campaign.

The article notes that Veselnitskaya brought with her to the meeting a "two-page document, one small part of which involved alleged DNC funding issues." That paragraph concluded by stressing that most of the document Veselnitskaya brought with her to the Trump Tower meeting "involved allegations against the Magnitsky sanctions, she [Veselnitskaya] said." The frame-up to prove Russian collusion was already rolling out, using the Magnitsky memo as exhibit number one.

The Democrats repeatedly criticized Trump during the 2016 election campaign for saying that as president, he wanted a closer relationship with Putin and Russia. Had Trump Jr. taken from Veselnitskaya the four-page memo she had been planning to plant at the highest level of the Trump campaign, the circle on the Russia-collusion-hoax narrative would have been completed.

If Trump Jr. had accepted from Veselnitskaya the memo as a courtesy to end an otherwise embarrassingly short meeting set up on false pretenses,

Mueller and company could have had "evidence" showing precisely why Putin preferred Trump to be president. President Obama had signed the Magnitsky Act into law, and Prevezon was being prosecuted even while the 2016 presidential campaign was ongoing. Browder had contributed to Clinton's campaign.

What possible reason could Putin have had to imagine that Clinton would repeal the Magnitsky Act once she were in the White House?

But if Trump Jr. had accepted the Veselnitskaya memo, the sting would have been successful. Mueller—or a similar person investigating Trump—would have "found" the memo in the Trump campaign's possession at the right time. This would then have been used by Mueller as "evidence" to "prove" that Trump secretly had promised Putin that he would repeal the Magnitsky Act once he was elected president.

Putin clearly wanted the Magnitsky Act repealed, as proven by the "unlimited" budget (millions of dollars) Putin gave Veselnitskaya to defend Prevezon in the U.S. federal court. Or consider the angry comments that Putin uttered in Helsinki, seeking revenge against Browder for getting the Magnitsky Act passed. And Putin's venom was not reserved just for Browder. He ended his diatribe by charging that Hillary Clinton was a beneficiary of the wealth Putin considered to be stolen by Browder from Russia.

Veselnitskaya's Magnitsky Act sting was calculated to be effective against Donald Trump precisely because the Russians knew the Clintons had joined Browder in supporting the passage of the Magnitsky Act and President Obama had signed it into law. All of them are Democrats. It would have been credible for Mueller to argue that Putin knew that Hillary Clinton as president would never repeal the Magnitsky Act, but Putin could easily have calculated that Trump as president might just seek to have the legislation repealed, if only to reverse the damage the Democrats had done to U.S. relations with Russia by passing the legislation. But Mueller could easily have concluded that Trump had promised Putin to repeal the Magnitsky Act, when and if he were president—an accusation that would have gained weight had Mueller found Veselnitskaya's four-page memo in the possession of the Trump campaign.

Goldstone Apologizes to Donald Trump Jr.

Robert Goldstone, in his testimony to the Senate Judiciary Committee on December 15, 2017, explained that he wrote the email to Donald Trump Jr. asking for a meeting because the morning he sent the email, he had received a phone call from Emin Agalarov.[283] "I received the call from Emin that morning, and he asked me if I could contact the Trumps with something interesting and said that a well-connected Russian attorney had met with his father that morning in his father's office and had told them that they had some interesting information that could potentially be damaging regarding funding by Russians to the Democrats and to its candidate, Hillary Clinton," Goldstone explained.

Agalarov's explanation seemed pretty thin to Goldstone. "Well-connected?" Goldstone asked. "What does that mean? Like into the power grid?" Agalarov tried his best, finally admitting that all he knew was that a Russian lawyer had "some potentially damaging" information about Clinton that would be of interest to the Trumps. Goldstone objected, explaining to Agalarov that he was a music publicist who basically knew nothing about politics. Agalarov's answer was, "I'm only asking you to get a meeting."

After the Trump Tower meeting had been concluded, Goldstone went back to his office and phoned Agalarov, telling him that setting up the meeting was "the most embarrassing thing you've ever asked me to do." Astounded at what had just happened, Goldstone explained to Agalarov in disbelief, "I just sat through a meeting that was about adoption."

Before leaving the meeting, Goldstone did what he could to repair the damage he knew setting up this fraudulent meeting would do to his relationship with Donald Trump Jr. "I said to him, 'Don, I really want to apologize. This was hugely embarrassing. I have no idea what this meeting was really about.'" Trump Jr. handled the situation gracefully; Goldstone told the Senate committee that Trump Jr. responded by saying, "'Don't worry. You know, we have so many meetings, and we go from one to the other. And I appreciate your friendship.'"

---

283 Testimony of Robert Goldstone, Senate Judiciary Committee, U.S. Senate, Washington, D.C., December 15, 2017.

From that moment forward, Veselnitskaya—a person Goldstone never wanted to see again—was suspect to Goldstone. Preet Bharara seems to have already come to that conclusion. Bharara had refused to renew Veselnitskaya's visa to allow her to return to the United States to resume her legal defense work for Prevezon in June 2016. The only way Veselnitskaya could get back into the country was to appeal to the Obama administration, very likely at the level of Attorney General Loretta Lynch, if not higher. Veselnitskaya was able to get the strings pulled within the Obama DOJ to get Bharara's decision reversed. After Bharara was fired by President Trump, his office—the U.S. Attorney's Office for the Southern District of New York—filed criminal charges against Veselnitskaya for the legal defense work she had done in the case.

Every aspect of the Veselnitskaya sting stunt has the earmarks of an intelligence operation. Veselnitskaya may have been paid by Putin, but she was working in the interests of the Clintons. Everyone attending that meeting on Veselnitskaya's side had close ties to the Clintons. Goldstone even explained to the Senate Judiciary Committee that the only reason he posted a photo of himself in the lobby of Trump Tower at 3:59 p.m. on June 9, 2016, was because he knew it would annoy 99.9 percent of his friends. Who were Goldstone's friends? They were Democrats, largely in L.A. and New York City. Goldstone was in the pop music business.

If Clinton had accepted campaign funds from Browder, as Putin accused, then why would the Democrats be working so hard to get Veselnitskaya into the United States and to arrange a meeting with the top level of Trump's campaign just to make the case Trump should come out as a candidate in favor of repealing the Magnitsky Act? Browder put the Magnitsky Act in place. He wouldn't want it repealed. Clearly, Browder supported the Democrats and Clinton, as evidenced by Obama signing the Magnitsky Act into law. But Browder may have approved Veselnitskaya's intel ruse to get Trump to accept her memo if Browder thought tricking Trump into opposing the Magnitsky Act may have helped Mueller drop the trap door on Trump in the Russia-collusion hoax.

John Brennan's attack on President Trump over the Helsinki meeting with Putin shows more about Brennan than Trump. It appears that in accusing Trump of treason, Brennan was subconsciously revealing something about himself. He had to be upset that Trump had allowed Putin's comments about Browder to stand without refutation, especially Putin's insistence that Clinton had received dirty money from Browder that could be traced back to the profits Browder made in Russia.

The full meaning of Putin's comments was that Clinton had accepted a foreign donation to her campaign, a direct violation of U.S. campaign finance laws. If Putin's comments were correct—and except for the amount of the donations, federal campaign finance records support Putin's claims—Brennan and the CIA had to know about it. This is every bit as certain as the assumption Mueller, Lynch, and Comey had to know at some level that HSBC was involved in illegal money laundering with drug dealers and terrorists. Money wire-transferred into and out of U.S. banks is monitored constantly by the U.S. Treasury Department, with information shared with the CIA and other intelligence agencies as necessary.

That Brennan has been unable to stop attacking Trump in the vilest manner betrays more than his hatred of Trump on ideological grounds. On subconscious grounds, Brennan's vituperative accusations that Trump is a traitor have the scent of Brennan blaming Trump for something Brennan fears he himself is guilty of having committed. Brennan's guilty conscience demands that he continue diverting attention from himself to Trump to cover up his personal involvement, as well as the CIA's involvement as an agency, in the Deep State plot to destroy Trump. Particularly damaging to Brennan is the Veselnitskaya sting designed to plant her four-page Magnitsky memo into the heart of Donald Trump's campaign. It is unimaginable that the Department of Justice in Washington overruled the U.S. Attorney's Office in the Southern District of New York to issue a special visa so Veselnitskaya could enter the country for the Trump Tower meeting without the CIA's being aware of what was going on.

Chapter Ten

RUSSIA! RUSSIA! RUSSIA!

On July 31, 2016, the Deep State coup d'état decisively changed direction, abandoning the idea the FBI would succeed by opening a formal criminal investigation to find evidence of crimes Donald Trump may have committed in his business dealings with Russia. Instead, the DOJ and FBI decided to open a counterintelligence investigation into alleged Trump campaign collusion with Russia. What the mainstream media intentionally failed to highlight was that this decision is proof that the FBI's criminal investigation on Trump had failed to find any probable-cause evidence of crimes Trump may have committed with his business dealings in Russia, including his negotiations to build a Trump Tower in Moscow. This was also a tacit admission that while the Steele dossier's accusations that Trump's allegedly perverted sexual activity in Russia may have compromised Trump, no violations of U.S. law were committed even had the never-verified "golden shower" incident been true. The only criminal investigation opened against Trump (not incident to the counterintelligence investigation) was in May 2017, when Acting FBI Director Andrew McCabe launched a criminal obstruction of justice investigation on the premise that Trump had obstructed the DOJ counterintelligence investigation into Russian collusion by firing Comey.

After July 31, 2016, by defining the coup d'état attack strategy as a counterintelligence investigation rather than a criminal investigation, the Obama administration avoided the rigorous probable cause standard of proof demanded in a criminal investigation to bring a criminal indictment.

The administration knew that a counterintelligence investigation would operate under less rigorous standards of proof, merely requiring that the conduct being investigated must have a legitimate national security concern. An FBI counterintelligence investigation is aimed at finding and convicting foreign spies operating in the United States, as well as U.S. citizens collaborating with the foreign spies. The Obama administration knew that a counterintelligence investigation was a national security case that would require only reasonable suspicion to reach across to involve foreign intelligence services. The question was no longer limited to whether Donald Trump had committed a crime under federal election laws, but now included whether he was a spy—specifically, whether he was acting as a Russian agent. Under the less rigorous standards of proof under which a counterintelligence investigation operates, the FBI's mission was merely to investigate whether or not Trump had colluded with Russia to defeat Clinton, with no requirement the FBI establish probable-cause evidence Donald Trump personally or his campaign officials had committed crimes in doing so.

But through the backdoor of a counterintelligence investigation, the Obama DOJ and FBI were also allowed to conduct a criminal investigation should any crimes be found in the espionage activity being investigated. In his closed-door testimony before the House Judiciary Committee, James A. Baker, the general counsel for the FBI in 2016, explained how counterintelligence investigations could also become criminal investigations. "The FBI always has all of its authorities in dealing with a counterintelligence matter," Baker testified. "And so to my mind, the FBI walks in with all of its options on the table. And it can pursue things in a strictly, you know, foreign intelligence channel, interacting with other intelligence agencies and things like that and never have anything to do with, you know, a grand jury subpoena or putting anybody in a courtroom or anything like that, or an indictment." Yet, Baker acknowledged, when a counterintelligence investigation transforms into a criminal investigation, the standard of proof becomes the more rigorous standard of probable cause. "But at the same time, if the facts and circumstances warrant going—using criminal tools, including up to and including prosecution, then the FBI can do that. And so I think it's just misleading to think of a counterintelligence investigation as not also being, in part, at least potentially a criminal investigation."[284]

This point disturbed former U.S. assistant attorney Andrew C. McCarthy, who has accused the DOJ and FBI of running a criminal investigation against Donald Trump under the pretext of a counterintelligence investigation. In his 2019 book, *Ball of Collusion*, McCarthy writes: "In the absence of a solid factual predicate for a criminal investigation, foreign-counterintelligence powers were used as a pretext to dig for criminal evidence that would support a hoped-for prosecution." McCarthy called this a major and abusive flaw of the Trump-Russia investigation.[285] McCarthy also comments the Obama administration "bent over backwards *not* to make a criminal case on Hillary Clinton—the candidate Obama heartily endorsed—despite a mountain of incriminating evidence." In sharp contrast, he noted the Obama administration "exploited every tool in its arsenal (surveillance, informants, foreign-intelligence agencies, moribund and constitutionally untenable criminal statutes) to try to make a criminal case on Trump—the candidate Obama deeply opposed—despite the absence of incriminating evidence."[286] McCarthy also explained this by noting that the Obama administration "notoriously political in its intelligence assessments and law-enforcement actions, used Trump contacts with Russia as a rationalization for a counterintelligence investigation because it saw Trump as a Neanderthal degenerate." At the same time, the Obama administration "ignored Clinton contacts with Russia, or assumed they simply must have been good-faith contacts, because it saw the Clintons as bien pensant transnational-progressives."[287]

The Deep State coup d'état planners calculated incorrectly that under a counterintelligence investigation, the FBI could get away with using the Steele dossier to get FISA Court approval to conduct electronic

---

284 Testimony of James A. Baker (Day 2), Executive Session, Committee on the Judiciary, Joint with the Committee on Government Reform and Oversight, U.S. House of Representatives, Washington, D.C., October 18, 2018.

285 McCarthy, *Ball of Collusion*, op. cit., p. 227.

286 Ibid., p. 178, italics in original.

287 Ibid., pp. 177-178.

surveillance. Using the Steele dossier to get FISA Court approval illegally was the central crime committed by the Deep State traitors.

But the coup d'état plotters didn't stop there. The Clinton-Obama traitors also miscalculated that the evidence the FBI and the White House had already obtained by abusing Section 702 of the FISA Court law would never become public knowledge. As we shall see later in this chapter, additional crimes were committed when Obama administration officials, including top-placed presidential advisors in the White House, unmasked the names of Trump campaign top officials gathered from illegal Section 702 queries designed to frame Trump as colluding with Putin. Yet another potential crime to add to the list is the willingness of John Brennan and James Clapper to use information gathered from British intelligence GCHQ electronic surveillance on U.S. citizens, including Trump campaign officials.

Starting on July 31, 2016, with the opening of the FBI's counterintelligence operation, the nonstop refrain the Clinton-Obama Deep State traitors tried to beat into the heads of the American people was this: "Russia! Russia! Russia!" This theme, designed to brand Trump as a traitor, was repeated over and over, 24/7, by the lapdog mainstream media, with volume added by the Trump-haters-in-chief, the talking heads at CNN and MSNBC.

What Does an FBI Counterintelligence Investigation Mean?

Many nations keep their national police force separate from agencies responsible for intelligence activities, but not the United States. The FBI website proclaims that the FBI is "the country's lead counterintelligence agency."[288] It says the FBI "is responsible for detecting and lawfully countering actions of foreign intelligence services and organizations that employ human and technical means to gather information about the U.S. that adversely affects our national interests." The FBI's Counterintelligence Division develops evidence to be handed over to the DOJ's Counterintelligence Division to convene grand juries, seek indictments, and prosecute criminal cases resulting from FBI investigations.

---

288 "What Is the FBI's Foreign Counterintelligence Responsibility?" FBI.gov, https://www.fbi.gov/about/faqs/what-is-the-fbis-foreign-counterintelligence-responsibility.

In a counterintelligence investigation, the FBI is empowered to investigate U.S. citizens when it has reason to believe they are working as spies for foreign nations. It was under the auspices of this authority that the DOJ and FBI worked together to pursue FISA Court authorization to conduct electronic surveillance on Carter Page, and to conduct electronic surveillance on his network of contacts—a network that may have reached to Donald Trump himself. FISA Court approval would never have been required if the investigation into Donald Trump had remained a criminal investigation. In a criminal investigation, when there is probable cause that someone has committed a crime, all the FBI has to do is to obtain a search warrant from a federal judge to authorize both physical search and seizure operations as well as electronic surveillance.

As noted above, FBI counterintelligence investigations may result in criminal charges against U.S. citizens. Typically, criminal charges in those cases include espionage charges. To bring criminal charges against a U.S. citizen, the FBI's counterintelligence investigation must produce evidence establishing sufficient probable cause to convince a federal grand jury to believe the citizen is engaged in spying activities. Spying-activity investigations in these cases usually involve allegations that those identified as spies have provided foreign entities with stolen classified, sensitive, or proprietary information from the U.S. government or U.S. companies, or have conspired with foreign sources to achieve a nefarious purpose—such as stealing emails to throw an election. Clearly, the theft of the DNC emails and the hacking of the NGP VAN system were used to justify the FBI opening a counterintelligence investigation on the premise that the Trump campaign had conspired or colluded with Russia to steal and publish sensitive and proprietary information from Hillary Clinton, her campaign, and the DNC to make sure she lost the presidential election.

Once begun, the counterintelligence campaign against Trump and Russia then became about finding or otherwise developing sufficient probable-cause evidence to convince a federal grand jury that criminal charges involving espionage should be filed against Trump. This evidence would have to establish probable cause that Trump had committed treason by working with Russian agents (like Guccifer 2.0 and/or Russia's military intelligence unit, the GRU) to steal or otherwise obtain information from the Democrats so sensitive and so proprietary that its public disclosure had the potential to destroy Clinton's presidential bid in 2016. That is what the FBI's counterintelligence investigation into Trump and Russia was all about. Added to the espionage theory would be evidence (for instance, obtained through the efforts of Russian attorney Natalia Veselnitskaya, as discussed in the previous chapter) that Trump had promised Putin to repeal the Magnitsky Act and end sanctions against Russia in exchange for Putin ordering the GRU to steal the Democrats' emails and to publish them through Julian Assange and WikiLeaks.

The Clinton-Obama Coup d'État Weaponized Counterintelligence

By definition, an FBI counterintelligence investigation presumes the active involvement of U.S. intelligence agencies—this is the full meaning of what can be read on the FBI website. Because spy activities involve foreign actors, an FBI counterintelligence investigation forces the DOJ and the FBI to expand their efforts internationally, working in conjunction with foreign law enforcement and intelligence agencies. The international investigations required of the DOJ in a counterintelligence operation further complicated the picture when DOJ officials and FBI agents took their Russia-collusion Operation Crossfire Hurricane activities overseas, infringing operations where the CIA and other U.S. intelligence agencies typically have jurisdiction under U.S. law.

That foreign intelligence agencies were involved expands the coup d'état into international dimensions. The FBI investigation of Trump not only was dishonest and politically motivated; it was also criminal, ultimately involving criminal efforts to deny a duly elected president the right to serve out his term in office, committing specifically the capital crime of treason.

What this chapter seeks to prove is that the highest levels of the Obama administration, including James Comey as head of the FBI, weaponized the FBI's counterintelligence capabilities for ideological purposes in their attempts to implicate Trump as a Russian spy. The FBI's goal became weaponized when FBI agents, in conjunction with rogue elements in the CIA and DOJ, plotted to develop and possibly even to plant incriminating information within the Trump campaign. The FBI shifted from a criminal investigation to a counterintelligence investigation because there was no evidence that Trump had broken any U.S. laws until June 2016, when Clinton used CrowdStrike to "prove" the Russians had hacked the DNC's computers.

But when the FBI, in its ideological zeal to keep Trump out of the White House, joined forces with rogue elements in the CIA, the DOJ, and the Obama White House to destroy Trump at any cost, the investigators themselves became criminals. This chapter is critical to establishing the basis for concluding that the rogue elements in the Clinton campaign and the Obama White House conspired in a traitorous coup d'état, going so far as to develop pretexts for impeaching and removing Donald Trump from office after he legitimately won a duly conducted presidential election.

As discussed in the previous chapters, the FBI concocted an international intelligence sting scheme designed to implicate Carter Page and George Papadopoulos in having "advance knowledge" that Russia possessed stolen Clinton emails. I will show in this chapter that the Obama administration and the Clinton campaign had confidence they would get away with this criminal plot because they blindly trusted that the DOJ and FBI's counterintelligence investigation would succeed in proving Trump was a Russian asset. When evidence of Russian collusion or criminal activity by Trump or his campaign could not be found, Comey and Brennan resorted to relying on the Steele dossier, a document they knew from the start was nothing more than a fabricated opinion research report financed by the Clinton campaign and the DNC, for "proof."

How the FBI Abused Section 702 of the FISA Law to Spy on Trump

What is known as Section 702 surveillance is a loophole that allows the FBI to conduct warrantless surveillance of U.S. citizens with practically no checks or accountability on the process. Obtaining a FISA Court warrant to authorize surveillance is supposed to be difficult under FISA law in that the DOJ's attorneys, working with FBI agents, need to convince the FISA Court that probable cause exists to believe a U.S. citizen is an agent of a foreign power. But Section 702 of the FISA legislation allows the FBI—and other entities within the federal government, including the White House—to query the NSA to obtain any information it may have on a U.S. citizen being monitored by the NSA because of suspicious contact with foreign agents acting against the United States.[289]

Just to be clear, under Section 702, the White House or the FBI can simply state a foreign intelligence concern, reviewed only internally if at all, to ask the NSA about any information it may have obtained on U.S. citizens believed to be involved in foreign espionage activities. Since it is likely that many Russian intelligence operatives and government officials were already under NSA electronic surveillance, FBI counterintelligence agents and various Obama administration officials who sought from as early as 2015 to monitor the Trump campaign could have asked the NSA for any information it may have collected on Trump campaign officials it was monitoring.

Thus, Section 702 has functioned as an FBI backdoor to conduct electronic surveillance on U.S. citizens dealing with Russians, without having to bother gathering (or, in the case of the Steele dossier, manufacturing) the probable cause required to get a warrant from a FISA Court authorizing electronic surveillance of the same U.S. citizens the FBI is targeting.

In 2016, Admiral Michael Rogers discovered that the NSA had not implemented sufficient safeguard measures to prevent the FBI and other investigative agencies of the federal government and the White House from abusing Section 702 to monitor the information on Trump campaign officials being collected by the NSA. Rogers brought this to the FISA Court as he undertook to investigate how extensive Section 702 abuses had become.

On April 26, 2017, as a result of Rogers's questioning, FISA Court judge Rosemary Collyer issued a ruling, disclosing that unwarranted and illegal surveillance of American citizens under Section 702 had reached the highest echelons of the Obama administration.[290] Collyer also dis-

---

289 Jake Laperruque, "Explaining Secret Surveillance," Pogo.com, July 25, 2018, https://www.pogo.org/analysis/2018/07/explaining-secret-surveillance/.

290 Rosemary M. Collyer, Judge, United States Foreign Intelligence (FISA) Court, Memorandum Opinion and Order, April 26, 2017.

closed that FBI director James Comey had allowed three unnamed federal contractors limitless, continuous, unlawful, and warrantless Section 702 access to NSA-collected data on U.S. citizens. Two of these unnamed contractors could have been Glenn Simpson of Fusion GPS and his contractor, Christopher Steele, the author of the Steele dossier.

Of the approximately five thousand searches of the NSA database from October 2016–April 2017 conducted by the National Security Division of the DOJ, Judge Collyer deemed that 4,250 were illegal or noncompliant under Section 702 rules. Collyer further revealed that the DOJ had shared this ill-gotten information on U.S. citizens with CIA Director John Brennan and Director of National Intelligence James Clapper.[291] At present, there is no way to know how many Trump associates were illegal targets of spying under Section 702 of the FISA law, or to determine whether or not Trump himself was also a target. But that the Obama DOJ used Section 702 to query illegally the NSA electronic surveillance database about Trump and his presidential campaign is well established.

Rogers Blows the Whistle

The hero of this story is once again NSA Director Michael Rogers. Rogers was the intelligence agency head who blew the whistle on the FBI using the NSA to spy on U.S. citizens through the illegal use of Section 702 of the FISA law. Rogers also warned Trump the Obama administration was spying upon him, going so far as to get FISA Court approval to conduct electronic surveillance of a computer in Trump's office in Trump Towers. Rogers was also the only intelligence agency chief with the sense of duty and the courage to risk his career by stepping outside his organizational responsibilities to warn Trump that his presidential transition team in

---

291 L.J. Keith, "FISA Court Exposes Obama's Abuse of NSA to Spy on Americans," Communities Digital News, May 28, 2019, https://www.commdiginews.com/politics-2/obama-white-house-fisa-nsa-prism-spy-americans-2012-119410/. See also: Jeff Carlson, "NSA Director Rogers Disclosed FISA Abuse Days After Page Warrant Was Issued," *The Epoch Times*, October 17, 2018, https://www.theepochtimes.com/nsa-director-rogers-disclosed-fisa-abuse-days-after-carter-page-fisa-was-issued_2692033.html.

Trump Tower was under FISA Court-authorized electronic surveillance, most likely in direct violation of federal law.

Judge Collyer, in her memorandum opinion of April 26, 2017, also disclosed that the Obama administration had begun using Section 702 to illegally spy on political opponents starting in 2012, in the run-up to President Obama's re-election campaign. The sheer volume of database abuse under Section 702 that Collyer documented as having happened during the Obama administration has led knowledgeable observers to conclude that there is no intellectually honest explanation other than that Obama weaponized the FBI's Counterintelligence Division, starting during his re-election campaign in 2012, to spy on political opponents.[292]

On November 17, 2016, acting on his own authority without notifying his authorities, Rogers broke ranks with Brennan and Clapper by going to visit President-Elect Donald Trump in his Trump Tower offices in New York City. In October 2016, the Obama administration submitted a new FISA Court application to gain permission to conduct electronic surveillance on a computer in Trump Tower that the FBI suspected was linked to Russian banks, in particular to Alfa Bank and SVB Bank. The electronic surveillance continued even after no evidence of criminal activity was found. Rogers did not want to participate in the Deep State spying, starting when he refused to sign on fully to the ICA that Brennan and Clapper orchestrated. Rogers explained to Trump that the FBI's Counterintelligence Division had the Trump transition team under electronic surveillance both through FISA Court-authorized electronic surveillance and through Section 702 queries to the NSA. On hearing this, Trump moved the transition team out of Trump Towers and into the more secure Trump National Golf Club in Bedminster, New Jersey.[293]

---

292 Blogger known as "sundance," "Evidence of Obama Administration Political Surveillance Beginning Mid 2012," The Conservative Treehouse, May 24, 2019, https://theconservativetreehouse.com/2019/05/24/evidence-of-obama-administration-political-surveillance-beginning-mid-2012/.

293 World Tribune Staff, "Who Is Adm. Mike Rogers? Unsung 'Hero' Alerted President Trump to Illegal Spying," *World Tribune*, May 1, 2019, https://www.worldtribune.com/who-is-adm-mike-rogers-unsung-hero-alerted-president-trump-to-illegal-spying/.

Then on November 19, 2016, the *Washington Post* reported, in what appeared to be sourced from an unnamed intelligence agency revenge leak, that Defense Secretary Ashton Carter and Director of National Intelligence James Clapper had recommended to President Obama that NSA Director Michael Rogers be removed.[294] At the time, President-Elect Trump was considering the nomination of Rogers to replace Clapper. Understandably, Obama never fired Rogers, a move that might have led to the revelation of Obama's many Section 702 abuses.

Rogers's warning was the basis for Trump's tweet on March 4, 2017, after Trump had been in the White House for forty-three days. Trump tweeted the common-sense understanding of what Rogers had told him: "Terrible! Just found out that Obama had my 'wires tapped' in Trump Tower just before the victory. Nothing found. This is McCarthyism!" Trump was right.

FISA Court Warrants Are Used to Cover Up Section 702 Abuses

The Obama DOJ and White House abused FISA Section 702 queries, accessing the NSA database of information on U.S. citizens with abandon. Why then did the DOJ and FBI bother seeking FISA Court warrants against Carter Page?

The answer appears to be that the FISA Court warrants were in large part designed to cover up the amount of intelligence the Obama administration had already obtained on Trump and his campaign officials through the NSA. Very possibly, the DOJ, the FBI, and the White House already had from the NSA most, if not all, of the intelligence gathered on Trump and his top associates that they needed. But the fact that the Obama administration gained this intelligence by abusing

---

294 Ellen Nakashima, "Pentagon and Intelligence Community Chiefs Have Urged Obama to Remove the Head of the NSA," *Washington Post*, November 19, 2016, https://www.washingtonpost.com/world/national-security/pentagon-and-intelligence-community-chiefs-have-urged-obama-to-remove-the-head-of-the-nsa/2016/11/19/44de6ea6-adff-11e6-977a-1030f822fc35_story.html?utm_term=.ee575bbd6b86&wpisrc=al_alert-national.

Section 702 queries could only remain secret if the intelligence the DOJ and FBI used against Trump and his campaign associates was attributed to the legal processes of obtaining FISA Court warrants to conduct electronic surveillance, not to NSA intelligence gathered by abusing Section 702.

Getting a FISA Court warrant on Carter Page also had one unique advantage. The FBI had no better way to fabricate evidence than to send double agents wearing wires into the heart of the Trump campaign and White House. These double agents working on behalf of the DOJ and FBI could then initiate conversations designed to plant "evidence" of wrongdoing on unsuspecting loyal Trump supporters. This entrapment scheme would bear additional fruit if the targets of the FBI not only were recorded by the operatives wearing wires, but also used their cell phones to send emails, text, or speak about the encounters.

The fact that George Papadopoulos suspected Sergei Millian was wearing a wire and the evidence that the FBI asked Papadopoulos to wear a wire to capture conversations with Mifsud raise questions regarding what laws authorized these activities. Or, by getting double agents to wear wires in their investigations of the GOP presidential candidate and his campaign officials, did the DOJ and FBI go rogue in a decision to act illegally?

The FBI Hides Three (or More) Secret FISA Court Warrants

In her closed-door testimony before the Senate Judiciary Committee on December 19, 2017, former attorney general Loretta Lynch was questioned by Democratic Representative Sheila Jackson Lee of Texas, in a manner suggesting that Carter Page was not the only Trump campaign associate to be the subject of an FBI/DOJ FISA Court application for electronic surveillance approval.[295] Consider the following exchange:

---

295   Brian Cates, "Just How Many Other Trump Campaign Members Were Targets of FISA Court Investigations?" *The Epoch Times*, May 26, 2019, https://www.theepochtimes.com/just-how-many-other-trump-campaign-members-were-targets-of-fisa-court-investigations_2937754.html.

Jackson: So, let me follow up with these questions that are basically yes or no. I want to talk about the spring, summer, and autumn of 2016. Carter Page, at that time, was suspected of being a Russian asset; George Papadopoulos had told the Australian ambassador that Russians had Hillary emails; Paul Manafort had been named Trump campaign manager; Michael Flynn was Trump's chief national security advisor and foreign policy advisor; and just yesterday, had a continuance in his sentencing.

One thing that all of these people had in common was that each was the subject of a FISA court investigation, which we now know, and all were directly connected to Trump. As attorney general, you had the authority to oversee FISA application process. Is that correct?

Lynch: Yes.

At this point, Lynch's attorney objected.

When Lynch resumed answering, she said, "Yes. The attorney general has the authority over the final signature on the FISA applications. It is delegated by regulation to the deputy attorney general, and the head of the national security division as well." Lynch never directly answered the question of whether, in addition to Carter Page, the FBI/DOJ sought FISA Court warrants to conduct electronic surveillance on George Papadopoulos, Paul Manafort, General Michael Flynn, and possibly others, including Donald Trump (for the computer in his Trump Tower office).

Throughout this exchange, Lynch's attorneys continued objecting, making sure Lynch never directly answered Jackson's question.

But it is hard to understand why Lynch's attorney objected so vigorously unless it was true that Page was not the only one subjected to FISA Court-approved electronic surveillance. The attorney general has authority over the final signature on the FISA applications. From the congressional transcript, it is clear that Lynch understood the importance of what she was being asked, yet she chose to keep the full extent of the Obama Justice Department's FISA Court applications secret from the American people.

The only reason Lynch did not answer the question directly is that she knew James Comey as FBI director had used extreme and possibly illegal measures to catch Donald Trump and his close associates in committing whatever crime the FBI could find. In the extreme, as discussed in previous chapters, the Obama FBI went so far as to fabricate evidence. Ironically, even when the Obama DOJ under Attorney General Loretta Lynch and FBI under Director Comey went rogue and committed crimes, the Obama justice system was incapable of manufacturing the evidence needed to destroy Trump.

Also being kept secret from the American public are the details of an apparent FISA Court application that was turned down in June 2016. Although it has not been confirmed, the application apparently named Trump and some of his associates. This could suggest that the FBI was seeking specific FISA Court permission to conduct electronic surveillance personally on presidential candidate Donald Trump. There is also speculation that the FBI application that was denied had alleged that Trump was a Russian agent that the FBI needed to surveil. In an article titled "The Obama Camp's Disingenuous Denials on FISA Surveillance of Trump," former assistant U.S. attorney Andrew McCarthy suggests that this sheds light on Trump's contention that his phones had been tapped. If Trump had been targeted for surveillance in the denied application, rather than just mentioned, the FBI almost certainly put him personally under electronic surveillance.[296]

Priestap Refuses to Answer

In his closed-door testimony to the House Judiciary Committee on June 5, 2018, Bill Priestap, the assistant director of the FBI's Counterintelligence Division, refused to discuss the FBI's counterintelligence investigation of Donald Trump.[297]

---

296 Andrew C. McCarthy, "The Obama Camp's Disingenuous Denials on FISA Surveillance of Trump," *National Review*, March 5, 2017, https://www.nationalreview.com/corner/obama-camp-disingenuous-denials-fisa-surveillance-trump/.

297 Lev Sugarman, "Document: Transcript of Bill Priestap Interview with House Judiciary Committee," LawfareBlog.com, April 2, 2019, https://www.lawfareblog.com/document-transcript-bill-priestap-interview-house-judiciary-committee.

The following exchange was repeated throughout Priestap's testimony to the House Judiciary Committee:

> Q. Can you describe the extent of your involvement in the FBI's investigation of whether there was any coordination between people associated with the Trump campaign and the Russians?
> Priestap: Yeah. I'm sorry. I'm not at liberty to discuss that today.
> Q. Are you part of that investigation?
> Priestap: Sorry. I'm just not…
> Q. Okay.
> Priestap: …at liberty to discuss that.

Priestap was also reluctant to discuss details of the international travel required by his FBI job. References to Priestap's travel to London appear to be part of the redacted sections of his testimony.

We know that Priestap was in London on May 6, 2016, when Australian intelligence operative Erika Thompson telephoned George Papadopoulos to set up a meeting with Australian Ambassador Alexander Downer, as discussed at length in Chapter 6. Details of Priestap's May 2016 trip to London came not from Priestap's testimony, but from text messages exchanged between FBI "lovebirds" Peter Strzok and Lisa Page.

On December 4, 2018, as Priestap reached his twenty-year mark with the FBI and became eligible to retire, he chose to do so, getting out while the *Wall Street Journal* could yet still announce with a straight face that his decision to retire was "unrelated to the controversies over the handling of the 2016 investigations."[298]

Priestap, Peter Strzok's boss and James Comey's confidant, shares an interesting characteristic with the FBI's Bruce Ohr, whose wife, as we saw, was a contractor to Fusion GPS. Priestap's wife, Sabina Menschel, is the

298 Byron Tau, "Another High-Ranking FBI Official to Retire," *Wall Street Journal*, December 4, 2018, https://www.wsj.com/articles/another-high-ranking-fbi-official-to-depart-1543964483.

current head of the Washington, D.C. office of Nardello & Co., a top private-eye firm in the Beltway.[299] "So the man the FBI has keeping all its secrets is married to the top private snoop in Washington," commented attorney Frank Friday. "A long time ago, a friend of mine who once worked in the intel community in D.C. told me all the agencies were just absolute cesspools of nepotism, and pretty much everyone advanced by playing leap-frog along with a spouse through the system," Friday wrote. "Use your connections to get your wife a better slot somewhere in the alphabet soup, then she does the same for you. A few detours on the way to congressional staffs, or well-connected private law and media firms, can be part of the track as well." Friday commented that Strzok was a variation of the game in that he appears to have used his mistress Lisa Page as "his ladder-climbing pal in the DOJ."[300]

Evidence that Flynn Was a Target of FISA Surveillance

In a 2017 congressional hearing, Senator Lindsey Graham asked then deputy attorney general Sally Yates and James Clapper, former director of national intelligence, how the intelligence community had gained the transcript of the controversial conversation between Russian Ambassador Sergey Kislyak and General Flynn on December 29, 2016. Yates and Clapper refused to answer Graham's direct question as to whether Flynn's name had been "unmasked," a process that involves leaking to the media the identity of a person discovered in a Section 702 query to the NSA. Text messages between Strzok and Page show that they were monitoring

---

299   Jones Harris, a longtime friend in New York City and one of the earliest and most diligent investigators of President John Kennedy's assassination, was the first to point out to me the importance in this drama of Bill Priestap. Harris also correctly insisted that when studying Washington political operatives it is imperative to understand the background and employment situation of their spouses.

300   Frank Friday, "How Husbands and Wives Figure in the Latest Scandal Revelations," *American Thinker*, December 16, 2017, https://www.americanthinker.com/blog/2017/12/how_husbands_and_wives_figure_in_the_latest_government_scandal_revelations.html.

Graham's questioning. The two indicated that by asking about Section 702 unmasking, Graham was off track.[301]

The correct assumption was that Flynn was being investigated as a named target of FISA Court-approved electronic surveillance prior to December 29, 2016, starting after the election, when Flynn began advising the Trump transition team. This is confirmed by a sentence in the Mueller report on page twenty-six indicating that prior to the discussion with Kislyak about sanctions, the FBI "had opened an investigation of Flynn based on his relationship with the Russian government." This is also validated by a report issued by the House Permanent Select Committee on Intelligence (HPSCI) on March 22, 2018, that indicates in an unredacted version that in the summer of 2016, there was an "FBI enterprise counterintelligence investigation into four Trump campaign associates: George Papadopoulos, Carter Page, Paul Manafort and General Michael Flynn." The HPSCI report further indicates that the FBI did not notify congressional leadership about these investigations during its regular counterintelligence briefings. The only one of these four under FISA surveillance in 2016 who was not indicted for a crime by Mueller's special counsel investigation was Page—the only one of the four working as an FBI informant when he was targeted by the FBI in a FISA Court application.[302]

This adds even more credibility to the argument that the FBI entrapped Flynn. McCabe sent Strzok, the deputy assistant director overseeing the FBI's Counterintelligence Division, and FBI Agent Joe Pientka to interview Flynn in his White House office on January 24, 2017, four days after Trump's inauguration and before the FBI had announced publicly that the FBI's Counterintelligence Division was investigating Trump. The FBI also

---

301　This section is drawn heavily from a blog post by "sundance," "Michael Flynn Was Not 'Unmasked'—Evidence Flynn Was Under Active, FISC Approved, Surveillance," The Conservative Treehouse, June 24, 2019, https://theconservativetreehouse.com/2019/06/24/michael-flynn-was-not-unmasked-evidence-flynn-was-under-active-fisc-authorized-surveillance/.

302　House Permanent Select Committee on Intelligence, "Report on Russian Active Measures," March 22, 2018, https://www.scribd.com/document/377590825/HPSCI-Final-Report-on-Russian-Active-Measures-Redacted-Release#.

did not inform Flynn that he was already under FISA surveillance. The meeting had been set up by McCabe after he reassured Flynn that Flynn did not need to have White House counsel or his personal attorney to attend the meeting.[303] On MSNBC, Comey took responsibility for the McCabe ruse, explaining he would not have bypassed the White House counsel in allowing McCabe to proceed with the plan, except that he had the opportunity to get away with it because the Trump White House was disorganized. This is "something I probably wouldn't have done or wouldn't have gotten away with in a more organized administration," Comey boasted on MSNBC.[304] Today, both McCabe and Strzok have been fired from the FBI for misconduct, and Comey, fired by President Trump, has been disgraced by two reports issued by DOJ Inspector General Michael Horowitz that charged Comey with acting unilaterally—in violation of his employment contract and well-established FBI rules and regulations.

Finally, in 2019, Flynn fired his legal counsel and retained as his attorney Sidney Powell, a former assistant U.S. attorney with experience exposing the history of prosecutorial misconduct by Andrew Weissmann and others involved in the Enron case.[305] Truthfully, Flynn pleaded guilty only after he was forced to sell the family home to raise money for his defense, and after Mueller's prosecutors threatened to investigate his son if Flynn refused to cooperate. Flynn is finally fighting back against the DOJ, but his efforts are hampered, given that he pleaded guilty to one count of lying to federal authorities about his meetings with Kislyak. Powell is forced to fight back against DOJ prosecutors who now are threatening to file additional criminal charges against Flynn if he does not cooperate. The

303 The Editorial Board, "The Flynn Entrapment," *Wall Street Journal*, December 12, 2018, https://www.wsj.com/articles/ the-flynn-entrapment-11544658915.

304 "New Comey Revelations on Flynn, Trump Legal Jeopardy, Blackmail Concerns," MSNBC.com, December 10, 2018, video of Comey's interview with MSNBC's Nicolle Wallace, https://www.msnbc.com/deadline-white-house/watch/new-comey-revelations-on-flynn-trump-legal-jeopardy-black-mail-concerns-1394141763963.

305 Sidney Powell, *Licensed to Lie: Exposing Corruption in the Department of Justice* (Dallas, Texas: Brown Books Publishing Group, 2014).

DOJ continues to threaten to file criminal charges against Flynn as a co-conspirator in a case the government filed against Bijan Rafiekian, Flynn's former consulting firm partner who failed to register under the Foreign Agents Registration Act, FARA, for the work Flynn and his partner did for the government of Turkey. Flynn is refusing to give the testimony the government is demanding because he believes that what the government wants him to say is not true.[306]

The fraudulent nature of Strzok and Pientka's interview of Flynn on January 24, 2017, was due to the fact that the FBI intercepted and recorded the call with Kislyak. Before McCabe set up Flynn to conduct the interview without legal representation, Deputy Attorney General Sally Yates had already concluded that Flynn had committed no crime in the discussion he had with Kislyak. The only mission Strzok and Pientka had was to quiz Flynn about the call to see if they could catch Flynn. Strzok and Pientka asked Flynn about the conversation he had had with Kislyak, without first sharing the FBI transcript of that call. Strzok and Page were positioned by Comey and McCabe to see if they could get Flynn to make statements that deviated from the transcript of the conversation that the FBI already had in their possession. In the FBI 302 report that Strzok and Pientka filed on the conversation with Flynn, the FBI admits as much. Strzok and Pientka were asking Flynn questions when they already knew the answers. By not first sharing with Flynn the transcript of the conversation he had with Kislyak, Strzok and Pientka had exploited an unfair advantage they manufactured. How this can be considered an honest FBI investigation technique defies comprehension.

Instead, intending to frame Flynn, the FBI had decided before the meeting that if "Flynn said he did not remember something they knew he said, they would use the exact words Flynn used…to try to refresh his recollection. If Flynn still would not confirm what he said…they would not confront him or talk about it."[307] Clearly, the FBI interview with Flynn

---

306 Sara Carter, "Michael Flynn's New Brief Shines Sunlight on Prosecutor's Tactics," SaraCarter.com, July 9, 2019, https://saraacarter.com/michael-flynns-new-brief-shines-sunlight-on-prosecutors-tactics/.

307 The Editorial Board, "The Flynn Entrapment," *Wall Street Journal*, op. cit.

was a setup in which Flynn's only crime arguably was a bad memory. As author Matt Palumbo noted in an article published on Dan Bongino's website, FBI agents were looking for any deviation from the script to claim that Flynn was lying to the FBI, even if unintentionally.[308]

Cambridge University academic Stefan Halper not only surfaces in the cases of Carter Page and George Papadopoulos; he also figures in Flynn's case. In May 2019, Svetlana Lokhova sued Halper and four major news outlets (the *Wall Street Journal,* the *New York Times,* the *Washington Post,* and MSNBC) for defaming her. Lokhova, a Russian-born British scholar, charged that Halper was responsible for spreading the false narrative that she approached then Defense Intelligence Agency director Michael Flynn on behalf of Russian intelligence at a Cambridge University seminar dinner in England in February 2014, as well as for spreading the false rumor that Flynn and Lokhova had an intimate relationship.[309]

As early as 2015, Halper had put a report on John Brennan's desk at the CIA linking Flynn and Lokhova from when they had first met at that seminar in 2014. "In 2015, as word of Flynn's interest in the Trump campaign spreads, the London-to-Langley spy ring fatten[ed] the file with more alarmist dreck—that Flynn had gone to a Russian Television gala and so forth," wrote author George Neumayr, a contributing editor for the *American Spectator.* Neumayr continued, noting that in February 2016, when it was reported that Flynn had joined the Trump campaign as an advisor, "the spy ring move[d] into more concerted action…extend[ing] its radar to Carter Page, George Papadopoulos, and Paul Manafort." Neumayr concluded that not only was British intelligence sending information to the CIA on Trump as early as 2015, but Peter Strzok, in his capacity as FBI liaison to the CIA, made sure Brennan was briefed on developments in the early stages of the FBI investigation of Trump.[310]

---

308   Matt Palumbo, "The Framing of Michael Flynn," Bongino.com, December 13, 2018, https://bongino.com/the-framing-of-michael-flynn/.

309   Josh Gerstein, "Intelligence Scholar Sues Cambridge Academic, U.S. News Outlets over Reports on Flynn Links," Politico, May 24, 2019, https://www.politico.com/blogs/under-the-radar/2019/05/24/cambridge-academic-news-outlets-flynn-links-1342943.

310   George Neumayr, "The London-to-Langley Spy Ring," *The American Spectator,* May 25, 2018, https://spectator.org/the-london-to-langley-spy-ring/.

The FBI's Counterintelligence Investigation of Trump Was Kept Secret Until After the Election

That the FBI was conducting a counterintelligence investigation of Donald Trump remained secret throughout the 2016 presidential campaign. The first public acknowledgement of the investigation occurred on March 20, 2017, some four months after Election Day 2016, when FBI director Comey appeared before the House Intelligence Committee.

Comey's announcement came as a surprise. He explained:

> As you know, our practice is not to confirm existence of ongoing investigations, and especially those investigations that involve classified matters. But in unusual circumstances where it is in the public interest, it may be appropriate to do so, as Justice Department policy has recognized. This is one of those circumstances.
>
> I've been authorized by the Department of Justice to confirm that the FBI, as part of our counterintelligence mission, is investigating the Russian government's efforts to interfere in the 2016 election. That includes the nature of any links between individuals associated with the Trump campaign and the Russian government, and whether there was any coordination between the campaign and Russia's efforts.
>
> As with any counterintelligence investigation, this will also include an assessment of whether any crimes were committed. Because it is an open, ongoing investigation, and is classified, I cannot say more about what we are doing and whose conduct we are examining.[311]

This was especially surprising because the *New York Times* had reported in October 2016 that the FBI had found no evidence of links between

---

311   Ben Mathis-Lilley, "Comey Confirms Trump-Russia Investigation, Says There's No Evidence of Trump Tower Wiretap," Slate.com, March 20, 2017, https://slate.com/news-and-politics/2017/03/james-comey-confirms-russia-trump-investigation.html.

the Trump campaign and Russian officials. In an article published on October 31, 2016, the *New York Times* reported:

> For much of the summer, the FBI pursued a widening investigation into a Russian role in the American presidential campaign. Agents scrutinized advisors close to Donald J. Trump, looked for financial connections with Russian financial figures, searched for those involved in the hacking of the computers of the Democrats, and even chased a lead—which they ultimately came to doubt—about a secret channel of email communication from the Trump Organization to a Russian bank.
>
> Law enforcement officials say that none of the investigations so far have found any conclusive or direct link between Mr. Trump and the Russian government. And even the hacking into Democratic emails, FBI and intelligence officials now believe, was aimed at disrupting the presidential election rather than electing Mr. Trump.[312]

The irony is that both reports are true. In October 2016, the *New York Times* was reporting the results of the FBI criminal investigation into Trump's involvement with Russia that came up empty and was shut down by the FBI at the end of July 2016. Comey was referring to the FBI counterintelligence investigation that the FBI began on July 31, 2016, transferring the investigation from the FBI's Criminal Investigative Division to its Counterintelligence Division, run by Bill Priestap.

Comey Hides the FBI's Counterintelligence Investigation from the "Gang of Eight"

Comey went so far as to hide the FBI's counterintelligence investigation of Trump and Russia from the congressional oversight group known as the

---

312 Eric Lichtblau and Steven Lee Myers, "Investigating Donald Trump, FBI Sees No Clear Link to Russia," *New York Times*, October 31, 2016, https://www.nytimes.com/2016/11/01/us/politics/fbi-russia-election-donald-trump.html.

"Gang of Eight." The compartmentalization of U.S. intelligence agencies into various units (the Defense Intelligence Agency, CIA, NSA, FBI, DOJ, and others) led the 9/11 Commission to recommend the creation of the Office of the Director of National Intelligence. In a similar fashion, congressional oversight created the "Gang of Eight" to oversee all the many and various compartmentalized intelligence agencies in the U.S. government.

In 2016, the Gang of Eight included the following: from the House Intelligence Committee, the chair, Representative Devin Nunes (Republican, California) and the ranking member, Representative Adam Schiff (Democrat, California); from the Senate Intelligence Committee, the chair, Senator Richard Burr (Republican, North Carolina) and the vice chair, Mark Warner (Democrat, Virginia); the speaker of the House, Representative Paul Ryan (Republican, Wisconsin); the House minority leader, Representative Nancy Pelosi (Democrat, California); the Senate majority leader, Mitch McConnell (Republican, Kentucky); and the Senate minority leader, Chuck Schumer (Democrat, New York).

During his closed-door testimony to the House Intelligence Committee on March 20, 2017, Comey testified that he did not notify the Gang of Eight during the 2016 presidential election that the FBI had opened a counterintelligence investigation involving a presidential candidate because Priestap, in his capacity as FBI counterintelligence director, suggested he not do so.[313] That conclusion is shocking because the DOJ and FBI weaponized their intelligence units to investigate a presidential candidate in a clandestine fashion designed to avoid congressional oversight. Neither the DOJ nor the FBI has congressional authorization to conduct counterintelligence investigations in secret, especially not one involving a presidential candidate during a presidential election year.

As compartmentalized intelligence units, the DOJ's National Security Division and the FBI's Counterintelligence Division hold proprietary intelligence they collect, with no requirement to share that information with

---

313 Blogger known as "sundance," "How the FBI and DOJ Intelligence Units Were Weaponized Around Congressional Oversight…," The Conservative Treehouse, January 8, 2018, https://theconservativetreehouse. com/2018/01/08/how-the-fbi-and-doj-intelligence-units-were-weaponized-around-congressional-oversight/.

other intelligence units. Although they also are permitted to receive intelligence from other agencies, including the CIA and NSA, this intelligence comes via a Sensitive Compartmented Information Facility (SCIF). Thus, the FBI counterintelligence investigation of Trump and Russia could easily be directed by the DOJ's National Security Division and run by the FBI's Counterintelligence Division without their sharing what they were doing with Congress or with other agencies of the government, including the CIA, the NSA, and the White House.[314]

Yet this should come as no surprise when we realize that in 2015, Sally Yates, in her capacity as deputy attorney general under Loretta Lynch, blocked DOJ Inspector General Michael Horowitz from gaining oversight over the DOJ's National Security Division.[315] On January 31, 2017, President Trump fired Yates, then serving as acting attorney general, over her refusal to enforce his Executive Order 13769, which restricted travel to the United States from seven predominantly Muslim countries. Yates on her own initiative believed the order to be unlawful, characterizing it as a racially motivated ban on Muslims entering the country, despite the fact Trump's executive order had a basis in previous similar executive orders issued by President Obama. In January 2017, Andrew Weissmann, before he joined the Mueller investigation as a prosecutor, praised Yates for standing up to President Trump. "I'm so proud," Weissmann wrote to Yates in an email Judicial Watch obtained through a Freedom of Information Act (FOIA) lawsuit. Weissmann concluded his email with lavish words of adulation: "And in awe. Thank you so much. All my deepest respects."[316]

Strzok and Page's Greatest Hits

Among the thousands of text messages FBI "lovebirds" Peter Strzok and Lisa Page exchanged, a few are important enough to merit comment here.

---

314 Ibid.

315 Ibid. See: Sally Quillian Yates, Deputy Attorney General, Department of Justice, "Memorandum for Sally Quillian Yates Deputy Attorney General," July 28, 2015.

316 Debra Heine, "Mueller Deputy Thanked DOJ Official Sally Yates after She Defied Trump on Travel Ban," *PJ Media*, December 5, 2017, https://pjmedia.com/trending/mueller-deputy-thanked-doj-official-defied-trump-travel-ban/.

Strzok headed the FBI investigation into Hillary Clinton's email server. Subsequently rising to the level of deputy assistant director of the FBI's Counterintelligence Division, Strzok led the FBI's investigation into Russian interference in the 2016 election. Page was an attorney in the FBI's Office of the General Counsel.

The FBI Recruits Overseas Intelligence Assets to Act as Double Agents against Trump in December 2015

On December 28, 2015, Strzok sent the following message to Page: "Did you get all our oconus lures approved?"

The term "oconus" is an intelligence term that specifies foreign intelligence agents operating outside the United States ("o" for "outside" and "conus" for "continental United States"). What Strzok appears to be asking Page is whether she had obtained approval for double agents (lures) from outside the United States to investigate Donald Trump.

December 2015 was before the FBI admitted to opening the criminal investigation of Donald Trump, and months before the FBI opened the counterintelligence investigation, on July 31, 2016. Strzok appears to be suggesting that as early as December 2015, the FBI was recruiting foreign intelligence (oconus) assets to penetrate the Trump organization as double agents (lures) appearing to be loyal to Trump while actually acting as FBI informants.

About twenty minutes later, Page responded: "No, it's just implicated a much bigger issue. I'll explain later. Might even be able to use as a pretext for a call… :)."

A likely conclusion is that as early as December 2015, Strzok and Page had begun the preplanning for what later became known as Spygate.[317] As noted earlier, both Joseph Mifsud and Stefan Halper appear to be "oconus lures" recruited by the CIA and used in conjunction with the FBI/DOJ to entrap George Papadopoulos.

---

317   Blogger known as "sundance," "#Spygate—President Trump Highlights Lou Dobbs Segment Outlining December 2015 Cointel Operation…," The Conservative Treehouse, June 5, 2018, https://theconservativetreehouse.com/2018/06/05/spygate-president-trump-highlights-lou-dobbs-segment-outlining-december-2015-fbi-cointel-operation/.

President Obama Personally Micromanages the FBI's Investigation of Trump and Russia

Included by Inspector General Michael Horowitz in the first report he issued on Comey and his handling of the Clinton email scandal was the following exchange of text messages between Strzok and Page on September 2, 2016. This was after Comey's announcement on July 5, 2016, that the FBI's investigation into Secretary Clinton's email server was closed and that his office was not recommending an indictment against her.[318]

At about 9:40 a.m. that day, Strzok began texting Page about a meeting he had scheduled for that day. Page responded that the meeting was not for the reason Strzok believed it to be. Instead, Page told Strzok, the meeting was being held because President Obama wanted "to know everything we are doing."

This is a critically important message in proving that President Obama had a hands-on role in overseeing and very possibly directing from the White House the FBI investigation into Trump and Russia.

Strzok Expresses to Page His Doubts That the Mueller Investigation Would Find Evidence Sufficient to Impeach President Trump

On May 17, 2017, Mueller was appointed special counsel. Almost immediately, both Strzok and Page realized they would be asked by Mueller to join his special prosecutor team. On May 18, 2017, Strzok sent a text message to Page stating: "[Y]ou and I both know the odds are nothing. If I thought it was likely I'd be there no question. I hesitate in part because my gut sense and concern there's no big there there."[319]

The obvious interpretation of this text message is that Strzok would be enthusiastic about joining Mueller only if he thought the Mueller investigation would be able to produce enough information to impeach

---

318 Inspector General Michael Horowitz, "A Review of Various Actions by the Federal Bureau of Investigation and the Department of Justice in Advance of the 2016 Election," Office of the Inspector General, U.S. Department of Justice https://www.justice.gov/file/1071991/download, June 2018, p. 409.
319 Ibid., p. 405.

President Trump. Strzok indicated he was hesitating only because he feared the Mueller investigation would fail, just as the FBI and DOJ had failed. Strzok implied that his concerns came from the experience he had directing the Trump-Russia investigation at the FBI, and because he knew the allegations of Russian collusion could not be substantiated.

Strzok and Page both finally decided to go ahead and were assigned by the FBI to join the Mueller investigation in June 2017. Strzok was the highest-ranking FBI official to join Mueller's team. In her testimony to the House Judiciary Committee on July 13, 2018, Page explained that Strzok finally resolved his doubts about joining Mueller when he realized that Mueller's special counsel probe might result in impeachment. "And so an investigation leading to impeachment is simply saying, like, that's a momentous thing," Page testified. "That doesn't happen a lot in American history. We're both nerds. We're both, you know, patriots. Being a part of something, like, that is cool. And in the same way that I said people who are on Watergate are still known as Watergate prosecutors whether they were, you know, the clerk who made copies, like, you're on Watergate."[320]

Strzok was dismissed from Mueller's Office of Special Counsel some two months later, in August 2017, when Mueller learned of his explosive hate-Trump text messages with Page.[321] After leaving Mueller's team, Strzok returned to the FBI, demoted to a position in human resources.[322] Page reportedly had completed her detail with Mueller when she left the Mueller probe approximately two weeks before Strzok was dismissed. Page

---

320 Testimony of Lisa Page, House Committee on the Judiciary, U.S. House of Representatives, Washington, D.C., July 13, 2018, op. cit.

321 Karoun Demirjian and Devlin Barrett, "Top FBI Official Assigned to Mueller's Russia Probe Said to Have Been Removed after Sending Anti-Trump Texts," *Washington Post*, December 2, 2017, https://www. washingtonpost.com/world/national-security/two-senior-fbi-officials-on-clinton-trump-probes-exchanged-politically-charged-texts-disparaging-trump/2017/12/02/9846421c-d707-11e7-a986-d0a9770d9a3e_story. html?utm_term=.ed3348bb31eb.

322 Debra Heine, "Strzok/Page Text Messages Are Even Worse Than You Thought," PJ Media, December 13, 2017, https://pjmedia.com/trending/ strzok-page-text-messages-even-worse-thought/.

resumed her work as an FBI attorney after she left Mueller's staff.[323] She resigned voluntarily from the FBI on May 5, 2018.[324] Finally, the FBI fired Strzok on August 13, 2018.[325]

Strzok and Page Discuss the FBI Counterintelligence Investigation as an "Insurance Policy" in Case Trump Gets Elected

In a text message dated August 15, 2016, after the FBI's counterintelligence investigation into Trump and Russia had been opened, Strzok told Page: "I want to believe the path you threw out for consideration in Andy's [FBI Deputy Director Andrew McCabe's] office—that there's no way he [Trump] gets elected—but I'm afraid we can't take that risk. It's like an insurance policy in the unlikely event you die before you're 40…"[326]

This text message appears to be saying that Strzok did not believe in August 2016 that it was safe to assume that Trump would lose to Hillary Clinton in the November election.

Strzok appears to be suggesting that the FBI's ongoing counterintelligence investigation should be used to develop information that would be sufficient to impeach Trump in the event that he won the election. The obvious idea would be to prove that Trump had colluded with Russia over the theft of the Democrats' emails. This, Strzok was suggesting, would prove that Trump had committed crimes—very possibly treason—in winning the election.

---

323 "FBI Agent Peter Strzok's Texts with Lisa Page Disparage Trump throughout Campaign," CBS, December 13, 2017, https://www.cbsnews.com/news/peter-strzok-lisa-page-texts-trump-idiot/.

324 Mary Kay Linge, "Lisa Page, FBI Agent Who Bashed Trump in Texts, Resigns," *New York Post*, May 5, 2018, https://nypost.com/2018/05/05/lisa-page-fbi-agent-who-bashed-trump-in-texts-resigns/.

325 Judson Berger and Brooke Singman, "FBI Fires Peter Strzok, Months after Anti-Trump Texts Revealed," Fox News, August 13, 2018, https://www.foxnews.com/politics/fbi-fires-peter-strzok-months-after-anti-trump-texts-revealed.

326 Inspector General Michael Horowitz, Office of the Inspector General, U.S. Department of Justice, "A Review of Various Actions by the Federal Bureau of Investigation and the Department of Justice in Advance of the 2016 Election," op. cit, p. 404.

At the very least, the text message demonstrates Strzok and Page's shared determination to make sure that Trump lost the 2016 election—or, if he did win, that the FBI counterintelligence investigation could be used as the basis for impeaching him and removing him from the presidency.

Strzok and Page Vow to Use the FBI Investigation to Stop Trump

In a text message on August 8, 2016, Page stated, "[Trump's] not ever going to become president, right? Right?!" Strzok responded, "No. No he's not. We'll stop it."[327]

This text message exchange leaves no doubt that Strzok and Page understood that the purpose of the FBI's counterintelligence investigation was to make sure Donald Trump lost the 2016 presidential election. This text message exchange demonstrates that they both allowed their personal political biases to influence how they conducted the FBI's investigation of Trump and Russia.

Strzok and Page could be confident that their FBI investigation would stop Trump only if they were assuming that somehow key findings of the FBI investigation would be leaked to the press to influence voting in Clinton's favor. Although Strzok and Page believed that Trump's collusion with Russia to influence the 2016 election was criminal, they excused their own desire to interfere in the election as being fully justified.

The question remains open: in the absence of evidence of serious crimes that would warrant impeachment, were Strzok and Page willing to fabricate it?

The record shows that they both knew that the FBI investigations, both the criminal investigation and the counterintelligence investigation, were coming up short. This is the implication of Page's answer to the question posed by Representative John Ratcliffe (Republican, Texas) in her closed-door testimony to the House Intelligence Committee on Friday, July 13, 2018. When Ratcliffe asked Page what she thought Strzok meant by saying there was "no there," she answered, "I think it's a reflection of us still not knowing."[328]

---

327 Ibid., loc. cit.

328 Testimony of Lisa Page, House Committee on the Judiciary, U.S. House of Representatives, Washington, D.C., July 13, 2018.

Investigative reporter John Solomon interpreted Page's comment as an admission that the FBI investigations were failing. Solomon wrote: "With that statement, Page acknowledged a momentous fact: After nine months of using some of the most awesome surveillance powers afforded to U.S. intelligence, the FBI still had not made a case connecting Trump or his campaign to Russian meddling."[329] In other words, the FBI had failed to prove Trump-Russia collusion before the Mueller appointment, yet Mueller was appointed anyway. Then, of course, Mueller failed, predictably, given the fact that the FBI had already failed.

On June 26, 2019, President Trump revealed in a tweet that Robert Mueller had scrubbed Strzok's and Page's iPhones when they left Mueller's Office of Special Counsel in August 2017. Documents from the DOJ's Office of the Inspector General indicate that Strzok's iPhone was reissued to another FBI agent following Strzok's departure, while Page's iPhone was reset to factory settings but not reissued to a new user. Trump fumed at the discovery: "Robert Mueller, they worked for him…they had texts back and forth…. Mueller terminated them illegally. He terminated them. They're gone. That's illegal. That's a crime."[330] When the FBI scrubbed the iPhones issued to Strzok and to Page by Mueller, any incriminating evidence that may have been there was destroyed—an action suggesting obstruction of justice charges should be considered.

Ironically, Mueller's prosecutors, as I noted earlier, threatened to charge me with criminal obstruction of justice charges for erasing emails from my laptop computer in 2016. I had so many thousands of emails saved on that laptop that I had to erase some at various times to open the email program. Besides, I had an external drive I used to back up all my emails using Apple's Time Machine application. Unlike with Hillary Clinton's email account and the iPhones issued to Strzok and Page, I erased emails on my device but backed them up first.

---

329   John Solomon, "Lisa Page Bombshell: FBI Couldn't Prove Trump-Russia Collusion before Mueller Appointment," *The Hill*, September 16, 2018, https://thehill.com/hilltv/rising/406881-lisa-page-bombshell-fbi-couldnt-prove-trump-russia-collusion-before-mueller.

330   Tyler Durden, "Trump Slams Mueller for 'Illegally Deleting Evidence' on Wiped Phones," ZeroHedge.com, June 26, 2019, https://www.zerohedge.com/news/2019-06-26/trump-slams-mueller-illegally-deleting-evidence-uncovered-oig.

The Obama Administration's "Enemy List" Unmasking Scandal

U.S. citizens who are surveilled by the NSA without a warrant because of their suspicious communications with a foreign citizen are routinely "masked," meaning their identities are kept secret unless there is a genuine and overwhelming national security interest justifying that the person be named—or, in intelligence terms, "unmasked." Under rules promulgated by President George H. W. Bush, unmasking U.S. citizens who were incidental targets caught up in NSA surveillance of suspicious foreign citizens was a limited practice that the intelligence communities frowned upon. This all changed not after the 9/11 attacks, but years later, when President Obama used the pretext of the need to fight a "War on Terror" to allow Director of National Intelligence James Clapper to revise rules in 2013 to make it easier to "unmask" the names of lawmakers and foreign staffers caught in foreign surveillance. The new rules specified that lawmakers' or staffers' names could be unmasked if an intelligence agency under the executive branch thought that "the identity of the Member of Congress or the Congressional staff is necessary to understand and assess the associated intelligence and further a lawful activity of the recipient agency." As reported by the *Washington Examiner* on July 31, 2017, the previous standard required the CIA director to give "prior written approval" that there was a legitimate foreign intelligence need that could only be met by having the names unmasked.[331]

---

331   Todd Shepherd, "James Clapper Eased Rules on 'Unmasking' Procedures in 2013: Report," *Washington Examiner*, July 31, 2017, https://www.washingtonexaminer.com/james-clapper-eased-rules-on-unmasking-procedures-in-2013-report. This paragraph also draws heavily upon the following: Editorial, "In Abusing NSA Intelligence, Did Obama White House Commit a crime?" *Investor's Business Daily*, August 2, 2017, https://www.investors.com/politics/editorials/in-abusing-nsa-intelligence-did-obama-white-house-commit-a-crime/. See also: Todd Shepherd, "James Clapper Eased Rules on 'Unmasking' Procedures in 2013 Report," *Washington Examiner*, July 31, 2017, https://www.washingtonexaminer.com/james-clapper-eased-rules-on-unmasking-procedures-in-2013-report.

Representative Devin Nunes, then the chairman of the House Intelligence Committee, wrote a letter to then director of national intelligence Dan Coats, dated July 27, 2017, in which he charged that he had found evidence that Obama administration officials had made hundreds of Section 702 requests to the NSA, seeking information on Donald Trump and his campaign officials. As reported by investigative reporter John Solomon, the Obama administration officials then took this NSA intelligence information, unmasked the names, and used this "easy access to U.S. person information" for partisan political purposes. Solomon noted that National Security Advisor Susan Rice and former CIA director John Brennan had acknowledged making such requests, though both insisted the requests were "for legitimate work reasons."[332]

The Nunes investigation into the Obama administration unmasking scandal also came to include Samantha Power, Obama's ambassador to the United Nations, and Ben Rhodes, Obama's deputy national security advisor in the White House. The apparent violation of Fourth Amendment rights did not end with the unmasking. Once the names of Trump campaign staffers and later of Trump transition officials were revealed in unredacted NSA intelligence reports obtained by these Obama officials through Section 702 queries, they were leaked to the press. Powers was reported to have averaged more than one Section 702 request every day in 2016.[333]

On April 3, 2017, Bloomberg reported that former national security advisor Susan Rice had requested, on dozens of occasions, the identities of U.S. persons connected to the Trump campaign and transition team

---

332 John Solomon, "Intelligence Chairman Accuses Obama Aides of Hundreds of Unmasking Requests," *The Hill*, July 27, 2017, https://thehill. com/policy/national-security/344226-intelligence-chairman-accuses-obama-aides-of-hundreds-of-unmasking.

333 Bret Baier, "Samantha Power Sought to Unmask Americans on Almost Daily Basis, Sources Say," Fox News, September 20, 2017, https://www. foxnews.com/politics/samantha-power-sought-to-unmask-americans-on-almost-daily-basis-sources-say.

found in raw NSA intelligence reports.[334] On April 4, 2017, in an interview with MSNBC's Andrea Mitchell, Rice denied that the Obama White House had ordered secret surveillance of the Trump campaign and transition teams as part of a political operation. "Absolutely false," Rice told Mitchell. Rice tried to position the practice as involving occasions when she received NSA intelligence reports and asked for the names of the U.S. persons involved so she could figure out the importance of each report and the name of the U.S. official involved. "I leaked nothing to nobody and never have and never would," Rice insisted.[335] But on September 18, 2017, CNN published a report that identified Rice as the former Obama official who had unmasked the identities of senior officials in the Trump administration to understand why the Crown Prince Sheikh Mohammed bin Zayed Al Nahyan of the United Arab Emirates arrived in New York at the end of 2016 for a meeting with Trump transition members Jared Kushner, Steve Bannon, and General Flynn. The meeting with the Crown Prince was undisclosed to President Obama, violating customary practices.[336] Rice subsequently admitted she was responsible for doing this unmasking.[337]

---

334   Eli Lake, "Top Obama Adviser Sought Names of Trump Associates in Intel," Bloomberg, April 3, 2017, https://www.bloomberg.com/opinion/articles/2017-04-03/top-obama-adviser-sought-names-of-trump-associates-in-intel.

335   Ken Dilanian and Corky Siemaszko, "Susan Rice Speaks Out on 'Unmasking' Accusations: 'I Leaked Nothing to Nobody," NBC News, April 4, 2017, https://www.nbcnews.com/politics/politics-news/susan-rice-speaks-out-unmasking-accusations-i-leaked-nothing-nobody-n742486.

336   Manu Raju, "Exclusive: Rice Told House Investigators Why She Unmasked Senior Trump Officials," CNN Politics, September 18, 2017, https://www.cnn.com/2017/09/13/politics/susan-rice-house-investigators-unmasked-trump-officials/index.html.

337   Elizabeth Preza, "Rice Told Investigator She Unmasked Members of the Trump Team after Clandestine Meeting with UAE Crown Prince," RawStory.com, September 13, 2017, https://www.rawstory.com/2017/09/rice-told-investigator-she-unmasked-members-of-the-trump-team-after-clandestine-meeting-with-uae-crown-prince/.

As noted earlier, regardless of how much intelligence the FBI derived from FISA Court-approved electronic surveillance, the likelihood is that the Obama administration already had this, and much more, though Section 702 queries to the NSA database. In my interrogation by Mueller's team, the prosecutors had details of my electronic communications, including my telephone communications, that suggested to me that I had been under FISA Court electronic surveillance during and following the 2016 election. Truthfully, I suspect I have been under NSA electronic surveillance since at least 2008, when I traveled to Kenya to research Obama's origins—if not as early as 2004, when I coauthored *Unfit for Command*, the Swift Boat book opposing John Kerry's presidential bid.

Obama Distributes the President's Daily Briefing with Unmasked Names

The president's daily briefing (PDB) is presented in a binder marked "Top Secret," with the contents prepared for "the president's eyes only." The PDB is a compilation document of the various intelligence reports of the federal government's many compartmentalized intelligence agencies (the NSA, FBI, DOJ, CIA, Department of Defense, Department of State, and so on) for the president's review. Traditionally, the PDB existed only in the White House's Sensitive Compartmented Information Facility (SCIF).

Also traditionally, a very small circle of readers (the vice president, the secretary of defense, the chairman of the Joint Chiefs of Staff, and a few White House staffers) was authorized by the president to review the PDB. In 2013, all this changed. President Obama expanded the PDB distribution list to more than thirty recipients. This expanded list included his top strategic communications aide and speechwriter, as well as deputy secretaries of national security departments.[338]

With the distribution list expanded, Susan Rice's unmasking of names of U.S. citizens mentioned in NSA intelligence reports increased the risk

---

338   David Priess, "Five Myths about the President's Daily Brief," *Washington Post*, December 29, 2016, https://www.washingtonpost.com/opinions/five-myths-about-the-presidents-daily-brief/2016/12/29/eeb4bbec-c862-11e6-8bee-54e800ef2a63_story.html?utm_term=.130afe3fbfb4.

that the unmasked information would be used for political purposes.[339] During an appearance on MSNBC on March 18, 2017, Obama administration Deputy Assistant Secretary of State Evelyn Farkas admitted that the administration had used intelligence information to spy on Donald Trump during the 2016 campaign and transition.

In that interview, Farkas even outed herself as the key source for a *New York Times* report that discussed White House officials' leaking classified information to the media.[340] The *New York Times* reported on March 1, 2017: "American allies, including the British and the Dutch, had provided information describing meetings in European cities between Russian officials—and others close to Russia's president, Vladimir V. Putin—and associates of President-elect Trump, according to three former American officials who requested anonymity in discussing classified information."[341] Farkas on MSNBC admitted to being one of these anonymous sources leaking to the *New York Times* about the Obama administration's misuse of classified information. This report also appears to provide additional confirmation that foreign intelligence agents were involved in the FBI's counterintelligence investigation of Trump.

---

339 This paragraph and the previous paragraph draw heavily from a post by a blogger known as "sundance," "Operation Condor—How NSA Director Mike Rogers Saved the U.S. From a Massive Constitutional Crisis," The Conservative Treehouse, January 5, 2018, https://theconservativetreehouse. com/2018/01/05/operation-condor-how-nsa-director-mike-rogers-saved-the-u-s-from-a-massive-constitutional-crisis/.

340 Blogger known as "sundance," "UPDATE: President Obama's Own Defense Deputy Admits Obama White House Spied on Candidate/President-Elect Trump," The Conservative Treehouse, March 28, 2017, https:// theconservativetreehouse.com/2017/03/28/oh-my-president-obamas-own-defense-deputy-admits-obama-white-house-spied-on-candidatepresident-elect-trump/.

341 Matthew Rosenberg, Adam Goldman, and Michael S. Schmidt, "Obama Administration Rushed to Preserve Intelligence of Russian Election Hacking," *New York Times*, March 1, 2017, https://www.nytimes. com/2017/03/01/us/politics/obama-trump-russia-election-hacking. html?_r=0.

On June 25, 2019, Jay Sekulow, an attorney on President Trump's legal defense team who also serves as the general counsel for the American Center for Law and Justice (ACLJ), obtained records showing that the office of the director of national intelligence, under Director James Clapper, took steps to undermine Trump and his incoming administration just two days before Trump was inaugurated. As Sekulow pointed out in an opinion piece published by Fox News, Clapper revised procedures to greatly expand access to classified raw intelligence to "unelected, unaccountable bureaucrats," paving the way "for a shadow government to leak classified information—endangering our national security and severely jeopardizing the integrity and reputation of our national security apparatus—in an attempt to undermine President Trump." Sekulow continued to point out that documents the ACLJ received under a Freedom of Information Act request show NSA officials were confident they would have the signature of Attorney General Loretta Lynch just days before Trump was sworn in as president on January 20, 2017. Sekulow concluded that all the evidence pointed "to a coordinated effort across agencies during the Obama administration to oppose the incoming Trump administration."[342]

---

342 Jay Sekulow, "Jay Sekulow: Obama Administration's Anti-Trump Actions Revealed in Newly Disclosed Documents," Fox News, June 25, 2019, https://www.foxnews.com/opinion/jay-sekulow-obama-administrations-anti-trump-actions-revealed-in-newly-disclosed-documents.

Conclusion

THE PLAN TO RE-ELECT PRESIDENT TRUMP

When I wrote *Killing the Deep State: The Fight to Save President Trump*,[343] the outcome of Mueller's special counsel investigation was far from certain. That book was published in March 2018, but it was months before the FBI knocked on my front door on August 28, 2018, three days before my seventy-second birthday, handing me a subpoena that ordered me to appear before Mueller's grand jury in Washington, D.C. Anyone who has reached this point in reading this book has seen overwhelming evidence that Mueller presided over a hugely partisan and, I would argue, extremely illegal investigation rife with prosecutorial misconduct. Truthfully, the Mueller investigation was a Department of Justice authorized investigation with a pre-determined conclusion (namely, that Trump had been compromised by Putin and, as a result, was a Russian asset seeking the presidency, the highest elected office in the United States), looking to find or manufacture "proof" on which to remove Trump from office and to convict him as a spy.

Encountering Mueller's prosecutors in person, I can attest that their only purpose was to "get Trump." Mueller did not investigate how the Steele dossier came to be, ignoring that the scurrilous and defamatory

---

343 Jerome R. Corsi, *Killing the Deep State: The Fight to Save President Trump* (West Palm Beach, Florida: Humanix Books, 2018), op. cit.

document was an unverifiable fraud. However, the Steele dossier was allowed by Attorney General Loretta Lynch to become the linchpin of the FBI's FISA Court application to conduct electronic surveillance on Donald Trump and his presidential campaign. Mueller refused to examine evidence that I have now presented here, which I believe proves Russia did not steal the DNC emails. I was astounded when Mueller's prosecutors—Jeannie Rhee, Aaron Zelinsky, and Andrew Goldstein—rebuffed my suggestion that they should go to London to interview Julian Assange.

When Mueller presented me with a plea deal that required me to lie by pleading guilty to a crime I did not commit, I realized his prosecutors were willing to suborn perjury to create the "proof" needed to perfect their treasonous coup d'état. I was "collateral damage," in that the Mueller prosecutors attempted to threaten and intimidate me into pleading before a federal judge that I was a felon for the process crime of "lying" to federal investigators. Clearly, Mueller's prosecutors know I did not lie, otherwise I would have been indicted once I refused to accept their fraudulent plea deal. The point is that Mueller's prosecutors were willing to create process crimes in their disdain of Donald Trump and all those, including me, who support him. George Papadopoulos and General Michael Flynn were victims of this same scheme that reduces to nothing more than criminal prosecutorial misconduct of the highest magnitude.

Only a criminal would have pressed me to accept a plea deal that fraudulent. If I had accepted the plea deal, Mueller would have demanded that I swear before God and a federal judge that I had knowingly and willfully given Mueller's team information on a material subject that I knew to be false, with the intent to deceive them. I had many memory mistakes, but I did not commit the crime of lying. I repeat that I rejected Mueller's "deal," and he never indicted me. That alone proves that the U.S. justice system is in the hands of criminals. Mueller was willing to see me die in prison if the president's attorneys led by Rudy Giuliani had not stormed the Department of Justice accusing Mueller of suborning perjury in my case, armed with the evidence I had arranged to get the White House of the "statement of offense" and "allocution" written for me to swear before a federal judge, as drafted under Weissmann's approval.

I argued in *Killing the Deep State* that hate-Trump Democrats have elevated the Russia-collusion hoax to the level of ideology, believing Trump must have colluded with Russia virtually as religious dogma, even when no credible evidence can be found to support that specious claim. In a chapter titled "How Trump Can Win the Propaganda War," I argued that propaganda rule number one for the Russia-collusion narrative is this: "Any facts that prove the disinformation meme to be factually false are rejected as not definitive because the investigation is continuing, and proof might yet be found." I define propaganda rule number two as follows: "Anyone attempting to disprove the truth of the disinformation meme is targeted for ridicule as part of the conspiracy theory." The point is that facts and evidence proving the falsity of an ideological belief are insufficient to dislodge that belief in the mind of a true believer.

Now the final Mueller report has concluded "no Russia collusion," and the attorney general has ruled that there will be no prosecutions for obstruction because Mueller found no probable-cause evidence that Trump or his associates committed obstruction of justice crimes. Trump has won, simply by following what I call in *Killing the Deep State* counterpropaganda rule number one, defined as follows: "A propaganda campaign can only be defeated by the passage of time, as the public will lose interest in the disinformation narrative if no criminal convictions can be achieved by a special prosecutor's resources after the expenditure of enormous government resources in the attempt to do so."

This has now happened. Yet the hate-Trump Democratic Party ideologues in Congress have re-doubled their efforts to impeach Trump, morphing Russiagate into Ukrainegate on the argument disproven by the transcript that Trump suspended USAID to Ukraine as a quid pro quo (morphed into "extortion effort," morphed into "bribe") held out until Ukraine agreed to investigate Hunter Biden, Vice President Joe Biden's son, for corruption in accepting a board position with Burisma, a likely corrupt Ukrainian natural gas firm. Detailing the impeachment hearings held by Representative Adam Schiff (Democrat, California) in the House Intelligence Committee is beyond the scope of this book. Suffice it to say that while the lying Steele dossier was at the heart of Russiagate, an equally suspect hearsay "whistleblower" report is at the heart of Ukrainegate.

As I write this, Donald Trump is in his first term and has been gaining month by month a mastery of the powers endowed by the Constitution to the presidency. In doing so, he is following what I call counterpropaganda rule number two: "Realizing that the presidency is endowed with enormous powers, a president must take action to change the subject by action aimed at addressing legitimate national security issues."

Look at all that President Trump has accomplished, despite the never-ending efforts of Democratic Never Trumpers in Congress to resist and obstruct his agenda. Trump has never dropped his emphasis on the need to build a wall and to eliminate immigration rules designed to create de facto amnesty if we are ever to have a chance of securing our southern border. The Trump administration has ended unfair international trade deals negotiated by previous presidents, including the NAFTA deal with Mexico and Canada and the one-sided trade deal with China. He has begun rebuilding the U.S. military while avoiding a war with North Korea. He has pulled out of President Obama's nuclear deal with Iran that was nothing but permission for that terror-supporting regime to rebuild economically and position itself to develop nuclear weapons in the not-too-distant future. How many billions of dollars in cash did President Obama really fly to Tehran in U.S. military cargo airplanes in a failed attempt to bribe a corrupt, terror-supporting regime? Or did Obama pay that cash in tribute? Perhaps most important, President Trump's tax cuts and dramatic reduction in burdensome regulations have stimulated the economy. Record numbers of new jobs have been created, including jobs for minorities and women.

President Trump won the presidency in 2016 proclaiming "Make America Great Again" (MAGA). I am predicting here he will win re-election in 2020, running on the theme "Keep America Great" (KAG).

The fight to save President Trump has succeeded, given that the Mueller investigation ended in disgrace, exposed as a partisan and corrupt criminal fraud. Now it is time to define a plan to re-elect him, so he can continue in his second term to fulfill his promise to "Keep America Great" (KAG 2020).

No American Participant, No Changed Outcome of Vote

How seriously did the Russians really intervene in the U.S. presidential election of 2016?

Mueller's Office of Special Counsel brought two sets of indictments against Russians for interfering in the 2016 presidential election.

On February 16, 2018, the Department of Justice announced that a grand jury had returned an indictment brought by the Office of Special Counsel, charging thirteen Russian nationals and three Russian companies with committing federal crimes while seeking to interfere in the U.S. political system, including the 2016 presidential election.[344] This indictment became known as the "Russian troll farm" indictment because of the focus on agents in Russia posting on social media to disrupt the election. Seldom noticed were two sentences in the press release announcing the indictments:

> There is no allegation in the indictment that any American was a knowing participant in the alleged unlawful activity. There is no allegation in the indictment that the charged conduct altered the outcome of the 2016 election.

What the DOJ admitted in this press release undermined the seeming importance of the indictment: one, no American citizen, including Donald Trump and his campaign officials, colluded with the Russians to interfere with the 2016 election; and two, the efforts by the indicted Russians to influence the 2016 election had no effect whatsoever on the outcome of the election.

Then came the second indictment against Russians allegedly interfering in the 2016 election. On July 13, 2018, the Department of Justice announced that a grand jury had returned an indictment presented by the

---

344 U.S. Department of Justice, "Grand Jury Indicts Thirteen Russian Individuals and Three Russian Companies for Scheme to Interfere in the United States Political System," Office of Public Affairs, February 16, 2018, https://www.justice.gov/opa/pr/grand-jury-indicts-thirteen-russian-individuals-and-three-russian-companies-scheme-interfere.

special counsel's office against twelve Russian nationals for committing federal crimes that were intended to interfere with the 2016 presidential election. The DOJ press release specified that all twelve defendants were members of the GRU.

The DOJ further specified that these twelve GRU officers had "engaged in a sustained effort" to hack into the emails of Hillary Clinton's campaign and the Democratic National Committee (DNC), releasing their information on the internet under the names DCLeaks and Guccifer 2.0. This second indictment was the special counsel's effort to identify the Russians working with Julian Assange and WikiLeaks, which made public the stolen DNC emails beginning on July 22, 2016, and emails stolen from Hillary Clinton's campaign chairman, John Podesta, beginning on November 6, 2016.[345]

This press release contains two sentences similar to those in the previous press release, again serving to undermine the importance of the indictment:

> There is no allegation in the indictment that any American was a knowing participant in the alleged unlawful activity or knew they were communicating with Russian intelligence officers. There is no allegation that the charged conduct altered the vote count or changed the outcome of the 2016 election.

This is remarkable in that with these two sentences, the DOJ admitted that the release of the stolen Democrats' emails by Julian Assange and WikiLeaks involved no U.S. citizen in the "crime" and had no effect whatsoever on the 2016 presidential election. If the DOJ could not prove that the WikiLeaks publication of emails stolen from the Democrats involved Russia, then a key premise of the Mueller investigation was undermined. But then, as discussed in Chapter 8, the DOJ chose not to indict Assange

345 U.S. Department of Justice, Office of Public Affairs, "Grand Jury Indicts 12 Russian Intelligence Officers for Hacking Offenses Related to the 2016 Election," July 13, 2018, https://www.justice.gov/opa/pr/grand-jury-indicts-12-russian-intelligence-officers-hacking-offenses-related-2016-election.

for the theft and publication of emails from the Democrats in 2016, but instead to indict him for crimes alleged in the 2010 WikiLeaks publication of classified documents stolen by Chelsea Manning.

Wasn't this an open admission that all the Deep State and Mueller hype about Julian Assange and WikiLeaks had no basis in fact? What appears the truth is the supposed link between Russia and Assange was also a fabrication that most likely originated with Hillary Clinton and John Podesta in the months between May 2016, when the last theft of Democratic emails occurred, and June 2016, when the DNC leaked the news of the email theft to the media. In those two months, Clinton and the DNC were able to recruit the Democratic-funded CrowdStrike to blame the email theft on Russia. But if the government had no proof Russia stole the emails, then why did Mueller threaten to put me in prison? I had no contact whatsoever with Julian Assange or WikiLeaks, I did not introduce Roger Stone to Julian Assange or WikiLeaks, and I refused to lie in a plea deal before God and a federal judge to swear differently. But the DOJ even today appears every bit as determined as it has been to imprison Julian Assange for the rest of his life, just as Mueller threatened to do to me.

The DOJ knew when the indictments were announced that none of the thirteen Russian nationals indicted on February 16, 2018, and none of the twelve alleged Russian intelligence agents indicted on July 13, 2018, would ever be extradited from Russia to face trial. By making a public spectacle of indicted Russians who the DOJ knew would never stand trial, the DOJ was attempting a "show indictment" fraud—suggesting that the indicted Russians were guilty but knowing that allegation would never get tested at trial. Under the principle of "innocent until proven guilty," the two DOJ indictments of Russians for "interfering" in the 2016 election have proven to be nothing at all—except they possibly prove that the DOJ was desperate to preserve the Russia-collusion attack on Trump, fearing that the Mueller investigation was in the process of crashing and burning.

Finally, if the two indictments are correct, and the Russians now charged with crimes did not change the vote count or affect the outcome of the 2016 election, all the Deep State and Mueller ruckus about "Russia, Russia, Russia" appears a pretext that could be used to save the necks of the Clinton-Obama coup d'état traitors. Mueller and others of his ilk in the

U.S. intelligence and justice system could claim their pursuit of Donald Trump was justified zeal given the seriousness of the Russian threat, not a covert plan to deny Donald Trump the presidency. As I will argue next, this is just another extension of the Deep State continuing their cover-up.

Mueller Shifts the Theme from Russian Collusion to Russian Interference

As the hate-Trumpers saw the Russia-collusion narrative fail, the political left predictably pivoted, morphing the narrative to Russian interference and dropping the implication that Trump and his campaign had been involved. The final Mueller report, as emphasized by Mueller's public comments about it on May 29, 2019, presented Russian interference as a serious threat to the integrity of U.S. elections. "As alleged by the grand jury in an indictment, Russian intelligence officers who are part of the Russian military launched a concerted attack on our political system," Mueller said. "The indictment alleges that they used sophisticated cybertechniques to hack into computers and networks used by the Clinton campaign. They stole private information and then released that information through fake online identities and the organization WikiLeaks." Mueller also referenced the first indictment, charging that the Russian troll farm operation involved "a private Russian entity engaged in a social media operation, where Russian citizens posed as Americans in order to influence the election."[346]

Aaron Maté, an opinion writer on the political left who is a surprisingly sharp critic of the failed Mueller investigation, borrowed a phrase from contributing editor Stephen F. Cohen of *The Nation*, saying that Mueller's railing against Russian interference in U.S. elections leaves us with a "Russiagate without Russia." Maté noted that the Mueller report details "a series of interactions where Trump associates speak with Russian nationals, people with ties to Russian nationals, or people who *claim* to have ties to the Russian government." But he noted that none of these links, ties, or associations ever involved a member of the Trump campaign

---

346 The New York Times Staff, "Full Transcript of Mueller's Statement on Russia Investigation," *New York Times*, May 29, 2019, https://www.ny-times.com/2019/05/29/us/politics/mueller-transcript.html.

interacting with a Kremlin intermediary. "Russiagate promoters have nonetheless fueled a dogged media effort to track every known instance in which someone in Trump's orbit interacted with 'the Russians,' or someone who can be linked to them," Maté noted. "There is nothing illegal or inherently suspect about speaking to a Russian national—but there is something xenophobic about implying as much."[347]

Maté correctly noted that Mueller's press conference on May 29, 2019, asserted that the "central allegation" of his two-year probe was that the Russian government had engaged in "multiple, systematic efforts to interfere in our election, and that allegation deserves the attention of every American." Maté also correctly observed that Mueller's comments echoed the ICA issued in January 2017, asserting with "high confidence" that Russia had conducted a sweeping 2016 influence campaign. The problem, Maté also argued correctly, was that a close examination of Mueller's final report shows that "none of those headlines are supported by the report's evidence or other publicly available sources."

Maté cited many of the deficiencies of the Mueller investigation detailed in this book. There is no proof that Guccifer 2.0 was a Russian cutout, nor that Guccifer 2.0 stole the emails from the Democrats, nor that Guccifer 2.0 supplied them to WikiLeaks, nor that WikiLeaks ever published the material Guccifer 2.0 stole out of the DNC's NGP VAN computers. That Mueller did not interview Assange indicated to Maté that Mueller was unwilling to explore avenues of evidence on fundamental questions. That the FBI never investigated the DNC server but instead relied on the forensics of CrowdStrike, a private contractor for the DNC that was not a neutral party, undermines the conclusion that the DNC server was hacked. That Mueller also relied on the Steele dossier puts two Democrat-hired contractors (CrowdStrike and Fusion GPS) "squarely behind underlying allegations in the affair"—a key circumstance that Mueller ignored. Maté noted that John Brennan "played a seminal role in all facets of what became Mueller's investigation: the suspicions that triggered

---

347 Aaron Maté, "The Mueller Report Indicts the Trump-Russia Conspiracy Theory," *The Nation*, April 26, 2019, https://www.thenation.com/article/russiagate-trump-mueller-report-no-collusion/.

the initial collusion probe; the allegations of Russian interference; and the intelligence assessment that purported to validate the interference allegations Brennan himself helped generate." Maté observed correctly that Brennan has revealed himself to be, like CrowdStrike and Steele, "hardly a neutral party—in fact a partisan with deep animus toward Trump."[348]

Maté's analysis, especially coming from the political left, is devastating to the integrity and credibility of the Mueller report. He pointed out that the final report contains crucial gaps in the evidence—for instance, in the way the Mueller report discusses the alleged GRU theft of DNC emails. Maté quotes the following sentence from pages forty to forty-one of the Mueller report:

> Between approximately May 25, 2016 and June 1, 2016, GRU officers accessed the DNC's mail server from a GRU-controlled computer leased inside the United States. During these connections, Unit 26165 officers *appear* [emphasis added] to have stolen thousands of emails and attachments, which were later released by WikiLeaks in July 2016.

Maté pointed out that Mueller's use of the word "appear" undercuts the report's suggestion that Mueller possessed convincing evidence that GRU officers stole "thousands of emails and attachments" from the DNC's email server.[349]

But, as always when the Deep State shifts ground on a losing argument, a careful analysis of the shift is needed to understand where exactly the political left is headed.

Will the Deep State Traitors Be Indicted?

Those who want the Clinton-Obama traitors to face justice have drawn encouragement that William Barr is now attorney general. Barr's various

---

348   Maté, "CrowdStrikeOut: Mueller's Own Report Undercuts Its Core Russia-Meddling Claims," Real Clear Investigations, July 5, 2019, https://www.realclearinvestigations.com/articles/2019/07/05/crowdstrikeout_muellers_own_report_undercuts_its_core_russia-meddling_claims.html.
349   Ibid.

statements indicate that he intends to get to the bottom of what caused the Russia-collusion hoax to be advanced in the first place. As noted above, a major concern is that Mueller's shift in emphasis away from the failed Russia-collusion argument and toward the threat to our elections from Russian interference is a ploy to establish a cover story that will be used to exonerate the Clinton-Obama traitors.

In the report DOJ Inspector General Michael Horowitz issued in June 2018, there was abundant evidence that Comey and many others in the DOJ and FBI conspired to give Hillary Clinton a pass on what appears to be obvious evidence of criminality in the apparent violation of national security laws regarding the handling of classified information that was occasioned by her decision to use a private email server while she was secretary of state. Over and over again, Horowitz excused the actions of Comey and others as being "policy judgments involving core prosecutorial discretion that were for the Department to make." Horowitz noted that although there were legitimate reasons to criticize judgments Comey and others made, they "did not substitute the OIG's [Office of Inspector General's] judgments for the judgments made by the Department, but rather sought to determine whether the decision was based on improper considerations, including political bias."[350]

Similarly, in the second report Horowitz released on Comey, issued on August 28, 2019, Horowitz made even more damning accusations regarding Comey's handling of seven memos he wrote to memorialize interactions with Donald Trump. Horowitz's conclusions disgraced Comey, justifying Trump's decision to fire him. The Horowitz report leveled the following judgment on Comey:

> By not safeguarding sensitive information obtained during the course of his FBI employment, and by using it to create public pressure for official action [i.e., to force the appointment of a special counsel], Comey set a dangerous example

---

350   Office of the Inspector General, U.S. Department of Justice, "A Review of Various Actions by the Federal Bureau of Investigations and the Department of Justice in Advance of the 2016 Election," June 2018, Executive Summary, p. vii, https://www.justice.gov/file/1071991/download.

for the over 35,000 current FBI employees—and the many thousands more former FBI employees—who have access to or knowledge of non-public information.

Horowitz continued:

> Comey said he was compelled to take these actions "if I love this country…and I love the Department of Justice, and I love the FBI." However, were current or former FBI employees to follow the former Director's example and disclose sensitive information in service of their own strongly held personal convictions, the FBI would be unable to dispatch its law enforcement duties properly, as Comey himself noted in his March 20, 2017 congressional testimony.

Horowitz noted that Comey's closest advisors used the words "surprised," "shocked," and "disappointment" to describe their reactions to learning that Comey handed one of the memos to his attorney, instructing the attorney to leak the memo to the press. Yet, while Horowitz found Comey's actions over the memos deplorable, he did not recommend criminal prosecution.[351]

In a separate report, Horowitz singled out former FBI Deputy Director Andrew McCabe for a special report issued in February 2018.[352] He found that McCabe was guilty of misconduct, of lying to FBI investigators—even under oath—regarding leaks made to the *Wall Street Journal* that clearly violated FBI policy. Horowitz referred McCabe to the U.S. attorney's office in Washington for possible criminal charges associated with lying to internal

---

351 Office of the Inspector General, U.S. Department of Justice, "Report of Investigation of Former Federal Bureau of Investigation Director James Comey's Disclosure of Sensitive Investigative Information and Handling of Certain Memoranda," August 2019, https://oig.justice.gov/reports/2019/o1902.pdf.

352 Office of the Inspector General, U.S. Department of Justice, "A Report of Investigation of Certain Allegations Relating to Former FBI Deputy Director Andrew McCabe," February 2018, https://oig.justice.gov/reports/2018/o20180413.pdf.

investigators and to the FBI for "such action as it deems appropriate."[353] Attorney General Jeff Sessions fired McCabe on March 16, 2016, with apparent malice, given that the firing was just hours before McCabe's scheduled retirement.

McCabe blamed his firing on politics, saying Sessions was politically motivated to get rid of him. Campaign finance records show that a political action committee tied to Governor Terry McAuliffe of Virginia, an influential Democratic political operative with longtime money ties to Bill and Hillary Clinton, donated $467,500 to Jill McCabe in 2015 to assist her in her losing race for a Virginia state Senate seat. Campaign finance records further demonstrate that the Virginia Democratic Party, over which Governor McAuliffe exerted considerable control, donated an additional $207,788 worth of support to McCabe's campaign in the form of mailers. This adds up to $675,000 donated by McAuliffe and the Democratic Party in Virginia to McCabe's wife while McCabe was associate deputy director of the FBI and one of a small group at the head of the FBI responsible during the 2016 presidential campaign for investigating the issue regarding Clinton's email server.[354]

On December 21, 2017, in his closed-door testimony to the House Judiciary Committee in a joint session with the House Committee on Oversight and Government Reform, McCabe denied that political bias had influenced key decisions the FBI made regarding Hillary Clinton's email server case.[355] Consider the following sequence in which Representative Raja Krishnamoorthi (Democrat, Illinois) questioned Andrew McCabe:

---

353 Pamela Brown and Laura Jarrett, "Justice Dept. Watchdog Sends McCabe Findings to Federal Prosecutors for Possible Charges," CNN, April 19, 2018, https://www.cnn.com/2018/04/19/politics/justice-mccabe-criminal-referral/index.html?sr=twCNN041918justice-mccabe-criminal-referral0155PMStory.

354 Devlin Barrett, "Clinton Ally Aided Campaign of FBI Official's Wife," *Wall Street Journal*, October 24, 2016, https://www.wsj.com/articles/clinton-ally-aids-campaign-of-fbi-officials-wife-1477266114.

355 Testimony of Andrew McCabe, Executive Session, Committee on the Judiciary, Joint with Committee on Government Reform and Oversight, U.S. House of Representatives, Washington, D.C., December 21, 2017.

Krishnamoorthi: First of all, did you harbor any bias in the handling of the investigation into Hillary Clinton's emails?
McCabe: Absolutely not, sir.
Krishnamoorthi: Do you believe that Director Comey harbored any bias in this particular investigation?
McCabe: No, sir.
Krishnamoorthi: Are you aware of anybody who harbored any political bias at the FBI in investigating Hillary Clinton's emails?
McCabe: I am not aware of any political bias during the course of that investigation in any way whatsoever.

That McCabe could claim with a straight face that his partisan Democratic Party allegiances and his resulting hate-Trump feelings did not constitute political bias is almost laughable. Clearly, we acknowledge that all people, including federal government employees, have political persuasions. Yet the public record now makes clear that senior officials in the Justice Department, including the FBI, were determined to excuse Hillary Clinton regardless of the probable-cause evidence that she had committed crimes, while being willing to go so far as to fabricate evidence and induce perjury to make sure Donald Trump's political ambitions were destroyed.

To date, no criminal indictments have been brought against McCabe. This is not surprising, given that the history of bureaucratic agencies investigating and policing from within is unfortunately dismal. Excuses within bureaucracies abound, even when senior officials commit crimes. Yes, as human beings, we all have political biases. But the record suggests the Deep State has rewarded McCabe. He collected over $500,000 on his GoFundMe site, supposedly to fund his legal defense. He will still get his pension and he has filed a federal lawsuit against the FBI and DOJ for firing him. He wrote a bestselling book—for which he received a handsome advance payment—and finally, he landed a consultant job with CNN.[356] Where is there justice in this?

356 Peggy Ryan, "The Deep State Will Face Justice Soon! Right?" *American Thinker*, August 31, 2019, https://www.americanthinker.com/articles/2019/08/the_deep_state_will_face_justice_soon_right.html.

Is the Deep State Still in Control?

The Obama administration's weaponizing of the DOJ, the FBI, the CIA, and the NSA to attack political enemies was a theme repeated throughout the Obama bureaucracy. Considering how the IRS under Lois Lerner screened out and rejected applications made by Tea Party groups for tax-advantaged status, McCabe's testimony—that the administration was not biased—is not credible. If Lerner had kept her job, the next step by the Deep State would have been to ask the FBI for a Justice Department criminal investigation into Tea Party officials, as well as other conservatives and Christians, for using tax-advantaged 401(c)(3) and 401(c)(4) organizations for political purposes proscribed by federal tax laws.

A report issued on May 14, 2013, by the U.S. Treasury inspector general for tax administration concluded that beginning early in calendar year 2010, the IRS "began using inappropriate criteria to identify organizations applying for tax-exempt status to review for significant political campaign intervention."[357] The inspector general's report established that in May 2010, the tax-exempt determination unit began developing a spreadsheet that became known as the "Be On the Lookout" (commonly known within the IRS as "BOLO") list, which targeted for additional scrutiny groups that included "Tea Party" or "Patriot" in their names, despite the fact that the law requires determination of tax status to be determinant on a group's activity, not its name. The report further found that organizations targeted for additional review because they were identified as "Tea Party" or "Patriot" groups experienced substantial processing delays. As of December 17, 2012, many of these organizations had not received an approval or denial letter more than two years after they had submitted their applications.

On July 22, 2015, Washington-based watchdog group Judicial Watch announced it had obtained documents from the IRS confirming that the IRS used lists of donors to conservative and libertarian groups to target

---

357 "Inappropriate Criteria Were Used to Identify Tax-Exempt Applications for Review," Treasury Inspector General for Tax Administration, May 14, 2013, Reference Number: 2013-10-053, http://www.cnn.com/interactive/2013/05/politics/irs-timeline/.

entities for audits.[358] In an interview on Fox News on October 27, 2017, Judicial Watch president Tom Fitton argued the Obama administration's goal in targeting conservative and libertarian tax-exempt groups was to limit the ability of the Tea Party to be the type of effective force in the 2012 presidential election that the group had been in the 2010 midterm elections when the Democrats lost control of the House of Representatives, with the Republicans registering a massive gain of sixty seats, for the biggest margin in sixty-two years. "That's how you steal an election in plain sight," Fitton commented, arguing that President Obama was cutting conservative and Christian groups off from collecting tax-favored contributions in his determination not to suffer a 2010-like setback in 2012, the year he was seeking re-election to the presidency.[359]

Then, in 2016, FBI director Comey usurped the authority of the attorney general, announcing a decision that Hillary Clinton would not be prosecuted despite clear evidence that she had been "extremely careless" in jeopardizing national security by her use of a private email server as secretary of state.

A similar pattern can be found in the Environmental Protection Agency (EPA). EPA leftist bureaucrats even today are prepared to reimpose regulations designed to impose a carbon tax on Americans in their effort to punish the use of hydrocarbon fuels under the rubric of protecting the earth against climate change, one of the hard left's ideologically driven bedrock beliefs.

The warnings by the Church Committee in the 1970s went unheeded. The Church Committee exposed that Richard Nixon had weaponized and politicized the federal government to go after the enemies on his list, as well as civil rights activists and antiwar Vietnam-era protestors. But

---

358 Judicial Watch, "Judicial Watch: New Documents Show IRS Used Donor Lists to Target Audits," July 22, 2015, https://www.judicialwatch.org/press-room/press-releases/judicial-watch-new-irs-documents-used-donor-lists-to-target-audits/.

359 "Tom Fitton on IRS Scandal: 'That's How You Steal an Election in Plain Sight,'" Fox News Insider, October 27, 2017, http://insider.foxnews.com/2017/10/27/judicial-watch-irs-scandal-lerner-helped-steal-election-targeting-conservative-groups.

Nixon was not impeached for this offense. He was impeached for the Watergate break-in and cover-up. As serious as the Deep State crimes revealed by the Church Committee were, the Nixon era pales in comparison to the extent to which the federal bureaucracy in 2016 was determined to retain its leftist orientation by giving Hillary Clinton a pass while attempting to destroy Donald Trump at any cost.

Why Government Investigations Typically Fail

All too often, internal investigations, including those conducted by DOJ Inspector General Michael Horowitz, have a history of whitewashing government secrets and covering up government illegal actions, regardless of how honest an investigator like Horowitz may be. When under attack, Deep State bureaucracies by nature tend to circle the wagons to protect their own, acting under the assumption that any given political crisis will pass, but that the bureaucracy must be kept intact to perpetuate political agendas and to preserve career jobs. Increasingly, the American people are catching on to the magnitude of the corruption that remains in the swamp known as Washington, D.C. All too often, the establishment GOP sides with those few moderate Democrats who yet exist to block everything President Trump attempts to get done. Yet rather than give up, those of us who support Trump are unafraid, resolving not to give up, especially when we appear to be holding ground, if not gaining ground.

The specific concern here is Mueller's shift to emphasize that Russian interference in the 2016 election can be used to provide excuses for the serious misconduct in the entire Russia-collusion investigation that this book documents, including the misconduct of Mueller's Office of Special Counsel. Excusing as overzealousness the obvious criminal offenses committed by Obama administration officials in their determination to protect national security interests in maintaining the integrity of elections is a patently weak excuse that will not restore the confidence of the American people in the U.S. justice system. Those wanting to excuse the Obama administration face major hurdles in that the use of the Steele dossier to obtain FISA Court warrants appears undeniably criminal, given that senior Justice Department officials knew the Steele dossier could never be verified. The willingness of the Obama justice system and intelligence agencies to join forces to fabricate testimony and induce perjury is demonstrated by my experience with Mueller's prosecutors and the cases of Carter Page and George Papadopoulos as presented in this book.

When and if the treason at the heart of the Obama administration is explored, another obstacle to promoting the Russian scare as an excuse for crimes committed by the Obama DOJ, FBI, CIA, and NSA is that President Obama gave a "stand down" order to counter Russian cyberattacks during the 2016 election. On June 20, 2018, former Obama administration National Security Council cybersecurity coordinator Michael Daniel confirmed during a Senate Intelligence Committee hearing that a "stand down" order was given to counter Russian cyberattacks during the 2016 election.

"There were many concerns about how many people were involved in the development of the options, so the decision at that point was to neck down the number of people that were involved in our ongoing response options," Daniel testified. "It's not accurate to say all activities ceased at that point." Daniel, then regarded as Obama's cyber chief, confirmed that in September and October 2016, a decision was made to shift U.S. cybersecurity efforts then being expended to counter Russian interference efforts in a different direction, "to focus heavily on better protecting and assisting the states in better protecting electoral infrastructure."[360]

If the Russia threat was as serious and pervasive as the Mueller report suggests, why did President Obama order his cyber chief to stand down from efforts to counter Russian cyberattacks on the 2016 presidential elections?

The Counteroffensive that Trump Has Begun Must Continue

When writing *Killing the Deep State* in 2018, I predicted that Trump would weather the storm, with the Mueller probe failing to produce any evidence of criminality or a politically convincing case justifying impeachment. I

---

360 Andrew Kugle, "Obama Cyber Chief Confirms 'Stand Down' Order Against Russian Cyberattacks," *Washington Free Beacon*, June 21, 2018, https://freebeacon.com/national-security/obama-cyber-chief-confirms-stand-order-russian-cyberattacks/.

predicted that Trump would triumph against the Deep State coup d'état, with his ultimate vindication developing in three distinct phases.

- Phase one, which required Mueller's Office of Special Counsel to fail, was accomplished successfully with the publication of the Mueller report on April 18, 2019. This marked the beginning of the Trump counteroffensive. Phase one demanded a combined effort by the Trump legal team in the White House to defeat Mueller's team on legal grounds and by Trump supporters in Congress to take initial steps to expose Deep State traitors trying to deny Trump the presidency. Phase one ended with Trump's vindication, both legally and politically.

- Phase two will involve Trump's launching criminal investigations against those in the Obama administration who took active steps to prevent him from winning the presidency and to remove him from office after he won the 2016 presidential election. If Attorney General William Barr fails to bring criminal indictments against the coup d'état traitors, President Trump will have to appoint a new attorney general or call for the appointment of a new special prosecutor to make sure justice is done. I predict that phase two will take Trump virtually the rest of his first term in office and will end successfully in his 2020 re-election.

- In phase three, I believe, enough credible information will be developed and published by Election Day, Tuesday, November 3, 2020, on the Deep State coup d'état traitors that the American people will have no doubt that Hillary Clinton and Barack Obama were the coconspirators in chief. Their treasonous coup d'état to remove President Trump from office, either by impeachment or by invoking the Twenty-Fifth Amendment, extended to many agencies of the U.S. intelligence and justice systems, including top officials at the FBI, DOJ, CIA, and NSA. The completion of phase three, bringing Clinton and Obama personally to justice for their roles in instigating, leading, and directing the coup d'état, will not be accomplished fully until the beginning of Trump's second term in office.

Despite the efforts of hate-Trump Democrats in Congress to begin impeachment proceedings, the American public appears largely to have decided that the Mueller report has vindicated Trump, both from Russia-collusion accusations and obstruction of justice allegations. The tables have turned on the now failed coup d'état. The Deep State traitors today have serious reasons to be afraid of being exposed, losing their government jobs, and possibly even facing criminal indictments.

In the hate-Trump fury that caused Democrats to commit the highest possible crimes against the republic, I believe that the Democratic Party of Franklin D. Roosevelt, Harry S. Truman, and John F. Kennedy has been destroyed. In the grip of "Never Trump" madness, the hard left has hijacked the Democratic Party so severely that the Democratic Party is rapidly transforming into a Democratic Socialist Party. This new "woke" Democratic Socialist Party is anti-American at its core, determined to destroy the Constitution as it transforms the republic into a totalitarian state in which parties and elections will no longer matter.

Democrats Turn against Russia, Become Democratic Socialists

One of the great ironies in the Deep State's Russia-collusion hoax is that the political left in the United States embraced Russia warmly from the first moments of Russia's 1917 revolution to 1989, when the Berlin Wall came down. The moment Russia was no longer Communist, the political left in the United States began demonizing Russia. Somehow, hard-left activists, always more Socialist Democrats than the Democrat Party has been willing to admit openly, could not hide their hatred of Russia for abandoning Communism with the fall of the Soviet Union.

For those of us old enough to have memories of U.S. politics in the 1950s, it is hard to believe that Saul Alinsky acolytes like Hillary Clinton and Barack Obama have become today's Joe McCarthy firebrands. But another great irony of the 2016 presidential election is that in true Alinsky fashion, Hillary Clinton blamed Donald Trump for colluding with Russia—a charge that appears designed to mask the reality that she and John Podesta were the ones raking in millions of dollars from their own collusion with Russia.

In *Killing the Deep State*, I document in detail how both Clinton and Podesta received millions of dollars in laundered payoffs from one of Russia's wealthiest oligarchs with close ties to Putin, who had become a multibillionaire through controlling the Renova Group, a Russian conglomerate with extensive investments in mining, oil, natural gas, and telecommunications.

There is now abundant, irrefutable evidence that the Clinton Foundation received millions of dollars in donations as apparent payoffs in the Uranium One scandal, in which the Clintons ended up placing some 20 percent of U.S. uranium production under the control of an energy company owned by the Russian government. We have never gotten a believable explanation as to why Robert Mueller as FBI director made a secret trip to deliver a uranium sample to Russia at the direction of Secretary of State Hillary Clinton. Mueller's Office of Special Counsel was one-sided and partisan, not interested in investigating any issue that risked incriminating Hillary or Bill Clinton.

Will America Become a Communist Country?

Since gaining seats in the House of Representatives in the 2018 midterm elections, the Democrats have gone increasingly hard left, with House Speaker Nancy Pelosi fighting hard to maintain leadership of the party against "The Squad." This group consists of four freshman members of Congress who identify themselves not only by their anti-American Socialist policies, but by race, identifying themselves as women of color: Representatives Alexandria Ocasio-Cortez (Democrat, New York), Ilhan Omar (Democrat-Farmer-Labor [DFL], Minnesota), Ayanna Pressley (Democrat, Massachusetts), and Rashida Tlaib (Democrat, Michigan). They are determined to resist and obstruct the Trump presidency.

Those few moderate Democrats who remain are frozen in ideological conflicts of their own making, unable to reverse the course as the Democratic Party rapidly abandons its traditional center-left political orientation. In the wake of the Democrats recapturing the majority in the 2018 midterm election, we are watching the Democratic Party transform into a European-style Democratic Socialist Party. Democrats have turned so far hard-left that Bernie Sanders has lost the unique status he held when he ran for president in 2016 as a Socialist. Today, all serious candidates for the Democratic Party presidential nomination are being forced by the hard left to compete with one another to be the most Socialist of all.

At the same time, Americans are witnessing the violent Antifa movement beating heads in the streets of Portland, Oregon, while the local police stand by and watch. Antifa anarchists and their violent tactics will almost certainly plague Trump rallies in an attempt to divert the attention of the partisan leftist mainstream media from covering President Trump's re-election campaign message. For many Americans, Antifa anarchists wearing black masks and openly engaging in violent criminal activity have become the vanguard of the new Democratic Socialist Party that is rapidly forming on the political hard left of the United States.

Increasingly, hate-Trump activists running social media companies like Facebook, Google, and Twitter have become open in their determination to censor conservatives and Christians from having a voice on their platforms, like the one Trump supporters had in 2016. As the Democratic Socialists accelerate their agenda and transform identity politics into criminalizing Christians who oppose, on Biblical grounds, the LGBT movement, we are rapidly losing both the freedom of speech and the freedom of religion protected by the First Amendment as the inalienable rights of all Americans. Today, George Soros-funded hard-left activists actively brand conservatives and Christians who dare to speak out as "racists" to be silenced by threatening advertisers, employers, and sponsors in a conscious effort to cut off the income and bankrupt those of us who refuse to go along with the hard left's agenda that is intolerant of criticism.

In his 2019 State of the Union address, President Trump made the following vow: "Tonight, we renew our resolve that America will never be a Socialist country." He said that the American people stand with the Venezuelan people "in their noble quest for freedom." He proclaimed that America rejects the brutality of the Nicolás Maduro regime in Venezuela, whose "Socialist policies have turned the nation from being wealthiest in South America into a state of abject poverty and despair." That the president of the United States would ever need to make such a statement shows how far left the Deep State traitors have turned in the aftermath of Hillary Clinton's defeat in 2016. "Here, in the United States, we are alarmed by new calls to adopt Socialism in our country," President Trump insisted. "America was founded on liberty and independence—not government coercion, domination, and control. We are born free, and we will stay free."[361]

Why President Trump Will Be Re-Elected in 2020

In 2020, President Trump will present American voters with a choice regarding what type of country we want the United States to be for ourselves, our children, and our grandchildren. The choice will be between Trump's America, in which he advances the theme "Keep America Great," or the path of the Democratic Socialists, as America follows Venezuela to be this hemisphere's next Communist country.

Following the path of the Democratic Socialists, Americans will be offered a raft of "free stuff"—Medicare for all, guaranteed college education for all, a guaranteed job paying a "living" wage, and a guaranteed universal basic income even for those not working. The Democratic Socialist candidates will insist that all these "positive rights" should be available to citizens and noncitizens alike living in the United States.

Democratic Socialist candidates for president will hide their Cloward-Piven ambitions to spend the federal government into bankruptcy. Also hidden in their campaign rhetoric will be the reality that along with these expanded government-funded "social justice" programs will come ever-expanding state and federal bureaucracies charged with promulgating regulations to implement them.

Law enforcement and judicial programs will be implemented to arrest and prosecute "thought criminals" who dare post opposition "hate speech" on social media. All of Hillary Clinton's "deplorables" will become outlawed as racism, sexism, homophobia, xenophobia, and Islamophobia will become crimes punishable by long prison sentences.

The Democratic Socialists will argue that their utopia of government-provided welfare can be accomplished by taxing the rich in a country like America, which has created the largest number of millionaires and

---

361   President Donald J. Trump's State of the Union Address, WhiteHouse. gov, February 5, 2019, https://www.whitehouse.gov/briefings-statements/ president-donald-j-trumps-state-union-address-2/.

billionaires in world history. Those of us objecting to another "income redistribution scheme" will be branded as reactionaries who deserve to be grouped with the "white men of privilege" whose ancestors wrote slavery into the Constitution.

Hard-left supporters of the Democratic Socialists running for president in 2020 will have a hard time hiding their support for redefining "pro-choice" as abortion on demand even if it involves infanticide of unwanted newly born infants. We are already hearing state and local initiatives to ban the Pledge of Allegiance from government, much as God has been banned from the public schools.

After a presidential win in 2020, the Democratic Socialists could easily move to hold a constitutional convention designed to shred the Constitution our founders ratified in 1776. Should Trump be defeated in 2020, will America as a nation cease to exist, as borders are erased and noncitizens afforded the same "social justice" welfare benefits extended to citizens?

To those of us who still believe in the Constitution and the United States of America that so many millions have fought and died to preserve, the Democratic Socialist vision of our future is the dystopian brave new world imagined by Aldous Huxley or the totalitarian 1984 envisioned by George Orwell.

There will be no First Amendment, Second Amendment, Fourth Amendment, or Fifth Amendment in a nation controlled by the hard-left Socialists and Communists currently in the vanguard taking control of the Democratic Party.

Already those on the hard left are destroying American history. Not content to rewrite the history books in Marxist terms, they are attacking statues of traditional American heroes, including George Washington and Thomas Jefferson.

Had Mueller succeeded in imprisoning me, this book would never have been written. Even now, should America become a Socialist nation advancing on the road to Communism, this book might yet be banned as criminal and subversive.

As I noted in concluding *Killing the Deep State*, the story of the 2016 election is that Clinton's "deplorables" won.

The story written in Donald Trump's first term as president is that those who voted for him expect him to keep on winning.

The story of the 2020 election, I believe, will be one in which voters embrace Donald Trump's proclamation of KAG as enthusiastically as voters embraced MAGA four years ago.

I predict that in 2020, the "deplorables" will rise up once again, this time to preserve the Constitution by re-electing Donald Trump.

Given the viciousness with which the Deep State has engaged in treason to destroy Donald Trump, we must all continue to pray fervently that God will save our land and our freedom.

While the battle will be fierce, I believe the "deplorables" are not about to quit winning, at least for now.

God willing, we the "deplorables" will never quit fighting to defend God, our freedoms under the U.S. Constitution, and the proud history and future of the United States of America.